The Centralia Tragedy of 1919
Elmer Smith and the Wobblies

How they say to me "Elmer, you are fanning the fire of discontent with your speeches!" Of course I am! Did ever anything worthwhile ever come to pass in the history of the world without fanning the fire of discontent? No! . . . By the Almighty I will fan the fire of discontent till I draw my last breath.

ELMER SMITH
May 1, 1923
Seattle, Washington

To my wife, Diane, for her unequivocal love and support

This book is published with the assistance of a grant from the Stroum Book Fund, established through the generosity of Samuel and Althea Stroum.

Copyright © 1993 by the University of Washington Press
Printed in the United States of America

Library of Congress Cataloging-in-Publication Data
Copeland, Tom.
   The Centralia tragedy of 1919 : Elmer Smith and the Wobblies / Tom Copeland ; foreword by Albert F. Gunns.
   p.   cm.
   "A Samuel and Althea Stroum book."
   Includes bibliographical references and index.
   ISBN 0-295-97211-4 (alk. paper). — ISBN 0-295-97274-2 (alk. paper)
   1. Trials (Murder)—Washington (State)   2. Trials (Riots)—Washington (State)
3. Riots—Washington (State)—Centralia—History.   4. Smith, Elmer.
5. Lawyers—Washington (State)—Biography.   6. Industrial Workers of the World—History.   I. Title.
KF221.M8C67   1993
345.797′02523—dc20   93-13453
[347.97052523]   CIP

The following songs from the *IWW Songbook* are quoted with permission of the Industrial Workers of the World, 1095 Market #204, San Francisco, CA 94103: "Fifty Thousand Lumberjacks," "There Is Power in a Union," "Hold the Fort," "The Popular Wobbly," "Christmas at War," "Hallelujah I'm a Bum," "Commonwealth of Toil," "Mourn Not the Dead."

"The Prisoner's Song" by Guy Massey (© 1929 Shapiro, Bernstein & Co., Inc., New York; copyright renewed), quoted by permission.

The Centralia Tragedy of 1919
Elmer Smith and the Wobblies

Tom Copeland

Introduction by Albert F. Gunns

A SAMUEL AND ALTHEA STROUM BOOK

University of Washington Press
Seattle and London

Contents

Illustrations

Map   2

Introduction

To most Americans in 1919 the death of four war veterans and a member of a radical labor union in a remote town in Washington state must have seemed to be yet another worrisome event in that already troubled "Red Scare" year. The months since the signing of the armistice on November 11, 1918, which terminated the carnage of World War I, had brought Americans not only the jubilation of victory but also the anxiety of domestic turmoil. Veterans who had fought to "make the world safe for democracy" streamed home to find that jobs were scarce and that it was difficult to re-establish a familiar way of life. Labor strikes in many industries disrupted an economy that was straining to return to peacetime production; and some strikes, such as the Seattle General Strike in February 1919 and the Boston police strike in September posed special threats to public order. U.S. Attorney General A. Mitchell Palmer seized on these and similar events to embark on a campaign that shrilly warned the public of the dangers of a Bolshevik-style revolution in the nation. Resting uneasily on thin legal ground, Palmer ordered a series of round-ups that netted thousands of suspected radicals, most of whom were later released after the public had raised an alarm.

This atmosphere promoted the belief that there was widespread lawlessness abroad in America—and there was. Unfortunately, much of it derived from official sources. Where established authority appeared to be helpless, citizens were emboldened to take authority into their own hands. During the police strike, armed citizens patrolled the streets of Boston; during the general strike in Seattle, a sort of citizen militia did the same.

What happened in Centralia, Washington, on November 11, 1919—the first Armistice Day—was a reflection of these anxieties. In that small lumber and railroad town, a radical labor organization, the Industrial Workers of the World (IWW), challenged the economic and social equilibrium of a sober, conservative business establishment. There was already a history of violent attacks by mobs of private citizens on the persons and property of union members, and there was a widespread expectation among townspeople in Centralia that the Armistice Day gathering of patriotic veterans would serve as the occasion for another confrontation. The clash occurred, and it resulted in death.

There have really been two Centralia cases: the case as fact and the case as symbol. It is the latter aspect that has dominated writings and discussions of the event. The earliest accounts of the events and the subsequent trial—even newspaper reportage—were highly partisan and in most instances written with the intent of influencing public sympathies to one side or the other. The American Legion commissioned Ben Hur Lampman to write its pamphlet, *Centralia: Tragedy and Trial*. Lampman had reported the case in the pages of the Portland *Oregonian* and did not need to alter significantly the anti-IWW, pro-Legion tone of those reports. For its part, the IWW enlisted the services of Ralph Chaplin and Walker C. Smith, whose respective accounts, *The Centralia Conspiracy: The Truth about the Armistice Day Tragedy* and *Was It Murder? The Truth about Centralia*, were equally propagandistic. It was Chaplin and Smith who fabricated, or at least first put in print, the story of Wesley Everest's alleged castration by members of the mob that lynched him. Both sides used their versions of the event for political purposes—the Legion and its supporters to argue the need for greater vigilance and more legislation restrictive of the activities of radicals, the supporters of the IWW and some groups such as the Communist Party to rally public sympathy to their cause.

These early, biased accounts have been the basis of much of the historical discussion of the event. From John Dos Passos (*1919*), who was promoting his own point of view, to later historians, who should have been more careful with their sources, these discussions have been used as the basis for creating a sort of modern-day "passion play" in which the Centralia events have become a symbol (or symbols) to be manipulated to produce the intended effect on the audience. Perhaps those who have been most honest in pursuing this approach have been the dramatists or "folklorists" who have frankly presented the Centralia outbreak as a subject for entertainment or as an example of powerful, popular myth.

Neither side among the early protagonists seemed content with a simple recitation of the known facts. Granted that much about the outbreak will never be known and is necessarily open to speculation; yet careful analysis of verifiable information yields insight into the personalities, passions, and events of those fateful days. DeWitt Wyckoff attempted it and published *The Centralia Case: A Joint Report*, a moderate and moderately influential account for the Federal Council of Churches in 1930; its principal failing was that it essentially matched the case for the prosecution against the case for the defense and concluded that neither case stood up very well. What was lacking was an impartial search for information that would provide an explanation and an understanding of these events.

One of the great strengths of Tom Copeland's account of the life of Elmer Smith is that he has done his homework on the Centralia case. He has gone far toward accomplishing what one wishes might have been done long ago. He has produced a factually accurate account that, without resorting to caricatures or shallow characterizations of persons on either side, shows the Centralia outbreak for the real tragedy that it was: ordinary people who perhaps should have known better but who were ultimately swept up by forces they only dimly understood. What emerges is a picture of a community driven by fear, intolerance, and the corrupt use of power that is far more gripping than the papier-maché cartoons of the myth-makers.

Copeland's real focus, of course, is on the life and career of Elmer Smith, the Centralia attorney whose association with the IWW led to his prosecution along with the other Centralia defendants as a co-conspirator. As a lawyer, Copeland argues, Smith was exceptional, not for his brains but for his heart. His poor advice was a contributing factor to the Centralia tragedy, but he was a faithful friend of the IWW and the downtrodden. His work on their behalf during the two decades following the Centralia trial was far-reaching and significant and accomplished at great personal sacrifice for both him and those who knew him.

Smith was one of a handful of contemporary lawyers who served the cause of political radicals and radical labor during the early part of the century, men of whom we know very little—George F. Vanderveer, Fred H. Moore, Ralph S. Pierce, Leslie B. Sulgrove, Irvin Goodman, even Clarence Darrow. These men were rarely members of the groups they defended; they were intellectually, professionally, educationally, and socially at a distance from their clients. They have been shadowy presences in these legal proceedings—magicians called in to save the day in court with some legal *leger-de-main* but who then disappeared from the scene as mysteriously as they appeared.

Elmer Smith was one of those men who sought to defend the legal rights of radicals. Such activity was generally disapproved by a legal profession that was astonishingly insensitive to the era's numerous threats to the civil liberties of American citizens. There was constant risk that the lawyer would be cast out with his client. Yet, some like Smith chose to take the chance.

ALBERT F. GUNNS
Long Beach, California

Acknowledgments

When I first read about Elmer Smith in 1970, I was a sophomore at his alma mater, Macalester College in St. Paul, Minnesota. My history professor, Steve Trimble, put a tape recorder in my hands and gave me the necessary encouragement to go out and begin recording the stories of Smith's surviving classmates. As my mentor, Steve inspired me to uncover the history of Smith's life. Without his support and enthusiasm this book would never have been written.

Four other friends were significant forces in influencing the shape of this book. Tracy Dalton conducted an important first interview with Smith's friend, Herb Edwards. She also provided me with a friendly, comfortable home base for my numerous trips to the Pacific Northwest as well as a much appreciated sympathetic ear. Al Gunns generously shared his insights into the Centralia tragedy, particularly concerning the raid and the trial. He encouraged me in my work and was a thoughtful host on several of my trips to California and Washington. Don Capron spent many dollars on long distance calls to me to discuss our mutual interest in the Centralia case. His comments on earlier drafts of the manuscript and his analysis of the Centralia raid and trial were invaluable to my understanding of events. Anne Kaplan gave the book much needed editorial criticism. Her rigorous review made substantial improvements in the style and presentation of this story.

I appreciate those who read earlier drafts of this book, spent time listening to me talk about my research, and offered many helpful comments: Craig Ledford, Milton Cantor, Cindy Cooper, Linda MacCracken, Pamelia L. Olson, Tom Grissom, Tom Churchill, John Fenn, Jill Breckenridge, Fred Thompson, Robert Tyler, Jim Stewart, Tony Velella, Susan Roth, Jerry Fisher, Peter Rachliff, Roy and Marjorie Hoover, and members of the Emma Steffens Commune, particularly Marisha Chamberlain, who cared deeply about my work. Thanks also to Marianne Keddington for her careful copy editing and to my editor Julidta C. Tarver at the University of Washington Press for her encouragement.

Many librarians and archivists responded to my requests for documents with a cooperative, professional spirit that saved me hours of research time: Karyl Winn, Janet Ness, and Richard Berner of the University of Washington Libraries; Thomas V. Hull, National Librarian, The American Legion; Carol A. Leadenham, Hoover Institution on War, Revolution and Peace; Dione Miles, Walter Reuther Library, Wayne State University; David Hastings, Division of Archives, Secretary of State, State of Washington; Dorothy Swanson, Tamiment Collection, New York University; Rebecca Campbell Gibson and Virginia Lowell Mauck, The Lilly Library, Indiana University; Edward Weber, Labadie Collection, The University of Michigan; George Rickerson, The Evergreen State College Library; and John Champagne, Clerk, The Supreme Court, State of Washington.

A number of individuals, with no motive except to be of some help to me, graciously provided introductions to new informants or access to additional information: the J. M. Cunningham family, Robert Venemon, Doris A. Huffman, D. Campbell Wyckoff, John Caughlan, John McClelland, Eleanor Walden, Frank Reid, Hamilton Cravens, and Dick Cowen. Charlotte Todes Stern, Charles Everest, Roger Baldwin, and Harvey O'Connor lived through part of the story described in this book and shared some of their memories in letters to me.

I am thankful for a 1972 grant from the National Endowment for the Humanities, Youthgrants in the Humanities Program, which enabled me to make my first trip to the Pacific Northwest and interview many of Smith's relatives and friends.

My love and appreciation go to my parents, Bruce and Carol Copeland, who provided financial support that allowed me to spend more time on research during the earlier years when I needed it the most.

Lastly, I want to recognize the contributions of the many individuals who allowed me to interview them for this book. The memories of Smith's relatives, friends, and adversaries are the bedrock of this biography. There would be no story to tell if they had not shared some of their past with me. I particularly want to acknowledge my debt to Herb Edwards, Edna Nelson, Lucy Anne Cloud, Virginia Waddell, Laura Willits, Edward Coll, Nora Beard, Mary Killen, Julie Ruuttila, Joe Murphy, Grace Skinner, and Stuart Smith. Although many of these people who loved Smith are now gone, their devotion endures in this book.

Although more articles, pamphlets, poems, and fiction have been written about the Centralia case than about any other event in IWW history, little has been written about Smith, probably for several reasons. He left almost no personal records, he fought on the losing side of battles all his life, and few serious studies of the Centralia case have been published. This biography draws heavily on interviews with Smith's surviving relatives and many of his friends, hundreds of pages of FBI records, previously sealed Washington State Supreme Court records on Smith's disbarment and reinstatement, and organizational records of the American Civil Liberties Union (ACLU).

TOM COPELAND
St. Paul, Minnesota

The Centralia Tragedy of 1919
Elmer Smith and the Wobblies

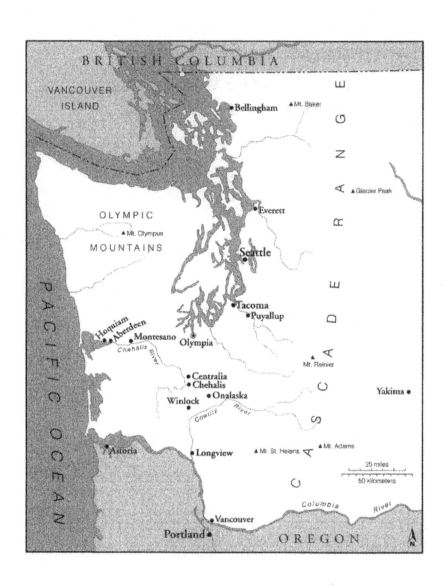

Prologue: The Determined Advocate

"God, Give Us Men!"—Josiah Gilbert Holland

God, give us men! A time like this demands
Strong minds, great hearts, true faith and ready hands;
Men whom the lust of office does not kill;
Men whom the spoils of office can not buy;
Men who possess opinions and a will;
Men who have honor; men who will not lie;
Men who can stand before a demagogue
And damn his treacherous flatteries without winking!
Tall men, sun-crowned, who live above the fog
In public duty, and in private thinking.[1]

The weather was chilly and the sky overcast when the parade line moved out at two o'clock from the city park in Centralia, Washington. It was Armistice Day, November 11, 1919, and the band played "Over There" to honor the veterans of World War I. Leading the march were members of the Elks Lodge, a patrol of Boy Scouts headed by the high school principal, and a few Marines and sailors. In the rear marched former soldiers who were members of the Centralia and Chehalis American Legion posts. The parade stretched for three blocks, with the parade marshal on horseback keeping the line under control. The marchers turned left on Tower Avenue and headed north toward the union hall of the Industrial Workers of the World. The crowd watched, most of them silent as they occasionally waved small American flags.

Elmer Smith came out of his law office on Tower Avenue to watch the parade pass a few blocks to the north. He stepped onto the street, trying to follow the parade line with his eyes as it curved with the street to the left and out of sight. After staring up the street for a moment, he turned and headed home to get his gun for the trouble that he knew was fast approaching.

Young and idealistic, the thirty-one-year-old attorney had struggled for three years to become established in his new career. Smith had already gained a reputation for aggressively representing union men and others in need against local lumber owners and businessmen. His fellow lawyers and prominent business leaders in the community did not quite know what to make of this upstart advocate who was committed to defending the underclass with a singular passion for justice. Several had advised Smith that his choice of clients was alienating him from his colleagues. In fact, Smith was not accepted by any group in town. Set apart from his colleagues, he was also set apart from those who came to him for help because of his educational background and profession.

Tensions were high in Centralia. Timber owners and town officials were violently hostile toward the IWW's attempts to improve working conditions in the forests and mines near Centralia. A weakened economy following World War I and a widely held fear that IWW radicalism threatened American values stiffened the employers' resistance to any change. When the American Legion announced that an Armistice Day parade would march past IWW headquarters, the Wobblies rightly feared that plans were being laid to drive them out of town. They remembered a Red Cross parade in 1918 that had ended in a raid on their hall, when union members had been run out of town.

Earlier in November, the secretary of the local IWW had come to Smith's office for advice. Smith had told him that the Wobblies had the right to defend their hall. Although Smith was not aware of what preparations the Wobblies had made for the coming parade, he knew that some of the union men were not afraid of a confrontation and that they were unlikely to back down in the face of violence. Smith was also stubborn enough to face danger calmly. But he had begun to worry about his own safety. He feared that if the parade turned into a raid on the IWW hall, his office would be next. When he went home that afternoon, he picked up his Colt .45 revolver, which he kept hidden in his dresser drawer. He told his wife Laura that he expected trouble and that he might be the target of attack. Frightened, Laura held their year-old baby close and tried to persuade Elmer not to go. Unable to stop him, she wept as he hurried out the front door.

A few minutes after returning to his office, Smith heard a knock on his door. A group of Boy Scouts and the high school principal told Smith that all hell had broken loose down the street. The IWW hall had been attacked, and several marchers in the parade had been shot and seriously wounded. The principal asked Smith to go with him, under his custody, to the police station. Smith went peacefully, leaving his gun in his top desk drawer.

Smith was put into jail with a dozen or more Wobblies. On the floor in the corridor lay a beaten body. Outside, a hostile mob of over a hundred people was howling for Wobbly blood. A little after five o'clock that afternoon, news began to circulate through town that three of the parade marchers had died from their wounds. Armed vigilante groups began rounding up all the Wobblies they could find. By nightfall twenty-two men had been thrown into cells built to hold less than ten. Two of Smith's brothers were among those arrested.

At seven-thirty, all the city lights in Centralia went out. A crowd marched to the jail through the night and entered without resistance. None of the prisoners spoke. The mob grabbed the bleeding man who was still on the floor and dragged him to a waiting car. The silence in the jail lasted until the noise of the cars driving away in the darkness faded.[2]

Elmer Smith was the central character in what became known as the Centralia Armistice Day tragedy, a confrontation that represents the high-water mark in the suppression of domestic labor radicalism during the World War I era. During the 1920s, the Centralia case was a national cause célèbre for labor supporters and liberals. To date, Smith has generally been perceived as a minor player in the Centralia case. In fact, he played a leading role in the Pacific Northwest labor movement during the 1920s and is one of the major figures in Washington state labor history. The Centralia case became the driving force in his career, and his work kept alive the cause of the IWW members who were imprisoned for their role in the shootings and eventually led to their freedom. Elmer Smith personified the Centralia tragedy, and we can best understand this event and the society that produced such intolerance and violence by examining his life.

Smith was a nonviolent man whose advice to the IWW helped precipitate violence. His lifelong efforts to free the imprisoned men ignited anti-radical passions wherever he went, often causing local officials to treat him without regard to his civil rights. He fervently believed in free speech and civil liberties, although his attempts to exercise those rights caused him to be arrested many times. The Bureau of Investigation of the Department of Justice considered Smith a dangerous radical and spied on him for years.

For carrying out his promise never to reject "the cause of the defenseless or oppressed" when he took his oath as an attorney, the Washington legal community rose up and disbarred him.[3]

Smith also stands out as one of the most important figures in IWW history during the 1920s. His defense work on the West Coast helped the union combat the attack on its right to organize working people. The IWW attracted notice because it offered hope for the future and a sense of self-respect and importance to its members. It gave a feeling of power to those who were poor, downtrodden, and alienated from society's institutions. Although Smith could not join the union because of his profession, he was "a determined advocate and an admirer of the men he defended."[4] He was a man of great courage who challenged the have-nots to claim their rightful share of wealth and power. A confident, charismatic spokesman, Smith provided leadership to the IWW at a time when it had few other active leaders and played a major role in turning back the tide of criminal syndicalism prosecutions against the Wobblies. He closely identified with his clients and fought for social justice during an era when the abridgement of civil liberties was commonplace. His personal life mirrored the optimism and crushing reality of IWW's fortunes in the Pacific Northwest during the turbulent decade after World War I.

Elmer Smith was also a man of many weaknesses. His rigid sense of morality caused him to have little regard for the consequences of his actions for himself or his family. He possessed only an average legal mind, and he was a poor provider for his family. He was also often naive, inflexible, judgmental, and driven by a measure of guilt for the role he played in the Centralia case. Although he was an outwardly confident and dynamic leader, Smith took on more responsibility than he could handle. He hid his personal doubts from his family, and the constant pressure of his work created tremendous stress that eventually ruined his health.

Despite these flaws, he was as admired by the working class as he was hated and feared by lumber owners and the American Legion. He displayed extraordinary fearlessness in standing up to intimidation and personal threats of violence, and he never responded in anger. "It was hard for Elmer to believe that a person could be a no-good-son-of-a-bitch," one of his friends remembered. "The weakness with Elmer is that he trusted too easy. His strength was also his weakness. He had an overwhelming faith in the goodness of his fellow man."[5]

"I'm Looking for Trouble"

"Come, Labor On"—Jane Laurie Borthwick, 1859

Come labor on. Who dares stand idle on the harvest plain
While all around him waves the golden grain?
And to each servant does the Master say, "Go work today."

Come labor on. No time for rest, 'til glows the western sky,
Till the long shadows o'er our pathway lie,
And a glad sound comes with the setting sun, "Well done, well done!"

In the fall of 1916, Elmer Smith opened his first law office on the
main street of Centralia, Washington. The town of ten thousand people
was nestled in a picturesque valley of green forests and cold rivers, watched
over by the snow-capped Cascade Mountains to the east. Centralia had
wide, tree-lined streets, comfortable residential homes, new sidewalks, and
a modern lighting system. Social life focused on several churches, the
YMCA, the Eagles and Elks Lodges, and three movie theaters. The Republican Party dominated the town's politics, and there was a growing
community pride among the residents.[1]

Centralia appeared to be an unlikely place for any labor conflict. A small but vital economic center, Centralia had the distinction of
being the fastest growing city in the state during 1900–10. The town had
grown up around the Northern Pacific Railroad division point, halfway
between Seattle and Portland. Situated at the confluence of the Chehalis
and Skookumchuck rivers, Centralia was also the hiring town for loggers
who worked in the nearby forests. The town was thriving, and the only
union activity was a small organization of trade unionists that posed no
threat to the status quo.

A sizable number of working people lived in several neighborhoods of Centralia, but the business community set the local standards. Chief among the capitalists was Franklin B. Hubbard, president of the Eastern Railway and Lumber Company. The company owned large tracts of timberland as well as sawmills, coal mines, and three railroad engines that hauled timber from the woods. Hubbard's Eastern Lumber Mill was the county's largest processing mill. He was an influential member of the local Chamber of Commerce and the Elks Lodge and bitterly opposed to union activity. Hubbard was actively involved in the anti-union Employers Association of Washington and the West Coast Lumber Manufacturers' Association, whose members owned the largest timber resources in southwestern Washington. His anti-union views were shared by the town's shopkeepers and by the businessmen who ran the Farmers and Merchants' Bank, the glove factory, and the boat company.

The timber industry was the lifeblood of Centralia, as it was for many Washington communities. The vast timber resources of the Pacific Northwest had contributed significantly to the economic development of the area during the first decade of the new century. Timber was an inexpensive, easily marketable raw material, and the demand had soared in 1906 after the San Francisco earthquake and fire. During the same period, the Northern Pacific Railroad opened up this vast natural resource to national markets. The transcontinental railroad and low-fare steamship lines brought new settlers to the Northwest. By 1910, the population of Washington had more than doubled to over a million people, with more than half living in urban areas. By 1914, lumbering ranked second only to farming in economic importance to the region.[2]

The timber industry was dominated by three corporations—the Weyerhaeuser Timber Company, the Northern Pacific Railroad Company, and the Southern Pacific Railroad Company—that owned 237 billion board feet of standing timber. Another seventeen thousand owners held 205 billion board feet.[3] The timber industry had a long tradition of a boom-and-bust existence because of ruinous competition, unstable markets, wide fluctuations in timber prices, and high transportation costs. Most timber and sawmill operators had chosen to go after quick profits and had extracted and processed timber without regard for the health of the land or the safety of their machinery. They felt little responsibility for the welfare of the workers, paid only a bare minimum in wages, and offered only temporary living quarters.

Elmer Smith's family, like many new settlers in Washington, had been lured west by the promise of steady work. In the summer of 1910, Tom and Isabelle Smith had moved from their North Dakota farm to Cumberland, Washington, a little mining town a few miles east of Seattle. Tom Smith, who had previously traveled west while working for the St. Paul, Minneapolis & Manitoba Railroad lines, found work repairing machines for a small mining company. The family moved into a logging camp bunkhouse that had been abandoned after crews had sawed through the valley and moved on. A mining company purchased the hilly, stump-littered land and operated a coal mine there. About a dozen other families who worked in the mine lived in shacks and tent houses in the small settlement.[4]

By the time Tom and Isabelle Smith settled in Washington they had traveled thousands of miles. A native of Ireland, Tom had immigrated to Toronto, Canada, in 1883 when he was nineteen. After four years of farming, he married seventeen-year-old Isabelle Smythe and they moved to a small homestead near Larimore, North Dakota. Tom was a tough-looking, strict, unrefined laborer with a crossed left eye and a short temper. He had a strong jaw and a tight lip, out of which he yelled at friend and stranger alike. A man of little compassion, Tom Smith was biased and self-centered. He would rather spend time with machinery and the soil than with other people, and he regularly complained about his own problems. He never had much success, but he worked hard and cared deeply for Isabelle.[5]

Isabelle Smythe was a hearty, outgoing, well-educated woman with strong forearms and beautiful long, light-red hair. Family members tell how Isabelle's mother was descended from the Stuarts of Scotland and describe how Isabelle's maternal grandparents fled to Scotland from England to avoid religious persecution. But Isabelle had no respect for her royal heritage and referred to her relatives as "those bloody Stuarts." When friends asked about her family history, Isabelle would dismiss the subject, saying, "We don't blow about that."[6] Isabelle's parents were disappointed when she married Tom. They considered it a setback for their daughter to marry an uneducated laborer, a common Smith. But Isabelle cared little about such things, and with her marriage and move to America she effectively severed all ties with her family.

Starting up a wheat farm on the flat, bleak landscape of eastern North Dakota proved discouraging for Isabelle and Tom. The winters were bitterly cold and the summer heat often oppressive. Drought, grasshoppers, and unfavorable market prices brought season after season of hard times. Between 1890 and 1900, North Dakota farmers enjoyed only four good crop years.[7] Many simply gave up and left. But more than the elements challenged the North Dakota wheat farmers. They were also highly dependent for their livelihood on the railroads and grain millers in Minneapolis and St. Paul. In the early 1880s, farmers began to organize to protect themselves from the monopolistic practices of the grain merchants, the extortionate interest rates of moneylenders, and the high freight rates and ruthless tactics of the railroad companies.[8]

Tom and Isabelle Smith were typical of the many North Dakotans who organized with other farmers to protect their rights. They were a stubborn, independent people, capable of enduring hardship and suffering. To supplement the meager income from their wheat crop, Tom took a job as a mechanic on the railroad while Isabelle managed the homestead and struggled with the task of raising their children. They both believed strongly in the democratic values that held out the promise of equal opportunity and success to everyone who worked hard and treated their neighbors fairly. They taught these basic values to their children.

Elmer Stuart Smith was born on the Larimore farm on January 22, 1888. An unusually severe blizzard earlier that month had killed scores of people across the state; and for several anxious days before the birth, the Smiths prayed that the doctor would be able to reach them through the deep snow. The doctor who did arrive was clumsy and inexperienced, however, and Isabelle suffered a painful birth.[9] Five other sons and a daughter were born, four in the first five years of the marriage (one brother later died). Until Elmer was old enough to help, Isabelle handled the domestic jobs alone. Tom was busy with his work and did not take pleasure in spending time with the children. After Isabelle's fourth child, she attended a lecture in nearby Lisbon about birth control. Birth control was not an accepted topic of conversation, and Isabelle received some criticism from her neighbors for going to the meeting, but she ignored them and also attended lectures on other progressive subjects.

Isabelle Smith was the driving force in the family. Her greatest pleasure was having her children close around her. Sitting around the fire in the evening, she read aloud to Elmer from the classics. When he grew older, Elmer did the reading, while she knit clothes for the younger children. There was a close bond of pride and loyalty between Isabelle and her first-born son. Elmer inherited more from her than his red hair and quick temper; she taught him to be self-reliant and not to count on help from anyone outside the family. She encouraged him in every way to develop his abilities, and he adored her.

Elmer loved the outdoors, and he spent many hours by himself hunting, fishing, and swimming. The great distances between neighboring farms gave Elmer little contact with other children, and he looked to his family for nearly all of his companionship and support. He rarely complained to his mother and learned to keep his feelings hidden. His mother encouraged this self-denial by teaching him to be more concerned about helping others than about expressing his own needs. By the time he was twelve, Elmer was responsible for looking after the six other youngsters.[10]

Elmer may have taken his responsibility too seriously. According to one family story, during a heavy spring blizzard in 1900 Isabelle told twelve-year-old Elmer to stay with the children while she went to the barn to check on the animals. When she was gone longer than Elmer had anticipated, he began to worry. He looked out the windows, but the blowing snow blotted out everything. Impatient, he took up a long rope, tied his five brothers and his sister together in a line, and led them outside toward the barn. Halfway there, he found his mother coming back toward the house. When they all returned indoors, Isabelle asked Elmer, "Why did you bring all the children outside with you?" He replied, "Well, you told me not to leave them."[11] Elmer was an aggressive actor in a time of crisis, and he had a fearless confidence in his ability to care for himself and others. His actions showed a willingness to risk his own safety and the safety of others and displayed a lack of common sense and judgment.

Family life in the Smith home embraced a large measure of religious instruction. Every Sunday, Isabelle took her family to a small Presbyterian church of some forty members, but she also made it clear to her children that it was even more important to read the Bible in their own home. They did not need ministers to understand God and his commandments. As a forceful but open-minded teacher, Isabelle taught Elmer well. He was a diligent pupil who learned a sense of duty to his family and a personal code of moral principles. For a while, Elmer even thought seriously about becoming a minister.

After a family tragedy in 1900, however, the world began to seem more arbitrary and uncertain to Elmer than the one he read about in his Bible. One day, Elmer's eleven-year-old brother Walter went to visit his cousin Alfred in a nearby field. Alfred was plowing with a horse, and he carried a gun to chase away crows. Walter had been with his cousin only a few minutes when Alfred stopped to rest, putting the gun against the plow. Suddenly, something caused the horse to bolt, the gun was jostled, and it fired. The blast hit Walter in the head, killing him instantly. From that day on, Elmer gave up hunting and said he would never carry a gun again.[12] He was also unable to reconcile a firm belief in God's love and his brother's death.

By the time Smith entered Lisbon's high school he was bored with the life of farming and was ready for a change. Studying did not come easily to him, but he was a conscientious, if restless, student. The physical activity

of football excited him more than his school books. He had a reputation
for high-spirited fun, as evidenced by the inscription on the folder cover of
his graduation picture, which read: "I'm Looking for Trouble."[13]

Smith wrote several romantic short stories while in high school.
In "Disguised Innocence," he clearly modeled the story's hero, Mr. Cole,
after himself. In the story, the hero falls in love with a woman named Grace
whom he meets while rowing on a lake. When Grace and her father fall into
the hands of an unscrupulous lawyer, Cole knocks the villain down, turns
him over to the police, and wins Grace's love. The story ends:

> There is happiness in the heart of anyone who does a brave deed
> but that happiness is small in comparison with the happiness
> that comes to a noble young man who has saved the idol of
> his heart from being hurt or dragged into misery. Not only had
> Mr. Cole saved his sweetheart's life, but he had helped to see
> that justice was administered to a feeble old man. It was right
> there, in the humble cottage on the lake shore, that Mr. Cole
> found out where the real pleasure of life came from, namely,
> from helping others.

One attorney in Smith's story is described as "a man of great ability
and had the reputation of being the most honest lawyer in N.Y. Unlike any
of his competitors, he spent his time working for the good of others and
not wholly for the almighty dollar." To Smith, lawyers are supposed to be
altruistic and bring evil men to justice without resorting to violence.[14]

There is much to speculate about Smith from this melodramatic
story. The hero, a fearless actor who is responsible for saving others, is
driven by an overpowering urge to do justice. He triumphs through his
physical strength, without the aid of any weapon. He is a man of action who
is not self-conscious or self-analytical. When the villain has been caught,
he asks Cole: "Under what authority do you do this?" The hero replies,
"Under the authority of justice and God." Smith clearly had a highly moralistic outlook on life and a strong belief that the law will ultimately make
things right in the world. The hero in the story experiences powerful emotions of love and anger, but outwardly he is polite and reserved. Other
characters express fear, sorrow, desire, anger, and joy, but not the hero. The
author appears to be a shy romantic, fighting against evil but also against
his own feelings and needs, which he has not yet learned to handle.

From the story, we can guess that Smith held an idealistic, chival-
rous view of women. Grace is the personification of innocence and good-

ness, and she is fiercely loyal to her father. The hero falls deeply in love with her when he first sees her hair and eyes. When the hero suspects that Grace is in trouble, he reflects: "So deep was his love for her that he never once thought of saving her for himself, but for justice sake and to make her happy. To take away from her all fear and sorrow." Beyond her beauty and helplessness, the hero sees little in Grace, and there is nothing realistic in their relationship. Although the two are planning their marriage at the end of the story, there seems to be little understanding between the two of what the other person is like or what they want in a relationship. This story portends in some ways Smith's own courtship and married life.

With the blessings of his high school teacher and his mother, Smith set his sights on college, having decided to make a living with his brains and not his hands. It was an ambitious goal, for no one in the family had ever gone to college. His father thought college was a foolish pastime for a farm boy, and he needed Elmer's labor on the farm. But Isabelle insisted that Elmer be given the opportunity, and she selected Macalester College in St. Paul, Minnesota, because of its strong Presbyterian orientation.

When Smith left North Dakota he stood nearly six feet tall and weighed close to 170 pounds. He had strong, calloused hands; a large face with coarse features; thick, red-brown hair combed to one side; and a determined set of jaw. The rugged look of his broad-shouldered body was softened by a generous mouth and a pair of large, expressive brown eyes that gave to those he met his undivided attention. His direct, but sympathetic gaze quickly put people at ease. He was judgmental and highly moralistic and was inclined to tackle problems head-on, without much flexibility of thought or action. An honest man, Smith had a positive outlook on life and did not abide pretense or deception. Taught to think independently by his mother, he also maintained a deep sense of loyalty to her and his family. When Smith went off to college in 1906, he left few friends behind.

Founded by Presbyterians in 1885 to educate aspiring ministers, teachers, and social workers, Macalester College was located three miles from downtown St. Paul. The grounds were laid out in a large rectangle, with the school's few buildings anchoring its corners and edges. Farmland surrounded the campus, and cattle grazed on the mall during the summer. The one imposing building, Old Main, housed a dormitory, most of the classrooms, and the chapel. Nearly every student at Macalester had to work his or her way through school. Although railroad magnate James J. Hill, lumber king Frederick Weyerhaeuser, and steel tycoon Andrew Carnegie contributed substantially to the college, Macalester still struggled to meet its expenses and keep its doors open.[15] Smith's parents had only given him enough money to get through the first semester. He worked as a gaslighter, lighting the street lamps up and down St. Paul's fashionable Summit Avenue each evening after dinner and returning to shut the lamps off in the morning before classes. He also shoveled snow, delivered papers, and carried groceries. Each summer, Smith went home to help with the wheat harvest and farm chores.[16]

As a student, Smith was "very dogged and persevering and thorough"—"just a plugger," his friends said. As a member of the men's Athenaen debating society, he attended the Friday night sessions where students gathered to discuss current social problems, from the Russo-Japanese war to Darwinian theory to Free Silver. Each week, the Athenaens took turns giving each other frank criticism. For variety, they staged a comedy or musical program or debated silly topics.[17] Smith's fellow Athenaens nicknamed him "Red" for his hair. When he was a senior, he was elected president of the society.

Smith may have excelled as a debater partly because he was not afraid of what others thought of him or his ideas. Stubborn and quick-thinking, he held down his side of an argument with a "bulldog grip." He was "a good faithful member, a good workhorse and a good clear thinker, and was not afraid of championing rather unpopular issues."[18] He made no personal enemies, even among those who did not share his more liberal views. Smith was a friendly, likable student who viewed the world as a place where differing ideas could be rationally debated among those who respected each other. He was optimistic that he could always change his opponents' views. In his sophomore year, Smith won a debate supporting the liberal position that Minnesota's primary election laws should allow a voter to vote a non–straight party ticket.[19] His short, forceful sentences and deep, clear voice won him a number of prizes at the state oratorical contests. The thrill of competition excited him and gave him confidence.

Despite his debating skills, Smith was personally very shy, although he won the part of a trusted attorney in the senior class play.[20] He talked little about himself, and his roommates never got to know him well. "He wasn't a backslapper type," one roommate remembered. "He was pretty serious." "I always liked Elmer but he was kind of an idealistic sort of a chap," another classmate said. None of his classmates could remember him ever going out on a date.[21] Smith's other preoccupation was sports. His favorite game was football, and he played one of the front line positions on defense. He pushed himself as hard as he could, not minding that his team lost most of their games, for he played primarily for the joy of physical activity. He also served as captain of the basketball team and spent many winter evenings ice skating behind Old Main.[22]

As the end of his college days approached, Smith gave more serious attention to making some practical decisions about his future. Most of his classmates planned careers as ministers, social workers, or teachers, but Smith was more intrigued by the study of law. As a lawyer, Smith would have the opportunity to use his skills as a debater, be in a position to help those in need, and achieve personal recognition. In the spring of his senior year, he applied to and was accepted at the St. Paul College of Law.

On June 8, 1910, Smith and twenty-six classmates attended Macalester's graduation ceremonies at the Central Presbyterian Church in downtown St. Paul. It was the twenty-fifth anniversary of the opening of the college, and the occasion was celebrated with a commencement speech by Booker T. Washington, president of the Tuskegee Institute. In his speech, entitled "From Servitude to Service," Washington told the students: "It is also true of the college as it is of the individual, that during the period of poverty and struggle it gets an experience and confidence that it would not get without hampered conditions." He concluded by calling on the graduating seniors to fight for everyone to be free, "because without the freedom of the lowest individual in the community, there cannot exist the highest degree of happiness in any part of the nation."[23] Those same altruistic ideals were beginning to shape Smith's life.

In 1910, the St. Paul College of Law described itself as "a lawyers' law school," because the faculty was composed entirely of practicing lawyers and judges. The college held classes in the evening on the second floor of a brick house in downtown St. Paul. Smith paid sixty dollars a year for tuition and twenty-five dollars for textbooks.[24] There was little social life outside the classroom, as most students held jobs during the day and went their own way after classes. Smith found a job teaching at South St. Paul High School, earning ninety-five dollars a month. During the summers, he worked as a clerk for the Northern Pacific Railroad.[25]

Smith often gathered with other students half an hour before classes to discuss cases and points of law. It was his favorite time to engage in friendly arguments and test his ability to defend his opinions. His classmates thought that he held his own and found that he would not back away from any argument. Despite having the reputation as a "liberal," Smith was known as a "gentleman."[26] Seemingly confident of his opinions, Smith advanced his reputation as an outspoken orator. Smith's professors generally used the Socratic method of teaching. They grilled each student with sharp, probing questions, forcing them to justify their opinions. Smith liked the method and thought it was a stimulating way to explore new ideas and weed out faulty thinking. He joined the school's debating society, The Judge Harlan Club, and was elected president in his second year.[27] In June 1913, Smith passed his final exams and was automatically admitted to the Minnesota Bar. On graduation night, he had less than ten dollars in his pocket.

Despite the apparently good prospects for getting a job in St. Paul, Smith quit his teaching post within weeks of his graduation and moved to Washington, probably at his mother's urging. He quickly lost all contact with his friends in St. Paul, and for the rest of his life he never lived more than a few miles away from his parents.

When Smith moved into the family's house in Cumberland, his father and eighteen-year-old brother, Glen, were working for the Rose Marshall Mining Company. Smith's sister, Dorothy, who was fifteen, and his youngest brother, Willard, eleven, stayed at home with Isabelle. His two other brothers, Harry, twenty-two, and Jim, twenty-one, had taken up adjoining 160-acre timber claims near Mendota, a small settlement sixty miles south of Cumberland. To acquire timber rights to the land, the brothers had to clear several acres for crops, build a house, and live on the land for three years. After only two months, Harry told Isabelle that it was too lonely for him to be away from his fiancée who lived in a nearby town and he was not going to prove up his claim.[28] At Isabelle's encouragement, Elmer took over Harry's homestead and moved to Mendota. He and Jim built their twelve-foot-square cabins, from the felling of the trees to the shaking of the hundreds of individual shingles for the roof. Both men had boundless energy for the hardy, practical work that homesteading required.[29]

Tom lost his job in the mine during the winter of 1913, and he moved the family to Mendota to be closer to Elmer and Jim. Jim, Tom, and Glen went to work for the Mendota Coal Mine Company. Even-tempered and enterprising, Jim was the brother most like Elmer. While Elmer was away at college, Jim assumed much of the responsibility for helping out at home, washing clothes and baking bread when Isabelle was sick. Elmer admired Jim's steadiness, and the brothers counted on each other for counsel and support. When Jim sold his timber rights to a lumber company, he discovered a deposit of coal under his land. Quitting his job at the mine company, he started a small-scale mining operation with the help of his father and his brothers Glen and Harry. The Smith men were a hardworking, boisterous, but mostly inefficient crew. Jim never made much money from his mine, since he reinvested most of the earnings either in machinery that kept breaking down or wages for the extra workers he hired. According to one worker, Jim paid every man the going union rate, which was higher than most employers offered. If he could not pay them fairly, he said, then it was not worth trying to keep the mine open. All of the Smith family carried the conviction that working people deserved a decent wage, even if it meant that the owners did not make much more than their laborers.[30]

Unlike Jim, Elmer had no plans to settle on his homestead, and just when he learned that there was coal under his land he showed no interest in developing it. Instead, he spent his free time studying for the state bar examination. In the fall of 1913, to make ends meet, he took a job as a teacher at the tiny country school in Kopiah, a short hike over the hill behind his land. Tom and Isabelle Smith sent their youngest son, Willard, to live with Elmer and attend his class. The seventh child, born four years after his sister Dorothy, Willard had been a surprise to his thirty-five-year-old mother, who had been practicing birth control. He was a listless fellow, who, when left to his own devices, became a discipline problem. Elmer took a stern tone with the boy and did not hesitate to rebuke him in class. Although Willard initially resented this punishment, he soon developed an interest in school and lost his chip-on-the-shoulder attitude.[31]

Huddling with his small group of students at the school's wood stove to shake off the early morning cold, Smith observed their threadbare clothes and calloused hands. When he visited the children's homes, he listened with sympathy as the parents described how scratching out a decent living on the land required almost as much good fortune as it did hard work. Many men took jobs in the sawmills to support their families, but work in the mills was back-breaking and low-paying. All too frequently lumber companies took advantage of inexperienced settlers and persuaded them to sell their timber for much less than it was worth. It was rumored that outright theft of timber was common.[32] In the bitterly cold winter of 1913, several of the families ran out of food. Smith walked into Centralia, seven miles away, to buy groceries for them, and he soon became known as an "honest man" and "a crusader for the underprivileged."[33]

In January 1914, Smith passed the bar exam and was licensed to practice law in Washington. That spring, he quit his teaching job in Kopiah, but he was not yet ready to begin his law practice—it would be two more years before he would be finished homesteading his land. During that time he worked on a logging crew, slashing out right-of-ways for logging roads. He also worked for a time at Jim's mine and, with the rest of the Smith men, joined the United Mine Workers, Mendota Local.[34] In the fall of 1916, he moved into Centralia and opened a law office on Tower Avenue, the town's principal street.

Timber Beasts and Soldiers

"Fifty Thousand Lumberjacks"—*IWW Songbook*, 1917

Fifty thousand lumberjacks, fifty thousand packs,
Fifty thousand dirty rolls of blankets on their backs.
Fifty thousand minds made up to strike and strike like men;
For fifty years they've packed a bed, but never will again.

"Such a lot of devils,"—that's what the papers say—
They've gone on strike for shorter hours and some increase
    in pay.
They left the camps, the lazy tramps, they all walked out
    as one;
They say they'll win the strike or put the bosses on the bum.

When Smith launched his law career in 1916, he was a stranger in Centralia. Seeking to meet people, he joined the First Presbyterian Church, but his appearance did little to impress. He was mostly indifferent about the clothes he wore: narrow ties, suspenders and a belt, scuffed shoes and white shirttails that refused to stay tucked in. His one or two dark suits looked rumpled and worn, as if he slept in them. His office was equally unimpressive. It contained the barest of furnishings: a desk, two chairs, one lamp, a wood stove, a typewriter, and a wooden wall shelf that held fewer than a dozen lawbooks. On the wall above his desk he hung a framed copy of his favorite poem, "God, Give Us Men!" His sister Dorothy came to work in his office on occasion to help him with typing.[1]

Smith was optimistic about his new career. In a letter to his brother Harry, he joked:

I do not intend to step immediately out into the limelight of publicity or mount the pinacle [*sic*] of fame or in fact do anything rash like that. You see the other members of the profession might all die of heart failure and I would have all the work to do alone.[2]

Nevertheless, Smith was nervous about starting out. An inexperienced lawyer did not find clients easily, so he handled several cases as a court-appointed attorney defending people who did not have enough money to hire a lawyer themselves.[3]

The few clients that Smith attracted were working-class people who either could not afford the more established lawyers in town or could not interest them in taking their cases. Smith's fees were low, and he was willing to defend wage-earners in cases against their employers. His first cases were damage suits and wage claims, and he collected hundreds of dollars in back pay for men and women who had been defrauded by their employers. In one case, a working man and his wife and child had fallen ill, and after several months the stricken family was heavily in debt to the doctor, the landlord, and a merchant. The Pacific Mercantile, a collection agency, was harassing the family to pay its bills. The desperate man turned to Smith and asked if the law did not provide him protection. Smith pointed out the option of bankruptcy, saying, "The bankruptcy law was invented by business men to save them in just such troubles. I don't see why it shouldn't be used for a workingman." With Smith's help, the worker successfully declared bankruptcy.[4]

Smith possessed only average legal skills, and he lacked the disciplined patience and sharp mind necessary to follow a legal argument through the complexities of the law. He was not interested in the fine points of legal reasoning, but in how the law affected people. Smith believed that the law should be used as a tool on behalf of common citizens. He chose to practice exclusively as a defense attorney, representing ordinary citizens against the sometimes strict consequences of the law. An emotional lawyer, Smith used his heart as much as his legal training in defending his clients. Unlike most other attorneys who cultivated a certain distance from their clients, Smith got personally involved in his cases. He showed uncommon respect for his clients, and they had high regard for this quality in him.

During his first year in practice, Smith had met a number of loggers while living in Mendota and he identified with the demanding physical labor and the poverty that the men endured. He still spent most of his time in the company of laboring men, frequenting the pool halls and cheap cafes of Centralia where he introduced himself and cultivated potential clients. He heard the news from nearby lumber camps and listened to the loggers talk about how working conditions should be improved. Working conditions *were* notoriously bad, with a six-day work week that lasted from daybreak until dark. The work was rough and dangerous. Men with giant handsaws and axes brought down Douglas fir, Sitka spruce, and Port Orford cedar that soared sometimes over two hundred feet tall. Then workers tied the trees with cables and dragged them by steam-powered machines, or "donkeys," to rail cars.

The work went on unceasingly. The men shouted over the noise of the falling trees and the pounding donkeys to warn each other or to call for help. The hazards of the rolling logs and unpredictable machines frequently exposed loggers to personal danger. A leading cause of death for loggers and sawmill workers was accidents on the job. Falling tree limbs were called "widow makers." At the end of the workday loggers returned to their miserable camps, where they slept in overcrowded, unventilated, lice-infested bunkhouses. With the rainy season lasting six months of the year and with no proper washing or drying facilities, clothes were impossible to keep clean. Camp food was sometimes good but often very poor, consisting mainly of potatoes, stringy meat, coffee, and mouldy bread. Most loggers were single, homeless, and young, and many were less than twenty-one years old. They traveled to wherever there were trees to be cut, carrying their rolled-up blankets, or "bindles," with them from job to job. Because hobos and workers were called "stiffs," lumber workers became known as "bindlestiffs."[5]

Loggers made up an outcast class in the Northwest. To many in the more "civilized" sections of Centralia, loggers were known as "timber beasts," and mill and camp owners often held a scornful attitude toward them. During the winter months, when work in the logging camps slackened, men without jobs drifted into town. Some found work with the railroad or in one of the local sawmills, but many hung around the cafes, saloons, and whorehouses waiting for the next job. If their money ran out before then, they usually took the next train out of town. The downtown civic leaders were always glad to see the loggers with their corked boots leave.

To combat the adversity that surrounded them and to improve working conditions in the woods, loggers and some sawmill workers joined the radical Industrial Workers of the World. As one logger explained:

> We want a break in the monotony of camp life. . . . We want
> amusement, comfort, leisure. We also want a clean and healthy
> environment composed of both sexes, we want a home, family,

children. . . . The I.W.W. seems to me . . . the only group offering me any sensible program under which I could operate with
a view to gaining these good things in life, and such changes in
society as I desired.[6]

Founded in Chicago in 1905, the IWW gained influence far beyond its
small numbers. "The working class and the employing class have nothing
in common," its preamble declared.

> There can be no peace so long as hunger and want are found
> among millions of working people and the few, who make up
> the employing class, have all the good things of life. Between
> these two classes a struggle must go on until the workers of the
> world organize as a class, take possession of the earth and the
> machinery of production, and abolish the wage system.[7]

Unlike the much larger and more conservative American Federation of Labor, which showed little interest in organizing any but the more
skilled class of workers into craft unions, the IWW organized industrially
into the "One Big Union." Under craft unionism, one factory could have
dozens of separate unions that displayed little or no solidarity with each
other. The IWW, or Wobblies, sought to unionize the unorganized sections of the working class—women, blacks, and immigrants and miners,
loggers, migrants, and textile workers. The bindlestiffs played an important role in setting the union's combative philosophy, setting the tone of
the organization during its formative years: "An injury to one is an injury
to all." Labor-management contracts, the IWW believed, interfered with
the exercise of labor's primary weapon, the strike. The workers wanted
nothing less than the overthrow of capitalism:

> The aim of the I.W.W. is industrial democracy, which means
> that those who run industry shall control industry and that every
> worker shall have a voice in its management. Control of industry
> by the workers means a social revolution—a complete turning
> over of the social system. With control of industry in the hands
> of the workers production will be carried on for use and not for
> profit.[8]

Any person who earned a wage could join the IWW regardless of
race, sex, religion, or job skill. Initiation fees and dues were low, and members could easily transfer from one local to another. The real power of the

organization was vested in the membership from the bottom up. More of a social movement than a labor union, the IWW offered workers hope for a better life, not just a better job. The Wobblies' optimistic spirit was reflected in their fearless rhetoric, irreverently funny songs, and bold claims that a new world was possible. Free thinkers, artists, songwriters, and poets filled IWW publications with commentary, cartoons, and opinions on a broad range of social issues. The IWW had a spirit and a take-on-all-comers attitude that sought to make the world a better place. Opponents of the union recognized the movement as a more serious threat to the social order for its ideas and spirit than for the number of its dues-paying members.

The IWW built its reputation as a powerful, radical union by helping to organize huge strikes in the textile and other industries on the East Coast. But these swift gains were often just as swiftly lost, as the union failed to consolidate its advantage and give continuing support to a core of union members. It could not resolve the contradiction between its role as a labor union that sought benefits for its members and its role as a revolutionary organization trying to change society. By 1913, the IWW was in decline in the East; the new frontier was in the fields, mines, and lumber camps of the West.

Between 1907 and 1912, when economic growth was declining and unemployment was rising, the IWW spread its name throughout Washington by spearheading strikes in sawmills and logging camps in Portland and Grays Harbor County and by fighting major battles over free speech in Spokane and Aberdeen. In almost every confrontation, local authorities used firehoses, raids on meeting halls, or mass arrests to beat back the union's efforts to organize.[9] The IWW was active in the logging camps near Centralia, where the number of ethnic groups and strong opposition from owners made organizing difficult. The union also had to contend with the stump ranchers, migrants to the area who logged only long enough to earn enough money to grubstake a farm and who showed little interest in improving working conditions in the woods. Membership in the IWW locals was always small, but the dedicated young men who did join dared to take leadership roles and attracted attention both inside and outside the ranks of labor.

The IWW was involved in only two encounters in Centralia before Smith moved into town, and he probably heard about them from his working-class friends soon after he opened his law office. The first occurred in 1914 when a Wobbly tried to organize the electrical workers in Centralia. The sheriff cut his stay short by throwing him out of town.[10] The second happened on a winter day in early 1915, during a strike at the

Eastern Railway and Lumber Company, when a group of hungry workers came to Centralia to demand bread from a bakery and apples from a grocery store (migratory workers typically asked for handouts as they moved from one job to another). Many of these "undesirables," as the *Centralia Chronicle* called them, were members of the IWW, and they hoped to bring food to their unemployed friends who were waiting outside town. After the merchants turned them down, the workers marched to the police station and told the chief that they would not leave town until they had been fed. The chief called for help and swore in one hundred citizens, including shopkeepers and a few attorneys, as special officers. Armed with pickaxe handles, the officers rounded up the Wobblies and their fifty friends and escorted them on foot to the neighboring town of Chehalis. Few in Chehalis welcomed the Wobblies, and even the local Trades and Labor Council denounced their appearance. After receiving food from a few sympathetic store owners, the Wobblies left on the next freight train.[11] For years, members of the "pick handle brigade" boasted of their success in ridding the town of labor agitators, and the *Centralia Daily Hub* warned: "Centralia has no need for or use for IWWism and our advice to those of the fraternity who intend coming here is that they don't. Centralia won't stand for IWWism."[12]

The union had been active in other ways as well. In the fall of 1916, the IWW staged a free-speech fight in Everett, a hundred miles north of Centralia. Shortly after a strike by the shingle weavers was defeated, the IWW stepped in to organize a membership drive. Violence quickly broke out when city officials and mill owners attacked participants at IWW street meetings and brutally beat the Wobblies with guns and clubs. When Everett police and a crowd of vigilantes fired on a group of Wobblies who were trying to enter the town by boat, at least five Wobblies and two vigilantes were killed. The jury acquitted the first Wobbly tried for the murder of the vigilantes, and the other seventy-three unionists who had been arrested were released. It was a notable victory for the IWW. Centralians followed news of the Everett case with particular interest. The locally based National Guard, Company M, 161st Infantry, which had just returned from patroling the Mexican border, was sent to Everett after the shootings to help preserve order.[13]

Smith was impressed by the fighting spirit and courage the Wobblies demonstrated in Everett. As a former union member, his sympathies were strongly on the side of the union men, and he began using his legal talents on their behalf. One day, several men came to his office to tell him about the severe injuries loggers suffered in the camps. They complained that the company would not pay on the insurance for injured men and that their families were in desperate financial straits. Smith took up the claims and won some judgments of liability against the company. When he went to the lumber camps to gather evidence, many loggers were at first hesitant to talk to him, fearing they might lose their jobs. They had never seen a lawyer in the woods before. But Smith's friendly manner and sincere concern for the loggers' plight soon earned him their trust.[14]

One day, Smith happened on the scene of an accident. A logger was lying on the ground with his leg crushed against a fallen tree. Smith tried to comfort the worker until medical help arrived. Fighting back his own tears, Smith went to the hospital with the logger and saw to it that the company paid his bill. After leaving the hospital, Smith visited the man's family and personally paid a few pressing bills. The young lawyer involved himself in many such cases. At a logging camp north of Centralia, near Olympia, a man's hips had been crushed between two logs. He lay in the hospital for sixty days while the company refused to pay on his insurance claim. Because the logger had no money, the hospital was about to evict him until Smith stepped in and successfully sued the company for the medical expenses. Smith never made much money from such cases. Often the men were unable to pay him because the insurance claims covered no more than the amount of their hospital bills. But Smith was gaining friends among the loggers and building his own confidence as a lawyer.

Smith's position in Centralia was a unique one. Because the social lines were tightly drawn, his choice of clients alienated him from many of Centralia's attorneys, while his education and vocation set him apart from the people he was helping. As a result, he was not completely accepted by either group. The town's attorneys attempted to persuade Smith to identify more closely with the interests of the businessmen and the more prominent citizens, pointing out that those who threatened the established order had always been made to feel unwelcome.[15]

Soon after Smith moved to Centralia he had a serious run-in with Franklin Hubbard, president of the Eastern Railway and Lumber Company and Centralia's most prominent citizen. Hubbard offered to buy the timber on Smith's land, but Smith told him he would not sell the timber for such a low price. According to several accounts, however, much more was behind Smith's decision. While Harry Smith was homesteading the land, Hubbard's company had illegally cut down several acres of trees on the land. Elmer Smith had patiently waited until he opened his law practice and his timber rights were secure before he sued Eastern Railway. But establishing proof was difficult, and Smith couldn't match the resources available to Hubbard's lawyers. He lost the case but, typically undaunted, he still stubbornly refused to sell his timber. Smith had quickly earned the enmity of the town's most powerful man.[16]

Although Smith was not afraid to champion the rights of ordinary people, he also sought out other attorneys for company and advice. Soon after opening his office, Smith met Warren Grimm. At twenty-seven, Grimm was a year younger than Smith, although his heavy cheeks and high forehead made him look several years older. Grimm was from a prominent, well-respected Centralia family, and his older brother was the city attorney. He had been a star football player while at the University of Washington, and he moved in Centralia's prominent social and business circles. Smith and Grimm regularly visited each other's offices to socialize and to talk about football and the law. They also enjoyed spirited political discussions in which Grimm identified closely with the interests of the powerful while Smith sided with the migrant loggers and the working poor. Their lives, which moved in opposite social and political directions, were to become inexorably linked by the conflict between the social classes they represented.[17]

Although Smith and Grimm disagreed over many things, they shared a common interest in getting married. After the death of his young wife, Grimm had become a popular figure at local dances, with his new open-topped Ford automobile. Smith, who was trying to conquer his own shyness, admired Grimm's easygoing manner with women. Smith had decided that it was time to think about starting his own family, and he moved in with his parents to save money. When his brother Harry married in 1914, Smith wrote the new bride: "I am certainly all joy over my brother's good fortune in getting a girl like you and I shall always be proud of my new sister. The biggest thing in this world, to my way of thinking is a real home. P.S. Shall send my wedding present later when I get some money."[18] Paying clients were still rare.

In the spring of 1917, Smith fell in love with Laura Magill, a new schoolteacher in town and the eldest daughter of a judge from Tacoma. Judge Magill had reared his children in a strict authoritarian manner, common in the days when girls were not expected to make major decisions or to take an active role in worldly affairs. Not until she was twenty-three was Laura allowed to leave home. A family friend in Centralia notified Judge Magill that a teaching job was available and at the same time offered to keep a parental eye on Laura. She moved into a respectable boardinghouse and began teaching third grade at Lincoln School. Laura later remembered: "No young woman should have 'left the nest' as unprepared as I was to face the world."[19]

Smith first noticed Laura singing in the choir at the First Presbyterian Church, where he led the youth group for high school boys. He admired her dark, thick hair, high cheekbones, and lovely voice. Smith's sister, Dorothy, who also sang in the choir, decided to assume the role of matchmaker. Laura had been dating a man from the local National Guard unit who had returned to Centralia following a skirmish along the Mexican border. When his unit was called into service again, the two agreed that the uncertainties of war made it unfair for Laura to await his return. When Dorothy learned of this, she told Laura that her brother very much wanted to meet her. Laura declined, saying she was not interested. Smith's mother strongly encouraged him to court Laura, and she let Elmer know that a marriage to Laura would be a promising match.[20]

Smith made his own introduction one spring morning while Laura was walking home from church with a friend. He was a determined suitor, and he urged Laura to marry him before summer vacation began. But Laura, who was five years younger than Smith, was not ready to consider marriage and refused his proposals several times. When the pressure became too great, she finally told him to talk to her father. Judge Magill opposed the match, both because he didn't think Smith had any good prospects as a struggling young lawyer and because he wanted Laura to get her permanent teaching certificate—still a year off. He told Smith to wait. But Laura was drawn to her confident, physically attractive suitor and, despite her father's advice, she finally agreed to become engaged. She later confided to one of Smith's sisters-in-law: "He was so persistent, I married him to get rid of the pestering." But Laura may have been protesting too much. She was attracted to Elmer probably as much as she was interested in getting away from her father's influence.[21]

On April 6, 1917, the United States entered World War I. Opposition to the nation's entry into the war was strongest in the West and Midwest, where there were many immigrants and a tradition of isolationism. A patriotic upheaval soon overwhelmed this opposition, and thousands displayed the flag, bought war bonds, and pledged themselves to "100% Americanism." The public pressed for conformity in support of the war effort, and domestic criticism and unrest were treated harshly. Immigrants were distrusted, and the Department of Justice worked closely with patriotic groups, principally the American Protective League, to ferret out spies, slackers, and saboteurs. The war unleashed hostile, anti-labor, anti-radical passions.

Elmer Smith strongly opposed the United States' involvement in the war, as did his mother, who sympathized with those men who were sent to jail because they refused to serve. Isabelle Smith openly criticized her minister at the Presbyterian church, saying that he was turning the church into a recruiting office with his weekly sermons on patriotism.[22] Smith was repelled by the violence on the battlefields, and he read works by pacifist Mohandas Gandhi and advocated nonviolence as the best way to resolve conflict. In conversations with clients and fellow lawyers, he said that the working class suffered most from the war while the bosses and war profiteers reaped great benefits.

It was shocking to hear these views expressed by a lawyer in a town like Centralia. Smith's fellow attorneys grew increasingly uncomfortable and began seeing less and less of him. Warren Grimm continued to talk with him whenever their paths crossed, but their discussions about the war put a great strain on their friendship. Grimm eagerly followed news of the war and voluntarily enlisted in the army after receiving an officer's commission, despite having just married the city librarian.

Just before the United States' declaration of war, President Wilson called on Company M to protect industries in Everett from domestic turbulence should war break out. A cheering, patriotic crowd wished the one hundred men well as they paraded through town before departing by train. In Everett, some of the men reported threats and "much insolence" from Wobblies around town. After an uneventful duty in Everett, Company M shipped out to France. Patriotic fever ran high in Centralia as newspapers urged citizens to support the Red Cross and buy Liberty Bonds and as the townspeople followed closely any news of their boys overseas. By the end of the war, sixteen hundred men from Lewis County had entered the service; forty-three had died.[23]

Not every eligible Centralian enlisted during the war. In the working-class section of town and in the lumber camps nearby, many union men saw no good reason for Americans to die in the trenches. The Wobblies were outspoken opponents of the war, and their periodicals constantly denounced it. "Don't be a soldier, be a man," advised one of many Wobbly stickers put up around working-class hangouts. "Join the I.W.W. and fight on the job for yourself and your class."[24] The IWW propaganda was anti-militarist, urging workers to fight the "class war" at home rather than the capitalist-created war abroad. The union never took an official stand against conscription but left the decision up to individual conscience. And despite their organization's strong rhetoric, the vast majority of Wobblies did register with their draft boards. In the general wartime hysteria, however, IWWism became a convenient scapegoat, a symbol of "anti-Americanism."

With the United States' entry into the war, the War Department sent out an order for 100 million board feet of spruce timber, which, because of its lightness and strength, was a principal material in the construction of airplanes and other vital wartime equipment. The major area of supply for spruce was Washington and Oregon. As the demand for timber surged, so did organizing efforts among the workers. During the early months of 1917, the IWW had formed the Lumber Workers Industrial Union No. 500, which quickly organized several thousand loggers and sawmill workers in lumber camps and towns from Montana to the Oregon coast. Although lumber and shingle prices had risen sharply during 1915 and 1916, owners refused to raise wages or improve working conditions. During the summer of 1917, the IWW called an industry-wide lumber strike in the Pacific Northwest. Loggers walked off their jobs by the thousands, and within a few weeks they had paralyzed much of the lumber industry. The ranks of the IWW swelled. Strikers demanded an eight-hour work day, a minimum of sixty dollars a month in wages, mattresses and bedding in all logging camps, showers, and better food. Even in camps where working conditions were relatively good, Wobblies struck for the right to join a union.[25]

It was the largest IWW-led strike ever organized in the West. Before long, there was a shortage of spruce, principally because of the tremendous demand and the logistical difficulty in harvesting the trees in remote forests. Employers were shrewd enough to blame the shortage on the IWW, claiming that the strike was a seditious interference with wartime production.[26] Newspapers charged—with no factual basis—that the strike was financed by German gold. "The I.W.W. are worse than the Germans . . . ," the *San Francisco Chronicle* editorialized on February 6, 1918. "The I.W.W. will never cease until persistently imprisoned or put out of existence."[27] During the strike, Centralia officials adopted a policy of arresting all Wobblies found riding freight trains into town or camping in "jungle" camps along the railroad right-of-way. The courts sentenced arrested men to thirty days labor in a stone quarry.[28]

Western timber company owners were hostile toward all unions, even the conservative trade unions. In July 1917, the owners formed the Lumbermen's Protective Association to resist union demands and pledged to maintain the ten-hour day. According to one newspaper report, "The operators frankly admitted that their opposition to the IWW was simply an expression of their general opposition to all attempts of organized labor to interfere with their exclusive management of their business."[29] Western businessmen missed no opportunity to encourage propaganda that linked organized labor with treason, and they pressured state and federal authorities to repress the IWW. The IWW was often accused of destroying employer property and committing other acts of sabotage, but evidence was never presented to give the charges credibility. Acts of violence by disgruntled individuals no doubt occurred, but not to the extent claimed by the strike's opponents. Although the Wobblies officially insisted on absolute passive resistance, wild rumors of IWW violence during the strike fed the public's paranoia about the Wobblies.

Washington's Democratic governor, Ernest Lister, allied himself with employers opposed to the IWW. He supported state-wide vigilante committees that searched for evidence of disloyalty, rounded up "irresponsible" IWW ringleaders, and held them for weeks in stockades. In Aberdeen, a mob of three hundred and fifty broke into the IWW hall and burned furniture and union records in the street. Across the state line in Hood River, Oregon, vigilantes threatened to lynch the IWW organizer and then drove him out of town. The police arrested dozens of Wobblies and closed down union halls in Spokane and Seattle. State authorities called in federal soldiers to deal with "German plots," and soldiers joined the vigilantes in arresting Wobblies by the hundreds. The Oregon National Guard, stationed in Washington, raided the IWW hall in North Yakima and held seventy-four Wobblies in a detention stockade. Many were kept there for months without formal charges, a clear violation of their civil liberties. Some local lawyers refused to come to their aid; others were denied access to the prisoners. Most Wobblies were later released and the charges dropped.[30]

With the initial success of the lumber strike threatening the economic solidarity of the home front, Secretary of War Newton Baker and Washington's two Republican senators urged the lumber companies to accept the eight-hour day. But the employers were steadfast and refused even the suggestion of mediation. Faced with such strong opposition, the IWW slowly lost support as the men began drifting back to the camps. Beating a strategic retreat, the unionists decided to go back to work and to deliberately slow down production. They caused endless delays by following orders exactly to the letter or by leaving camp at the end of eight hours. These tactics were highly effective in continuing to disrupt the industry, particularly since there was a labor shortage during the war.

In an effort to settle the lumber strike, President Wilson ordered a Mediation Commission in the late fall of 1917 to investigate and hold hearings on labor conditions. The commission determined that the cause of the strike lay with the dangerous social conditions in the lumber camps, not with the "sinister influences and extremist doctrines" of the IWW. Members of the commission reported that the employers were taking advantage of wartime hysteria to reap excessive profits and to fight *all* unions, not just the IWW. The commission recommended an eight-hour day, the elimination of war profiteering, and an agreement by the employers to work together with labor in the future. The IWW leafletted lumber camps and western cities with this favorable report.[31]

Despite the commission's report, the owners refused to negotiate and the shortage continued. In November 1917, representatives of sixteen of the region's largest lumber companies met in Centralia and agreed to sponsor units in a new labor union to be called the "Loyal Legion of Loggers and Lumbermen," or the Four L's. The new union would be founded on the principle of "mutuality of interest as between employer and employee"—the exact opposite of IWW philosophy. The idea for the Four L's originated in the War Department, which wanted to eliminate discontent in the woods and increase spruce production. One hundred War Department officers were sent out to recruit men by the thousands and to extract their pledge not to strike until the war was over. The recruiters approached loggers with a basic patriotic appeal: "Are you a loyal citizen? If so, why not wear the Four L button and sign the pledge of allegiance?" With free membership and heavy pressure from fellow workers, the loggers found it difficult to turn down the Four L's and few dared risk it. Twenty thousand members signed up during the last two months of 1917.[32] The army also sent thousands of soldiers into the lumber camps to meet the government timber quotas. The men received civilian pay while working under military discipline, and they helped raise logging camp conditions to the level of army camps. The soldiers solved the labor shortage problem and helped undercut the influence of the IWW. An army officer from nearby Camp Lewis, a Four L recruiter, visited Centralia in early 1918 and spoke at several local sawmills to sign up employees. Those who refused to join were singled out for special observation by their bosses.[33]

By March 1918 the lumber owners had finally agreed to institute the eight-hour day and to improve working conditions. The strike was over. The Four L's claimed the victory for itself, but the success of the strike was largely due to the organizing activities and the direct action of the IWW. After the end of the war, the Four L's faded away. In a successful postscript to the strike, on May Day 1918, many Wobblies burned their blanket rolls and forced employers to provide bedding and sheets for their workers. The days of the bindlestiff were over.

The IWW was not the only union on strike in 1917. There were

4,450 strikes that year, more than any other year in United States history.[34] The AFL and other labor unions called many more strikes during the war than the IWW did, but none of them attracted the insistent opposition and accusations of disloyalty that accompanied IWW-led strikes. Such reactions were largely due to the hostility of authorities and other unions to the class-conscious outlook and revolutionary rhetoric of the IWW. The IWW also organized in industries that were not accustomed to unions or collective bargaining. The IWW efforts in the lumber industry had introduced owners to serious unionism for the first time.

All across the country, federal and local officials attempted to crush the One Big Union. In July, members of the Bisbee Loyalty League forced twelve hundred striking copper miners out of Bisbee, Arizona. The miners were put on a train at gunpoint and dumped in the middle of the desert, where they were taken to a federal stockade and held without charges for three months. In August, vigilantes lynched IWW organizer Frank Little while he was trying to organize a copper strike in Butte, Montana. They pinned a note on his body warning others not to try to unionize copper workers. In September, coordinated raids by the federal government closed down dozens of IWW halls. The tons of records and literature taken in these raids were used to put the IWW on trial for treason and sedition for propagandizing against the war. Subsequently, hundreds of Wobblies were brought to trial in Chicago, Sacramento, and Wichita. Many organizers were found guilty on the sole evidence that they were members of an organization that was said to advance violence and revolution. It was a severe blow to the national leadership of the IWW. As a result, subsequent Wobbly activities in small towns such as Centralia were carried out without the national direction or support that had marked earlier successful IWW strikes in the East.[35]

During the first few months of the lumber strike in the Northwest, the War Department enacted new laws, including the Espionage Act, to stamp out criticism of the war. Many of those prosecuted under the act were in western states where the IWW was most active, and local authorities arbitrarily applied the law to suppress dissent. By 1920, the army had put down twenty-nine domestic disorders without regard for individual civil liberties or due process. Many left-wing newspapers and magazines were censored, including *The Nation*, the *Milwaukee Leader*, and the *New York Call*.[36]

International events fueled the public's fear of labor and radicalism. In October 1917, news of the Russian Revolution burst into the headlines. It was the first proletarian revolution, the first regime in history to try to construct a new socialist order. In March 1918, Russia withdrew from the war after signing a truce with Germany, causing great apprehension in United States, and many accused Russia of being a traitor to the Allied cause.

Many Wobblies and other radicals viewed the events in Russia as the beginning of world revolution. The IWW was sympathetic to the workers' revolution, but close ties with Russia were never officially established. Some Wobblies were attracted by the instant success of the Russians and drifted away to join the American Communist Party, which was founded in 1919. But most were reluctant to believe that the nonindustrial Russian experiences could be repeated in industrial America. Despite this, the American press accused all Wobblies of being Russian agents and constantly referred to them as "Bolsheviks" and "reds."

Although no records exist on this point, Smith was probably a strong supporter of the IWW throughout the timber strike. With his union credentials and working-class sympathies, it is likely that he identified closely with the strikers. He followed news of the war and the strike with interest, and he handled more cases for the IWW loggers as the strike wore on. Despite his opposition to the war, Smith strongly believed in the rule of law, so when he was called up for military service in early 1918 he reported for his induction physical. The medical examination revealed extensive scar tissue on his lungs, disqualifying him from the service.[37]

When Laura Magill returned to her parents' home for the summer of 1917, Smith missed her terribly. He wrote her one, sometimes two, passionate letters a day. Exasperated that Laura was so concerned about the practical details of their future, he wrote:

> I have tried to be very frank about my financial affairs, and let you know that I am quite poverty stricken but if that makes any difference I don't want you at all. I have needed your sympathy and love and help so the last few days—and if you don't want to give me that when I most need it I don't think you are worthy of sharing my good fortune when it comes, if it ever does come.[38]

Smith's impatience at Laura's reservations about marriage and the subsequent delay in the wedding date was undoubtedly deepened by his frustration with the relative powerlessness of the people he defended in court. Driven to correct the injustices facing his clients, he felt stifled by the rigid rules and formalities of the law, which favored the few against the many. In late August, he confided to Laura:

> Tonight I feel much like I think a certain lawyer must have felt when the judge said to him—'Sir are you trying to show your contempt for this court?' In answer he replied, 'No, your honor, I am trying to conceal it.'[39]

In September 1917, convinced that he could not get Laura to set a wedding date unless he was more financially secure, Smith became a substitute teacher at Centralia High School. He taught physics, chemistry, and geometry at ninety-five dollars a month and kept his law office open on weekends and evenings.[40] Smith approached his teaching with enthusiastic intensity and was soon a favorite among the students. After school he coached the football team and spurred his players on to a winning season. Through his friendly manner he gained the trust of many students. He also gained a reputation as a strict disciplinarian and a sharp questioner. He would casually lean sideways with one hand on his desk and direct questions at students: "How do we know if the air in this room is hot or cold?" or "What have we learned from this experiment?" He asked question after question, using the Socratic method much as he had experienced it in law school. Most students enjoyed the challenge.[41]

Elmer continued to pressure Laura about setting a wedding date after she returned to teach school in the fall, telling her that he could not settle down until she married him. Laura's reservations lessened after the draft board rejected Elmer, and she finally agreed to marry him at their minister's study on February 16, 1918. The only other person present was a church custodian, who was the witness. Before he began the service, the minister asked Laura, "Do your parents know about this?" "No!" she replied. Surprised, the minister still proceeded with the ceremony. As the minister pronounced them man and wife, Laura later remembered, she thought, "What have I done?" Although overwhelmed by the experience, she was in love and happy to be married. The couple immediately left for their honeymoon, a night in Olympia, and the news of the marriage was made public the next day. When they returned to Centralia, Laura learned that Elmer had arranged for them to stay at his parents' house until the school year ended in order to save money.[42]

Back in his classroom, Smith's students joked that he was much better natured since his marriage. But the outspoken Smith was still eager to express his opinions and philosophy. One student later remembered Smith's favorite story:

> A man was walking down the street when another man came up to him and hit him in the nose. When the first man protested, the second man said, 'Well this is a free country isn't it?' The first man replied, 'Yes, but your freedom stops where my nose begins!'[43]

Things grew more serious when Smith spoke out against the war. He generated considerable controversy when he told his students that the war was being run for the sole benefit of the capitalists and that America had no business in it. When word of this got back to the school principal, W. G. Graham, he visited Smith's law office one day after school. Smith repeated to Graham his opinion that the common people were being killed off in the interests of capitalism. He cited the huge profits being made by munitions makers and other suppliers of war materiel, and he denounced the violence of war. Graham was furious, and he ordered Smith either to change his views or to keep silent about them. Smith refused to do either.[44]

At the next school board meeting, Graham recommended that all teachers be required to sign an oath of allegiance before they returned to teach the following year and asked teachers to promise not to speak out against the war. The demand for loyalty oaths was not uncommon in the United States, and many communities banned the teaching of German and suppressed those teachers who held unpopular opinions and had unclear loyalties. The board adopted Graham's recommendation without opposition.[45]

Smith refused to sign the oath, and he quit his teaching job at the end of the school year. Before the semester ended, he encouraged other teachers not to sign the oath, but they all did.[46] Smith's behavior stirred up some public sentiment against him, but he had no regrets. The law was his primary interest, and with a little money saved from his teaching he looked forward to resuming his legal career full time. But events in Centralia would soon make it hazardous to earn a living by defending working-class clients.

Lawlessness Leads to Bloodshed

"There Is Power in a Union"—Joe Hill, *IWW Songbook*, 1913

There is pow'r, there is pow'r
In a band of workingmen,
When they stand hand in hand,
That's a pow'r, that's a pow'r
That must rule in every land—
One Industrial Union Grand.

With the end of the timber strike in the spring of 1918, some of the Wobblies from the lumber camps and sawmills near Centralia redirected their energies and initiated a campaign of education and recruitment in town. Several loggers, dressed in woolen shirts and heavy boots, passed out IWW literature downtown, trying to sign up new recruits. A year earlier, in March 1917, the IWW had rented a hall in Centralia for the first time. Business leaders from the Commercial Club had demanded that city officers rid the town of the unionists, but the officers had said they were powerless as long as the Wobblies committed no crime. Under threats that the businessmen might "take matters into their own hands," the owner of the hall had evicted the IWW, with the *Chronicle*'s editorial approval.[1] The Wobblies quickly found another hall, a narrow, wooden, two-story building just off Tower Avenue. Again, threats were made, but no further action was taken.

Other IWW union halls had opened earlier on the Pacific Northwest coast, and they served as a welcome haven to itinerant workers. They were places where men could sit by a fire and fraternize with fellow workers and attend educational meetings. Jobs were listed on a blackboard, and there was IWW and other labor literature to read. The more inquisitive men could find a selection of pulp novels and worn volumes on economics and history.[2] By early 1918, because of wartime suppression and poor economic times, only two Wobbly halls remained open in Washington—one in Seattle and the one in Centralia.

To many townspeople, the presence of the IWW hall was an unpleasant reminder that the hated Wobblies were recruiting members while the town's sons were facing death in Europe. Each week the *Chronicle* printed the letters of hometown boy Dale Hubbard, describing in detail his experiences in France.[3] Compared to such fighting heroes as Hubbard and Warren Grimm, the Wobblies in town were seen as slackers and malcontents, a shame to the community. As the war dragged on and the casualty list grew, the hostility against the loggers intensified.

In early March, Centralia police arrested a Wobbly for distributing IWW literature. Convicted of stirring up opposition to the government by selling a seditious newspaper that promoted anti-war positions and supported the lumber strike, the unionist was fined and then released. During one night at the end of the month, someone demolished the IWW sign in front of the hall.[4]

On April 5, Centralia's Red Cross fund drive wound up with a bazaar, a parade, and a patriotic speech by F. B. Hubbard in the town square. After the festivities, the chief of police, along with the mayor and the governor, led a parade composed of a company of the National Guard and the Elks Lodge members. As the parade line approached the union hall, someone called out, "Let's raid the I.W.W. Hall!" The crowd surged forward. The marchers stormed the building, shattering windows and smashing in the door and seizing the men inside. They took furniture, records, and books outside and burned them in the street. They also destroyed an American flag hanging on the wall.[5] Members of the mob carried a Victrola and a desk out to the middle of the street and auctioned them off for the Red Cross. F. B. Hubbard won the desk and gave it to the Chamber of Commerce. The mob shoved the captured Wobblies into vehicles amid cries from the mob to have them lynched. The men were dumped across the county line and threatened with more serious harm if they dared to return to Centralia. The next day, the *Chronicle* ran an article with the headline, "Local I.W.W. Headquarters Are Effectively Closed Up":

> The raid was orderly, the citizens who made it showed no violence. No property was damaged other than that of the IWWs. No opposition was encountered by the half dozen IWWs who were in the place when the determined citizens entered.

"I am glad to get away with my life," the IWW secretary remarked.[6]

Elmer Smith was probably the only lawyer in town who was outraged by the attack. No one else in the legal community seemed to be concerned that the Wobblies had broken no laws and the mob had taken the law into its own hands. Smith's working-class friends privately denounced the raid, but there was little they could do.

Tensions in the Smith household were not nearly as high as those in town, but the first six months of married life proved to be a difficult time for Elmer and Laura. Laura was not prepared for the sudden intimacies and responsibilities of marriage, even though she was a realist and extremely practical about everyday affairs, to which Elmer paid little attention.[7] A retiring, private person, Laura found herself thrust into the middle of a noisy, crowded household with Smith's parents and their two youngest children, Willard and Dorothy. When Jim, Harry, and Glen traveled in from Mendota with their wives, they added to the generally chaotic living conditions.[8] When Glen's wife, Mabel, was about to have her baby, she also moved into the family's household. On the day of her delivery, Laura and Elmer had to move into a hotel for a night. Laura could only escape the disorder when she taught school. With Elmer absorbed in his work, Laura was left alone much of the time to adjust to her "new life."[9]

Life for the Smith clan, as for most other small-town families, centered on the home. Elmer loved to liven up family gatherings with jokes and funny stories. He was a terrible tease, and no relative was safe from his barbs. He led rousing discussions among the men around the dinner or card table. Isabelle often joined in the fun, but the other women did not share so easily in the fellowship. Dorothy, just twenty years old, was a proud woman with long, black hair that she braided and pinned on top of her head. She was extremely rigid about her convictions and rarely participated in the family's friendly debates. Although quiet in comparison to her outgoing and physically energetic brothers, Dorothy was stubborn and lazy and often expected others to do her work for her.[10]

Laura also had a hard time joining in the camaraderie. She felt intimidated by Isabelle, who did not want to share her son, and the two were never close. In an atmosphere that fluctuated between smothering affections and shouting matches, Laura felt out of place and unaccepted. Then, to her embarrassment, she discovered that she was pregnant. Tightening her corset, she made every effort to hide the evidence from her students.[11] But Elmer was thrilled about Laura's pregnancy. He could not understand her unhappiness and assumed that she was merely nervous about the baby. When the school year ended in May, Laura and Elmer moved onto their land in Mendota, and Laura breathed a sigh of relief. They both loved being out in the country, where she had privacy and he could work out-doors. Laura was especially relieved to get out of Centralia. She feared the flu epidemic that raged across the nation, striking one out of every four people.

That summer, Laura and Mary Smith, Jim's wife, became close friends. Both women were pregnant, and the two shared their discom-forts during the slow summer. In Mary, Laura finally found someone who understood her well, and the two couples spent many weekends together at nearby Deep Lake swimming and having picnics. That fall, Laura and Elmer returned to Centralia and rented a bungalow on Walnut Street. Laura had persuaded Elmer that moving out of his parents' house would give them more time together after the baby arrived. Having already quit her teaching job, she was pleased to have a house to manage herself. She settled in to prepare for the baby, while Elmer, tanned and feeling fit, returned to his law practice.

As Elmer Smith brought more and more cases to court on be-half of working people, he began making a name for himself as a lawyer who was unafraid of a challenge. He took up and won the case of a young woman employee of the *Centralia Chronicle* who made only three dollars a week, a violation of the state's minimum wage law for women. And he suc-cessfully sued a local automobile firm that was in the practice of defrauding customers who came in for repairs. The company replaced the new Ford engines with old ones, defacing the engine numbers so that they could not be identified.[12] Smith suffered the wrath of local lawyers when he took the case of a coal miner who had worked for F. B. Hubbard's Eastern Railway and Lumber Company. Hubbard's lawyers had denied the miner his back wages on a legal technicality; as a result, the man's large family became destitute and one of his daughters died of malnutrition. Smith heard about the tragedy, filed suit against the company, and brashly charged the com-pany lawyers with the child's death. Centralia's attorneys were outraged, and several sued Smith for libel and tried to have him disbarred. Neverthe-less, Smith was able to win a little relief from the company for the miner's family. Nothing came of the disbarment talk or the lawsuit.

Despite this unusual case, Smith's legal career showed promise. He conducted himself with great determination and courage as he battled powerful opponents and resourceful lawyers. But he also lost his share of cases. Sometimes his legal defenses were weak, and sometimes he took on a hopeless case and did what he could. But he was generally respected by his colleagues for his honest and open-handed dealings.

In November 1918, Smith went to court to defend his brother,

Glen, on a charge of third degree assault for hitting another man. Glen was found guilty and fined one dollar. But even over such a minor incident, Smith decided to go all out. He filed a motion for a new trial, where he planned to subpoena eleven witnesses to testify. The prosecutor, who believed that both sides were probably at fault and wanted to save the county the expense of a retrial, persuaded the judge to dismiss the case.[13]

As the time approached for Laura to deliver her baby, she began suffering terrible cramps and diarrhea. Smith nervously begged her to let him call his mother to help. Although she preferred not to fall under Isabelle's dominating influence, under the circumstances she could not refuse. In late November, the doctor was summoned to Laura's bedside where he told Isabelle there was nothing to do but let "nature take its course" and promptly left. Hours later he returned to deliver an eight and one-fourth pound girl, Virginia, from a very frightened and exhausted mother. A short time later, Smith took out a life insurance policy with a fraternal organization, Woodsmen of the World.[14]

It was at this time that Smith began to publicly speak his views on a number of social and economic issues. He attended labor meetings and community lectures, such as those sponsored by the Lewis County Triple Alliance, a nonpartisan organization whose goal was to unite liberals into a state-wide political force of laborites, farmers, and railroad workers. Smith's working-class background and his credentials as an attorney won him the presidency of the county chapter within a year.[15] But the Alliance had few friends outside of labor circles. Meanwhile, the war ended and the American troops came home. Warren Grimm, Dale Hubbard, and dozens of other local servicemen received a hero's welcome in Centralia. The veterans held fast to the wartime values of national unity and common sacrifice, and they resented the critics who found fault with the society they had so recently defended.

In February 1919, several Wobblies reappeared in town to rent a building and reopen their union hall. Finding that no one would rent to them, they occupied a vacant building until local authorities drove them out.[16] Although this incident received little attention, the four-day Seattle General Strike that became headline news the same month shocked and alarmed Centralia's veterans. The Seattle Central Labor Council, with the support of the IWW, called the strike to support striking shipyard workers. Since the end of the war, prices had gone up but workers' wages had not. The first general strike in United States history paralyzed Seattle. Although the twenty-five thousand strikers were peaceful, the police and National Guard eventually forced the Labor Council to end the strike.

The *Chronicle* echoed the views of many when it editorialized, "The revolutionist, the I.W.W., the Bolshevik should be banished from our shores forevermore."[17]

The strike in Seattle was only the beginning of a long series of strikes and violent encounters in 1919. By the end of the year, one in five workers in the nation had gone out on strike, more than at any other time in American history. A rising cost-of-living following years of wartime economic cutbacks and low wage levels created widespread labor unrest, and more than half of the strikes were for wage increases.[18] Before the year ended, the steel and coal industry experienced two bitter nationwide strikes, and even the police briefly went out on strike in Boston. Labor discontent reached into hundreds of American communities. On May Day, patriotic zealots in New York, Boston, and Cleveland attacked peaceful parades of workers. During May and June, a series of bombs aimed at prominent industrialists and state and federal officials, including Attorney General A. Mitchell Palmer, exploded in cities across the nation. Against this backdrop of violence and public outcry, Palmer asked for and received half a million dollars from Congress to help the Justice Department round up those who sought to undermine law and order. He established the General Intelligence Division and appointed young J. Edgar Hoover as its head to gather and coordinate all information concerning domestic radical activities. The war on radicalism became the Justice Department's number-one concern.[19] Before long, Elmer Smith would become one of its casualties.

Joining in the national crusade against radicalism and the IWW was the American Legion. Formed in May 1919, the organization of ex-servicemen pledged to "maintain law and order: to foster and perpetuate a 100% Americanism." By 1920 the Legion had one million members. It was dedicated to combatting left-wing doctrines that it feared would infect and radicalize the restless troops returning home. Often, this meant acting as strikebreakers. The Legion took a formal stand against violence and vigilante action, but it nevertheless encouraged patriotic emotionalism and never actually discouraged its members from participating in acts of violence. In June 1919, the Grant Hodge American Legion Post #17 was formed in Centralia and elected William Scales, a grocer, as commanding officer and Warren Grimm as a trustee. The local Legion post members marched in the Fourth of July parade in full uniform, carrying the American flag.[20]

National labor unrest and radicalism caught the attention of many people in Centralia. Servicemen returning home found the state deep in recession. Inflation was high, and a labor glut created hard times as well as bad feelings between working people and employers. In April 1919, Washington Congressman Albert Johnson spoke in Centralia about the "menace" of radicalism and the IWW. The Wobblies were bomb throwers, anarchists, and reds, he warned, and advised the crowd that those who did not get melted in the immigration melting pot should get out. "Don't get the idea that this country will be run by Bolsheviks," he concluded. "We will let them go so far; then we will rise up against them." [21]

Although the Wobblies had been driven from Centralia four times, some Centralians kept a vigilant watch for signs of their return. The only public IWW presence in town was maintained by Tom Lassiter, a forty-three-year-old Wobbly who had been almost blinded in an industrial accident. To support his wife and young child, Lassiter sold newspapers on the street: the *Seattle Union Record* (which had supported the Seattle strike), a number of IWW papers, as well as the *Centralia Chronicle*, the *San Francisco Chronicle*, and the *Chicago Tribune*. In June 1919, raiders broke into his newsstand, burned his papers and belongings, and used his American flag to tie the newsstand door shut as they left. They also left this note: "You leave town in 24 hours,—U.S. Returned Soldiers, Sailors and Marines of Centralia, Wash." [22]

The next day Lassiter called on Smith for legal help and announced that he was going to remain in Centralia "as long as I damn please." Lassiter had no funds and had a reputation for being belligerent, but Smith promised to help. He had a difficult time getting local authorities to take the incident seriously. Smith requested protection for Lassiter from the chief of police and County Attorney Herman Allen, but they both turned a deaf ear. [23]

Lassiter reopened his newsstand, but one night a week later soldiers broke in again. The *Chronicle* later printed excerpts from one of the radical pamphlets the thieves seized. After meeting with Lassiter the following afternoon, Smith called on the chief of police. While Lassiter waited outside on a corner of Tower Avenue, several men jumped him, pushed him into a car, and drove him out to the country where they dropped him in a ditch. Smith learned where Lassiter was from an anonymous call, and he and several friends drove out to pick up his helpless client. Smith advised him to stay away from Centralia for a while, but Lassiter ignored his suggestion and returned within a week. [24]

Many people in town knew the identities of those who had tormented Lassiter. County Attorney Allen made a superficial investigation of the kidnapping but said he was too busy to bother with a "third degree assault." Smith secured fifteen sworn statements recounting the facts of the case and submitted them directly to the governor in Olympia. Smith told his secretary: "We in Centralia demand that the people who kidnapped Lassiter be prosecuted. I very much fear that this lawlessness is going to lead to bloodshed unless curbed." The governor replied a few days later: "There is nothing I can do."[25] The only thing the authorities did manage to do was arrest Lassiter for distributing IWW literature that advocated using violence to accomplish social change. The unionist was convicted, and he served several months in prison. Smith probably represented Lassiter, although there is no record of who defended him in court.

Smith's relationship with his old friend Grimm became strained when Grimm returned to Centralia after the war. As deputy prosecuting attorney, Grimm found himself increasingly on the opposite side of the courtroom from Smith. One day, in a discussion with Smith, Grimm asked, "How would you feel if one of your clients, in his dirty overalls, were to come up to you in public, slap you on the back and say, 'Hello, Elmer?'" "Very proud," replied Smith. Grimm cautioned Smith about defending clients such as Lassiter. "Handle the IWW cases if you want to," he said, "but sooner or later they're all going to be hanged or deported anyway. You'll get along all right if you will come in with us." Smith strongly disagreed and argued that free speech was one of the fundamental rights of all citizens. If Lassiter's kidnappers were not prosecuted, he reasoned, people will know that they can get away with breaking the law. "I can't agree with you," Grimm replied. "That's the proper way to treat such a fellow."[26]

"A lawyer with a heart is as dangerous as a working man with brains," wrote Wobbly Ralph Chaplin about Smith in a 1920 pamphlet about the Centralia case.[27] Despite troubles with collecting money from his clients (at which he never worked very hard), Smith was determined to defend the town's outcasts. He had become isolated from much of Centralia's legal and business community, and in the spring of 1919 Smith told his landlord, Dan Sulzer, that it would be only a short time before the "gang" (the town's businessmen) tried to evict him for his handling of labor cases. Even though Smith had only a verbal lease, Sulzer promised to stand by him. As it happened, several bankers did apply financial pressure on Sulzer to get Smith out, and Sulzer notified Smith in July that he must vacate his office. Smith refused. In September, Sulzer instituted eviction proceedings, and Smith was compelled to move temporarily into a small room in the Centralia branch offices of the *Seattle Union Record*. The *Record* reported:

> Business men admit they object to Smith only because of his "associations." Fear of the business men is now causing some of

the working people to desert the attorney, but . . . Smith says
this will not drive him into submission to the gang.[28]

In July, George F. Russell, secretary-manager of the anti-union Employers'
Association of Washington, came to Centralia to meet with local businessmen at the Chamber of Commerce. He advised the town's business
leaders that the IWW and other labor unions should be crushed. After only
brief discussion, the group formed a temporary organization, with F. B.
Hubbard as the chair, to address the Wobbly problem.[29]

Shortly after the Chamber's meeting, a traveling labor union lecturer came to town to speak at the park next to the public library. During
the speech, hecklers grouped in the back of the large crowd and tried
to shout down the speaker. Fearing trouble, Smith bravely stepped onto
the stage at the end of the lecture to shake hands with the speaker. He
then walked the man safely back to the train depot. "That young man was
headed for a ride out of town on a different kind of rail," Elmer told Laura
afterward. The next morning Smith found a cardboard sign taped to his
office door: "Are you American? You had Better Say So. Citizens Committee." Across the bottom was scrawled: "No More I.W.W. Meetings for
you." Laura feared for Elmer's safety when he showed her the sign, but he
shrugged it off.[30]

Labor Day in Centralia was marked by two entirely different
gatherings. After a parade, the official ceremony was held at Riverside Park,
a half mile from town across the Chehalis River bridge. In the welcoming
address, Warren Grimm remembered his war experiences with American
forces in Siberia and he warned of the dangers of Bolshevism. He attacked
union activity in the United States as "unAmerican" and admonished his
audience to beware the sinister influences of "The American Bolsheviki—
the Industrial Workers of the World." Smith listened from the back of
the crowd.[31]

After Grimm finished his speech, Smith left to attend the other
Labor Day celebration, the one put on by the Triple Alliance. Some five
thousand workers and labor sympathizers from nearby lumber camps and
sawmills gathered in another part of town to discuss what kind of political
organization they might support. Labor activity in the area was not dominated by the IWW; there was also the more conservative Central Trades
Council, with several thousand members, which had announced plans that
summer to build a new Labor Temple in Centralia. The Triple Alliance
hoped to attract broader support from these ranks.[32]

But on that Labor Day, a far more important event was taking place in Centralia. A Wobbly named Britt Smith was making final arrangements to lease the ground floor of the Roderick Hotel near the railroad tracks on Tower Avenue.[33] The owners of the hotel, James and Marie McAllister, were a sixty-year old couple sympathetic to the IWW cause. IWW membership in the woods had increased over the summer, and Britt Smith felt that the time was right for another attempt to open a hall. The secretary and main organizer of the local IWW, Smith had been born in Bucoda, a few miles from Centralia. He was a likable logger who walked with a limp from an injured right leg and who talked with a fast, nervous voice. His middle-class parents had long since given up on him as the black sheep of the family. At thirty-seven years of age, he was an old-timer to most of his fellow loggers.[34] After signing the lease, Britt set up living quarters in a back room and put up a sign identifying the IWW headquarters. The Wobblies had returned. Rumors began to circulate immediately of planned reprisals against the hall.

Several days after Labor Day, Elmer Smith stopped by Grimm's office, told him that he thought his speech was plain "rotten," and corrected a few of the historical inaccuracies he had made about the Bolsheviks. He also said flatly that he could not agree with Grimm's anti-labor conception of Americanism.[35] There was little more to say and Smith left abruptly. It may have been the last time the two talked to each other.

On October 1, F. B. Hubbard called a meeting at the Elks Club that was open "to all citizens desiring to see law and order maintained." A hundred businessmen showed up and formally organized the Centralia Citizens Protective Association to "combat I.W.W. activities in this vicinity." On October 16, the Legion post met to plan a celebration of the first anniversary of the signing of the Armistice on November 11. The group decided to have a parade followed by patriotic speeches, a banquet, and a dance. Governor Louis F. Hart later declared the day as a state holiday.[36]

The reopening of the IWW hall brought the Protective Association into action. The front page of the *Centralia Hub* announced a meeting on October 20: "Employers—Your presence at the Elks Club Monday evening at 8 o'clock to discuss the IWW problem is earnestly requested."[37] Over a hundred businessmen were present, but so was a small group of workers that included Smith's brother Harry and at least one Wobbly. They were there to watch for any trouble.

F. B. Hubbard opened the meeting with a call to drive the IWW out of town. Many in the crowd agreed; they were enraged that an IWW hall existed at all in downtown Centralia. But the chief of police dampened the crowd's spirit when he reminded them that the IWW had violated no laws and had a legal right to occupy its hall. The city attorney, Warren Grimm's brother, spoke in support of the chief, repeating that no law allowed them to close the hall. Hubbard then declared that if he were chief of police, he would rid the town of Wobblies within twenty-four hours. If the law would not handle the problem, he said, then it was up to the citizens to do it. A chorus of voices cheered with approval. William Scales, the local American Legion post's commanding officer, opposed a raid on the hall but stated that no jury in the land would convict anyone who did. At the meeting's end, a secret action committee was formed. It was rumored that the chair of the committee was Warren Grimm and that both William Scales and F. B. Hubbard were members. Many speculated that the committee's first priority was getting the names of all Wobblies in town so that they could be rounded up.[38]

During one of the first days of November, Britt Smith entered Elmer Smith's office. A raid on his IWW hall had become an open topic of discussion in town, and he was worried that events were getting out of control. Wobblies were always moving in and out of the logging camps, and nobody could predict what might happen if one or two hotheads started some trouble. Smith knew some of the Wobblies as clients, but he was not involved in their organizational activities. Only a week earlier, a twenty-one-year-old Wobbly, Loren Roberts, had come to see him about the feared raid. Smith told him that if the hall was raided and the front door broken down, then it was just like someone breaking into a man's home. "If someone comes into your home and breaks in the door you have a right to shoot," Smith told him.[39] Britt Smith had the same question on his mind. What could be done to prevent a raid on the IWW hall, and could the Wobblies defend themselves if they were attacked?

During their brief meeting, Smith told Britt that the Wobblies had the right to defend their hall, their lives, and their property if they were attacked first.[40] He suggested that Britt seek help through proper channels by talking to the mayor and appealing directly to the townspeople, which Britt later did. There is no evidence that Smith advised Britt to either use or not use guns in the defense of the hall. But according to his later trial testimony, Britt left his meeting with Smith convinced that the Wobblies were entitled to use violence in self-defense. Britt Smith also knew that the Wobblies would not back away from trouble.

Smith's legal advice to Britt Smith might have been the turning point that led to the violent events that followed. Certainly, his advice contributed to the tragedy. In this case, Smith fell short of his responsibility to advise his client of the probable consequences of alternative courses of action and to recommend the one that best served his client's interests. By any reasonable estimate, the probable consequences of a physical resistance to a raid on the hall would have been a serious defeat for the Wobblies, given that they were heavily outnumbered. Yet, Smith apparently did not point out the perilous position the unionists would be in if a raid occurred.

Smith's major failure was his misjudgment of how serious the situation was in Centralia. He particularly misjudged the growing sentiment among some of the Wobblies to fight back. Perhaps he failed to see the dangers facing others because he had a fearless disregard for his own personal safety. Or his negligence could have been the result of his inexperience as a lawyer. Whatever the reason, Smith apparently did not advise Britt Smith to avoid a violent confrontation.

Elmer Smith did urge Britt to seek out police protection, but he also could have encouraged the Wobblies to lie low during the parade so as not to provoke trouble. Smith knew that the Wobblies were stubborn, independent-minded men who would not go out of their way to avoid a fight. He also knew that the Wobblies were likely to offer resistance to any attack as a matter of self-respect, in defense of their union. Given this, Smith should have done all in his power to explain to the Wobblies the consequences of physical resistance. It appears that Smith led Britt and the others to believe that the law supported any actions they might take to defend their hall. This was clearly bad legal advice. Violent resistance could not have been too far from their minds. On the day of the raid, both Elmer and Britt Smith handled guns, but Elmer did nothing to warn against their use or explain the limited legal justification of armed self-defense.

Prominently displayed guns might have served as an equalizing force for the outnumbered Wobblies, but they could not serve as a deterrent because the public did not know of their planned use. Some Wobblies were afraid that without an armed defense they would be overwhelmed, but they could not achieve consensus. According to Smith's trial testimony, he did not advise Britt Smith about the use of guns in the Wobblies' defense of the hall. It will never be known if a strong plea by Smith against using them would have made any difference, but surely his failure to do so encouraged the Wobblies in their ill-fated plans.

On November 4, Britt Smith called a meeting at the IWW hall to discuss distributing a handbill that sought support from the townspeople. A thousand copies were printed in Tacoma because no Centralia printer would take the job, and for the next two days the men delivered handbills door-to-door in the residential parts of town. The flyer acknowledged the rumors to close down the hall and mob the occupants:

> We implore the law abiding citizens to prevent this. . . . Let
> the law take its course, our manhood revolts at mob violence
> coming from the hands of the lumber barons. Let the officers
> do their duty if we have violated the law.[41]

On November 7, the anniversary of the Bolshevik revolution, the Bureau
of Investigation and Immigration Service of the Labor Department conducted raids in twelve cities across the nation to round up foreign-born
radicals and deport them. Hundreds were arrested. Complaints to J. Edgar
Hoover of brutality and the destruction of property went unheeded.

On the same day in Centralia, the parade route was announced. It
would proceed from the park to Tower Avenue, then up to Third Street;
at Third it would reverse its course and return down Tower. It would pass
the IWW hall twice. Never before had a parade traveled so far uptown,
and many Wobblies believed that the route had been designed to allow the
paraders to raid their hall. That same day, Warren Grimm was elected commander of the Legion Post, replacing William Scales, who, it was rumored,
had resigned because of his opposition to a raid on the IWW hall.[42]

On one of the few days left before the parade, a Legionnaire complained to Marie McAllister about a red Wobbly songbook in the window
of her hotel. He warned her that the Legion was going to "clean them [the
Wobblies] out." When McAllister asked Chief of Police A. C. Hughes to
protect her property, he told her the Legionnaires had not done anything
yet so he could not do anything. If they raided the hall, he told her, "As far
as the Wobblies are concerned, they wouldn't last fifteen minutes."[43] Britt
Smith had even less luck when he tried to seek help from the mayor. The
mayor was not in.

On Sunday, November 9, the Wobblies held their regular weekly
meeting and listened to John Foss, a Spanish War veteran and member of
the General Executive Board of the IWW. The audience of some twenty-
five to thirty men listened restlessly as Foss talked about union organizing
and raising bail money for Wobblies who were in prison. Throughout the
speech, several loggers paced nervously in the back of the meetingroom.
After Foss finished, Britt Smith spoke briefly and passed out copies of the
handbill that had been distributed in town. He announced that attorney
Elmer Smith had advised him that the Wobblies had a right to defend their
hall, and the men discussed what course of action should be taken.

Many of the Wobblies gathered in the hall that night did not know
one another. Most of them worked as loggers in the isolated camps near
town. Some of them lived in town—several sharing Britt's living quarters
in the back of the IWW hall—others had just arrived in Centralia and knew

little or nothing about the tense atmosphere there. Some were family men; others slept in the blankets they carried on their backs. With no time to get to know each other, there was little progress toward reaching a common policy and course of action. As a result, they reached no consensus on the best defense strategy to take on the day of the parade.

After Britt Smith, the best-known Wobbly in the group was Wesley Everest, a handsome, twenty-nine-year-old logger of medium build and reddish hair. Everest was one of nine children of a pioneering family that lived on a farm in Oregon. His father, a schoolteacher and postmaster, had died when Everest was twelve and his mother had died two years later. Soon after being sent to a relative's farm outside Portland, he had run away and had made his living ever since as a logger and railroad construction worker. In May 1913, Everest participated in a lumber strike near Coos Bay, Oregon, that was marred by raids on the IWW hall. Strikers were beaten and arrested, and Marshfield police arrested Everest and another Wobbly organizer on a vagrancy charge. A large crowd of businessmen took them from jail and forced them to kneel and kiss the American flag. The two men were then deported on a boat to a town eight miles away.[44]

During the war, Everest was drafted into the U.S. Army Spruce Production Division in Vancouver, Washington, where he reportedly spent sixteen months in and out of the stockade for refusing to salute the flag. After he was discharged in the spring of 1919, he moved into a rooming-house in Centralia. His few possessions included a blue serge suit, a bundle of law books, and a .32-20 Colt revolver. Everest liked to wear his army uniform around town, and he was wearing it when he attended the October 20 meeting of the Protective Association.

Everest, who had worked closely with Britt Smith organizing local Wobbly activities and putting out the handbill, was one of the more hotheaded men in discussions about how to defend the hall. He spoke up more than once, saying that if their hall was raided he did not figure a man's life was worth much if they did not defend it. "When those fellows come," he warned, "they will come prepared to clean us out and this building will be honeycombed with bullets inside of ten minutes." Loren Roberts, another Wobbly at the meeting, later described Everest as "a man that didn't give a God-damned for nothing. . . . He was really a desperate character and he didn't give a God-damned what happened to him or what he done." Britt Smith and Everest expected the raiders to be armed, but some of the others in the room were opposed to taking up guns. At the end of the meeting it was understood that the hall would be defended and that some men would be armed. It was also understood that no shootings would take place unless the raiders tried to destroy the hall.[45]

The Essence of Law and Order

"The Tragedy of Sunset Land"—Loren Roberts

There's a little Western city in the shadow of the hills
    Where sleeps a brave young rebel 'neath the dew;
Now he's free from life's long struggle his name is with us still;
    We know that he was fearless, tried and true.

Now the moonbeams in the dell linger there in sad farewell,
    In memory of that fateful autumn day;
And some day we're coming home in the Sunset Land to roam,
    Where the old Chehalis River flows its way.[1]

On the morning of November 11, Elmer Smith was working in his office, his mind on the upcoming parade. A friend came in to say that a Legionnaire, Arthur McElfresh, had told him that the IWW hall was going to be raided after the parade was over. Leaving his law books behind, Smith decided to go over to the hall and talk to Britt Smith. Wobblies had been gathering at the hall throughout the morning. By noon, thirty to forty men, some carrying guns, had been in and out. Britt Smith was checking with everyone to see that those who wanted guns were armed. He directed several men to take positions in buildings across the street.

Smith arrived at the hall around one-thirty that afternoon. Addressing the group of fewer than twenty men, he asked casually, "Well, boys, are you ready for a raid?" Most avoided Smith's gaze and no one replied. When Smith told Britt that it looked like there was going to be a raid, Britt replied, "Well, if there is, we are going to defend our hall." Although he did not see anyone carrying a gun, Smith said he did not think there were enough men present to defend the hall, but Britt didn't answer. Worried about the Wobblies' and his own safety, Smith told Britt he was going back to defend his office: "If they raid this place they may come down and raid mine too." As Smith walked back to his office, he met a friend and the two talked briefly about the atmosphere of violence in town. "It is hard to tell what will happen," said Smith. "It is hard to tell what these fellows will do."[2]

By the time Smith returned to his office, the parade had begun. With the band playing "Over There," the parade line moved out from the city park at two o'clock. Members of the Elks Lodge, Marines, sailors, and a patrol of Boy Scouts led by high school principal Graham led the march, with veterans from the Centralia and Chehalis American Legion posts bringing up the rear. Under Warren Grimm's leadership, men from the Centralia Post, many in civilian clothes, stepped out in eight platoons of ten men each. Other veterans also marched in the parade, but only about half of them were members of the American Legion. The parade marshal, Adrian Cormier, rode horseback up and down the length of the parade, attempting to keep everyone moving along the parade line that stretched for three blocks. The parade turned left on Tower Avenue and headed north on the right side of the street. A mostly silent crowd watched, occasionally waving small American flags.[3] After watching the parade pass out of sight a few blocks away, Smith headed home to get his gun.

As the parade crossed Second Street it passed the IWW hall on its left. As the first marchers reached Third Street they turned and headed back down Tower on the right side of the street. This maneuver spread the line thin, and to compensate Grimm ordered the Legionnaires at the end of the parade to stop and close up ranks. They regrouped directly in front of the IWW hall.

Wobblies were watching the parade from four locations. Several men were stationed in the Avalon and Arnold hotels, across the street from the IWW hall. Three men looked down on the parade from Seminary Hill, four hundred yards behind the two hotels and seventy-five feet above the street. As the parade line halted, one of the men on the hill said he "hope[d] to Jesus" there would not be any trouble.[4]

In the street, there was a moment of indecision. Some of the men in the parade began talking about who would lead the raid. Cormier rode up and, according to some witnesses, blew his whistle, giving the signal to charge. With shouts of "Let's get them!" a group of veterans broke ranks and rushed toward the hall. A few reached the front door and started to kick it in. The Wobblies watched as the front plate-glass window was smashed in and the door was broken open. Then, from inside the hall, gunshots exploded through the doorway, and the raiders doubled back to avoid the bullets. Hearing the gunfire, the Wobblies stationed at the Avalon Hotel and Seminary Hill started shooting and caught the raiders in a crossfire. Directly in front of the hall a bullet struck Arthur McElfresh near his left ear and he fell to the ground. Farther away, Warren Grimm was hit in the left side of his chest. He doubled over and staggered for a few feet before collapsing in the street. Ben Cassagranda caught a bullet in the stomach as he ran for cover down Second Street. Several others were wounded before the firing stopped. It had lasted less than a minute.[5]

In the street, everyone dashed for cover. A few men helped the wounded into cars and drove quickly to the hospital. A number of Wobblies ran from their posts and attempted to escape. While many of the former servicemen rushed home for weapons, others forced open hardware stores and began distributing guns and cartridges. Within a few minutes, enraged and determined men had regrouped and stormed the hall, destroying everything in their way. The mob captured Britt Smith, Ray Becker, Mike Sheehan, James McInerney, Tom Morgan, and Bert Faulkner, most of whom had retreated into a large unused icebox in the rear of the hall. The mob ripped down a porch attached to the front of the hall and set fire to financial records, books, stacks of newspapers, and mattresses.[6]

Wesley Everest escaped through the back door as soon as the mob had entered the building. Several veterans saw him running away, mistook him for Britt Smith, and gave chase. Everest fled toward the woods to the Skookumchuck River, trading shots with his pursuers. He waded out into the river a few feet but then stopped in the swift current. As he turned back, the mob moved in closer. Everest yelled that he would surrender only to the police, but the mob kept coming. Legionnaire Dale Hubbard drew closer, and Everest fired, hitting him several times in the chest. The mob quickly overpowered and subdued Everest, kicking and beating him. With a belt around his neck, they started dragging him back to town with an angry crowd gathering along the way. Many demanded that he be hanged over a telephone pole, and a few stepped forward to do the deed. But the police stopped the lynching and took Everest safely to jail. They threw him onto the concrete floor in the corridor next to the jail cells, where he lay still.[7]

Beyond the sound of the guns when the shooting broke out, Smith was at home when the hall was raided. As he picked up his small Colt .45 revolver, which he had hidden in the dresser drawer in his bedroom, he spoke briefly with Laura, telling her he expected trouble and might be attacked. Laura tried to persuade Elmer not to go, but he was adamant. She wept as he hurried out the front door.[8]

Back at his office, Smith met principal Graham and a group of Boy

Scouts. Graham told him that all hell had broken loose and asked Smith to come with them to the police station. "Where is your warrant?" Smith asked. When Graham said he did not have one, Smith replied that no one but an officer could make him leave. During the tense pause that followed, Smith recognized several of the scouts as his former pupils from school and decided that this was not the time for a violent confrontation. Smith was put into the city jail at around four-thirty that afternoon, where he joined a dozen or more Wobblies. Outside, a mob of over a hundred people was howling for Wobbly blood, making it hard for the men packed in the jail cells to hear each other talk. With Everest lying in a heap on the floor, Smith listened with dismay to the news of the afternoon's bloodshed.[9]

At the hospital, McElfresh was pronounced dead on arrival. Grimm was still conscious and talking to the doctors as they tended him. He told them to hurry up and do something, but at five o'clock he died. A short time later Cassagranda also died.[10]

Word passed quickly through Centralia about the deaths of the three men. The police were doing little to establish order, and the Legion took control of the streets and formed vigilante groups to round up all Wobblies. Armed with pistols, shotguns, and rifles, the Legionnaires spread out through the town. They approached workers, stuck guns in their stomachs, and demanded, "Are you a Wobbly?" They raided the local pool halls, lined up the occupants, and searched them for red IWW membership cards. At the train station, they stopped one eyewitness to the raid, seized his camera, and told him, "If you know when you are well of[f] you will keep your damn mouth shut about anything you saw here today." By nightfall, twenty-two men had been thrown in the city jail, which had been built to hold fewer than ten. Those arrested included Smith's brothers Jim and Harry and Tom Lassiter.[11]

Just before five o'clock that afternoon, while the roundup was in progress, a group of men gathered at the Elks Club hall. Someone told the men to go to the Armory, get the guns held there, and be back in an hour. At six o'clock about seventy-five people met again at the Elks hall. Those who were not members of either the Elks or the American Legion were asked to leave, and thirty to forty men did so. The meeting lasted until seven o'clock.[12]

At seven-thirty all the city lights in Centralia went out for about fifteen minutes.[13] On the streets, Legionnaires stopped motorists and ordered them to extinguish their auto lamps. The crowd from the Elks Club marched through the dark and entered the jail without resistance. Inside, Smith and the other men could hear the mob move toward the jail cells. None of the prisoners spoke. Several armed men stepped over the trail of blood running across the corridor from Everest's mouth, picked him up and dragged him out to a waiting car. The silence in the jail lasted until the noise of cars driving away in the darkness had faded.

Six cars with their headlights off drove west to the Chehalis River bridge. The men hauled Everest from the car and put a noose around his neck. An eyewitness reported that Everest mustered the strength to speak and said, "I got my man and done my duty. String me up now if you want to, damn you!" The lynchers worked without a word. They tied one end of the rope to a bridge crossbeam girder and pushed Everest over the side. After a few minutes, they heard moans in the darkness, and they realized that the rope had not been long enough to snap their victim's neck. They pulled Everest's body back onto the bridge and substituted a longer rope. For a second time they pushed him over the side. This time there was silence. After watching the body swaying below for a moment, the lynchers returned to their cars and flashed their headlights on the corpse. From a distance they fired their guns at the dangling body. By the time the mob returned to town the lights were back on. News that Dale Hubbard had just died quickly circulated in the semi-darkened streets.[14]

The large crowd milling outside the jail continued to yell and curse at the terrified prisoners. Someone pushed a rope through the window bars and threatened to lynch them. Britt Smith later remembered, "Everytime I heard a footstep or the clanking of keys I thought the mob was coming after more of us." James McInerney came close to death: "I thought it was my last night on earth and had reconciled myself to an early death of some kind, perhaps hanging. I was taken out once by the mob, and a rope was placed around my neck and thrown over a crossbar. I waited for them to pull the rope. But they didn't."[15] Instead, cooler heads convinced the crowd that one lynching was enough and McInerney was beaten and pushed back into his cell. At around midnight, after several hours of terrorizing the prisoners, the crowd grew tired and broke up. No one inside slept.

Laura waited anxiously for Elmer to return home that day. When dinnertime passed without any word, she grew frightened and went to a friend's house where she asked if her daughter could spend the night. Laura was not in touch with the rest of the Smith family, which was perhaps just as well. After dark that night, an armed posse barged into the elder Smith's home and at bayonet point lined up Isabelle, Tom, Dorothy, and Willard in their nightclothes against the fireplace. While the trembling family watched, the posse searched the house for Wobblies. The next day they returned and took Tom off to jail.[16]

Just before midnight on November 11, sixty troops from the Washington National Guard at Fort Lewis arrived in Centralia. Governor Hart had sent them to keep a lid on further outbreaks of violence and to prevent more lynchings. Legionnaires were still rounding up the Wobblies. The *Chronicle* published an editorial calling the IWW "despicable parasites of humanity" and praising the recent mobism:

> The episode of last night is but the natural result of a red-handed revolutionist getting his just deserts without loss of time or the painfully slow process of law. . . . The apparent infringement of the law last night was the essence of law and order.[17]

The next morning, the Lewis County commissioners appointed Clifford Cunningham associate prosecuting attorney, and he began to identify the Wobblies who had participated in the shooting and to question those who had already been arrested. He interrogated Nora Dishong who was arrested that day because she was Smith's secretary. Cunningham tried to get her to implicate Smith directly in the shootings, but she insisted that Smith was not a member of the IWW and did not take orders from them. Dishong was released after the questioning was over.[18]

Sometime during the early morning hours of November 12, someone finally cut the rope holding up Everest's body, which fell to the shallow river bottom, where it lay all day. At sunset, the body was brought back to the jail, with the rope still around its neck, and thrown on the floor in full view of the prisoners. The town's two undertakers refused to accept the body, and it remained there throughout the night. Smith was not there to see Everest's body. To ease the overcrowding, he and some other prisoners had been transferred to the Thurston County jail in Olympia. Laura learned from a good friend who was a court reporter that Smith had been arrested, and she attempted to visit her husband before he was transferred, but the police chief refused.[19]

In the Olympia jail, Smith protested loudly about being locked up without being formally charged and about being moved. But feelings were running high against the lawyer in Centralia. The November 13 *Chronicle* reported: "One of the central figures in the 'red' plot is the I.W.W. attorney Elmer S. Smith."[20] The atmosphere was little different in Olympia, where the *Olympia Daily Record* regarded him as the

> chief conspirator and guiding factor in the Armistice Day massacre. . . . Smith is now believed to be the brains back of the red activities in Centralia, and as evidence of his connections with

the outrage became more conclusive, feeling in the community
is said to have become intensified in its bitterness.[21]

Within hours of Smith's arrival in Olympia, reports reached the
authorities there that a group of Wobblies was gathering in a nearby town
to prepare an attack on the Olympia jail to release the men. Many local
citizens came to the jail and offered to help defend it. To avoid a confrontation, the three prisoners were taken away by car to a state reformatory
school at Monroe. The police arrested eighteen suspected Wobblies who
were on their way to Olympia by train, although no evidence ever surfaced
to tie the men to the planned raid.[22]

Also on November 13, Everest's body was removed from the Centralia jail and examined by a coroner's jury. After a brief examination and
without calling any witnesses, the jury concluded: "We find that deceased
came to his death by gunshot wounds and by strangulation caused by persons unknown." Until that point, the dead man had been identified in the
press as "Brick" Smith. Britt Smith set the record straight after identifying the body, and the newspapers reported that Wesley Everest had been
the victim of the lynch mob. Shortly after the inquest, Everest's body was
put in a wooden box and loaded onto James Lynch's moving van, which
carried a painted sign on its side that read, "Lynch, for quick work call
us."[23] Seventeen armed National Guardsmen, four Wobblies from the jail,
and a handful of newspapermen and curious onlookers escorted the van
to a local cemetery. The Wobblies dug a grave in the pauper's section and,
without ceremony, Everest's body was finally laid to rest.

Meanwhile, the hunt for Wobblies continued, spreading out into
the countryside near Centralia. Armed vigilantes combed the woods and
hills and broke into the homes of suspected labor sympathizers. All of
Smith's relatives were targets of the manhunt, and police had arrested
Harry and Jim Smith on the streets of Centralia within hours of the raid.
The vigilantes raided the brothers' homesteads and Glen's as well, looking
for Wobblies on the run. When the vigilantes forced their way into the
homesteads looking for guns, radical literature, and Wobblies, they found
the women washing baby clothes and making doughnuts. Concerned about
the fate of their husbands, the women moved into the elder Smiths' house
in town. Any relative of Elmer Smith's was presumed to be a Wobbly, but
in fact, only Glen was a member, and he managed to flee to Seattle to seek
help for the defense of his family.[24]

The morning after Grace and Mary Smith arrived in town, they
tried to visit their husbands in jail. When the officer on duty refused them
entrance, Mary angrily responded:

> You have made more IWWs and radicals in the last forty-eight
> hours in Centralia than the IWW themselves could make in a
> year's time. It's this kind of thing that makes people radical![25]

Later, the women were allowed in for a brief visit. Tom Smith was tired and irritable. "They can't do this to me! I'm not an IWW!" he complained.[26] By November 14, Jim, Harry, and Tom had been released because of lack of evidence. Elmer remained behind bars in Monroe and received the news of their release with mixed emotions. He was undoubtedly happy that his father and brothers were free, but he had to know that his continued imprisonment meant that serious charges would soon be brought against him.

The violence continued. On November 14, a millworker driving through Chehalis disregarded an order to stop and was shot in the shoulder by a Legionnaire. Several days later two armed posses collided in the woods, mistook each other for fugitive Wobblies, and opened fire. John Haney was killed in the confusion and became the last casualty of the Centralia tragedy.[27]

The Armistice Day events in Centralia gained national attention and condemnation. Most people accepted the American Legion's version of events, that a group of radicals conspired to fire without provocation on a peaceful parade of former servicemen. Press reports described the shootings as "An Act of War Against the United States." Little mention was made of the lynching, the raid in 1918, or the atmosphere of violence that pervaded the town. Instead, newspapers reported that the rifles of the radicals "were aimed at the heart of democracy," headlined their stories "Radicalism Run Mad," and advised that "the sooner the firing squad is got into action the better." "To even sympathize with the perpetrators of the tragedy," the *Chronicle* judged, "is proof evident that the sympathizer is a traitor to his country." The Centralia tragedy placed the IWW squarely on the center stage of anti-radical hysteria. Centralia's congressman, Albert Johnson, accused the IWW of attempting armed revolution. And World War I hero General John Pershing declared: "Too drastic measures cannot be taken to rid our country of the class of criminals who inspire or commit such crimes."[28]

As the news of the Centralia shootings spread, law enforcement authorities in the Pacific Northwest moved quickly to smash local IWW organizations. Federal prosecutors in Seattle declared war on the IWW "to the death."[29] Fearing further violence, police and vigilante groups rounded up Wobblies in raids in Seattle, Aberdeen, Yakima, Tacoma, Spokane, and

Portland. Washington Governor Hart urged President Woodrow Wilson to deport alien IWW leaders as the only efficient way to deal with the problem. State Attorney General L. L. Thompson advised a meeting of the prosecutors of thirty-nine counties to rush the IWW cases through the courts in mass trials to prevent the Wobblies from finding enough lawyers to defend them properly. Authorities used the Centralia incident to conduct multiple prosecutions under the state's new criminal syndicalism law and sent many Wobblies to prison.[30]

Not all of the public reaction to the tragedy was anti-IWW. The *Seattle Union Record* editorialized: "Both sides have earned the severest condemnation of law-abiding people. We advise all to await with us the development of the truth about the whole affair." The *Union Record* had reported on the previous attacks against the IWW in Centralia and gave the attacks as one reason for the retaliatory violence. But the *Union Record* was not to be allowed to counsel moderation. The police raided its offices, shut down the presses, and arrested the editor and several staff members, charging them with sedition. After a week, the courts ruled that the *Union Record* had been unlawfully seized and the plant was returned to the owners. The charges of sedition were dropped after two months, but in such an atmosphere few dared speak out.[31]

Only the IWW press and a few radical papers expressed any support for the Centralia Wobblies. The ACLU issued a pamphlet appealing for funds for the Wobblies' defense and describing the confrontation as the result of a bitter battle between labor and lumber owners. *The New Solidarity*, an IWW paper in Chicago, declared that the Wobblies "were decidedly not the aggressors."[32] The commander of the American Legion Post in Butte, Montana, attracted attention when he announced that the IWW members were fully justified in their act because they had fired in self-defense in the face of a mob attack.[33] But such statements of support were rare. Most newspapers agreed with the *Literary Digest* when it judged the confrontation to be an attack by "sinister forces of revolution and anarchy."[34]

Two days after the raid, however, a different interpretation of the events was presented at the coroner's inquest on the dead Legionnaires. The county coroner, Dr. David Livingstone—who, it was rumored, had participated in the lynching of Everest—was not present. Instead, another local doctor testified that Grimm, McElfresh, and Cassagranda were killed from bullets that passed downward into their bodies, suggesting that the firing came from over their heads. Other witnesses from the parade told of seeing gunfire coming from the Avalon Hotel. But the testimony that undermined the public consensus of events came from Frank Bickford, a forty-nine-year-old surgeon who had lived in Centralia for ten years and who had marched with Centralia's Legionnaires on Armistice Day. Bickford told the jury that he had offered to lead a raid while the veterans were marking time in front of the hall. He also said that the doors of the hall had been forced open before any shooting began. Another marcher corroborated Bickford's testimony. In the end, the jury concluded that Grimm had been killed by a bullet fired from the Avalon Hotel and that McElfresh and Cassagranda had been killed by gunfire from the IWW hall or surrounding territory. No IWW member was identified as a participant in any of the shooting. After the inquest, an Associated Press correspondent who had reported Bickford's testimony was run out of town by an armed mob and told never to return.[35]

Centralia's citizens were profoundly shaken by the November 11 tragedy. Just about everyone in town knew at least one of the dead men. Warren Grimm, one of Centralia's favorite sons, had left a young wife and a year-old child. Dale Hubbard, also very popular, had been married for only a few weeks, as had twenty-nine-year-old Ben Cassagranda. Arthur McElfresh, twenty-six years old and unmarried, had worked as a druggist in town. Many of their friends and the news media believed that the men had died as heroes, just as though they had fallen on the battlefields of France. Thousands of people from nearby communities attended a memorial service on November 14, when Grimm and McElfresh were buried. Funeral services were held the next day for Hubbard and Cassagranda.[36]

A grand jury indicted twelve Wobblies and Elmer Smith for the murder of Warren Grimm. The Wobblies were Britt Smith, Ray Becker, Bert Faulkner, James McInerney, and Mike Sheehan, who were captured in the IWW hall; O.C. Bland and John Lamb, who were in the Arnold Hotel during the raid; Bert Bland, Loren Roberts, and Ole Hanson, who were on Seminary Hill; Eugene Barnett and John Doe Davis, who the prosecution claimed were in the Avalon Hotel. Hanson and Davis had escaped after the shooting and were never found, and those who were captured refused to reveal the names of other Wobblies who had escaped from the IWW hall after the shooting. The rest of the men nabbed in the manhunt were released. All of the prisoners were charged with first-degree murder, and Elmer Smith was charged as an accessory for advising the Wobblies to kill Grimm. No one was ever charged with the murder of Wesley Everest.

Cunningham focused on Grimm's murder for several reasons. Hubbard's killer was already dead. The preliminary evidence seemed to indicate that McElfresh was killed in close proximity to the front of the IWW hall, and some eyewitnesses placed him in the group that broke down the front door. It would be easier to make a case that Grimm and Cassagranda were innocent victims. Grimm's entry wound was one-and-a-half inches higher than the exit wound, which seemed to clearly indicate that he was killed from a bullet fired from either the Avalon Hotel or Seminary Hill. Having the lethal bullet come from somewhere besides the IWW hall also strengthened the prosecution's charge that the Wobblies had conspired to fire on the parade. And finally, Grimm had been Cunningham's close friend, and his prominence in the community would influence a sympathetic jury.

Knowing that the eleven men faced great obstacles to a fair trial, the IWW General Defense Committee in Chicago hired George Vanderveer, the nationally known labor attorney who had led the defense during the IWW trials in Everett, Washington, and Chicago. Because of Vanderveer's reputation, Smith and the other prisoners believed that he was the best possible lawyer for their case. Vanderveer sent his law partner, Ralph Pierce, to Washington to begin the investigation for the defense while he finished up some legal work for the IWW in Chicago. Pierce took the train south from Seattle, where he had served nine years as city attorney, but two uniformed men prevented him from getting off the train in Centralia. This tactic was repeated on several occasions. In Chehalis, the police prevented Pierce from seeing the prisoners until November 18.[37]

Although the prisoners finally had legal counsel, the Lewis County Bar Association passed a resolution on November 17 that none of its members would defend the "numerous assassins who directly or indirectly were concerned in that atrocious deed." This was a clear violation of the oath every Washington attorney had taken to never reject "the cause of the defenseless or oppressed."[38] The dominant social and political powers in Centralia were lining up in solid opposition to the prisoners. On the Sunday following the raid, one Centralia minister's sermon, "The Cure for IWW-ism," was blunt:

> First of all, let us have the surgeon's knife. Let us cut out this cancerous growth. If we have laws, then enforce them. Apprehend every murderer: send them to the gallows. This is God's law. . . .[39]

A week later, Centralia's mayor and two city commissioners published a flyer charging that there was a "preconceived plan to kill the ex-servicemen" and that the "attack was unprovoked and without justification."[40]

On November 20, the defendants were arraigned before Judge

W. A. Reynolds in the Lewis County Superior Court; they all pleaded not guilty. Pierce filed a motion of prejudice against Reynolds (who was notorious in IWW circles for his anti-union views), who disqualified himself and was replaced by Judge George D. Abel. Pierce also filed for a change of venue to have the trial moved to another county because of the intense prejudice against the IWW in Lewis County. Pierce and Vanderveer wanted the trial held in as large a city as possible, such as Tacoma, in order to gain a better chance of finding neutral jurors. The change of venue motion was supported by a petition signed by 315 people. The petition also protested charges filed against Elmer Smith and Faulkner, saying that the two men were not involved in the killings. Despite the general hysteria in Centralia, a number of citizens were still sympathetic to Smith.

Cunningham fought the change of venue with affidavits signed by other Centralia citizens, including F. B. Hubbard, claiming that there was no prejudice against the defendants in Lewis County. In December, Judge Abel granted the change of venue to Montesano, the county seat of Grays Harbor County, northwest of Centralia. But the atmosphere in Montesano, which was heavily influenced by the lumber industry, was little different from that in Centralia. After the shootings, the leading Montesano newspaper ran an editorial on its front page calling the IWW "a nest of copperheads. . . . We have no sympathy for such human reptiles. . . . They must be destroyed."[41]

In the middle of December, the prosecution tried to strengthen its hand by hiring as an assistant W. H. Abel, the brother of the judge. They then filed a motion to have the judge removed because of a conflict of interest. Governor Hart passed over a judge that labor had supported during the last election and appointed John M. Wilson, whose views on labor and the IWW were anything but neutral. Shortly after the raid, Wilson had spoken at a memorial service held at the Elks Club Lodge each year to honor its deceased members. The most recent additions to that list were Warren Grimm, Dale Hubbard, and Arthur McElfresh. In June 1919, Wilson had also delivered an address at Tenino, Washington, in which he assailed the IWW and said that it was up to the returned soldiers to get rid of the radicals.[42]

By now, Vanderveer had arrived on the scene. Realizing that there was little advantage to having the trial moved to Montesano, he filed a motion for change of venue to Tacoma on the grounds that Montesano lacked accommodations for the defense and prosecution witnesses. Judge Wilson agreed but then reversed himself when Cunningham pointed out that the Tacoma jails were full and that a second change of venue could be allowed only if there was sufficient evidence of excitement or prejudice.[43] Vanderveer had failed to show this in his motion, and a hearing on the issue of prejudice against the IWW failed to change Wilson's ruling.

To counter some of the anti-IWW prejudice in the region's newspapers, the Seattle Central Labor Council and a number of other AFL organizations throughout the Pacific Northwest endorsed a resolution that sent six craft union representatives to Montesano to serve as a silent "Labor Jury." The men were to sit in the courtroom as spectators and then arrive at their own verdict. Despite their opposition to some IWW activities, the craft unions viewed the upcoming proceedings as a class trial that threatened all organized labor.[44]

With the trial finally set, the defendants were moved into the county jail near the Montesano courthouse. Smith and the others watched helplessly as the tide of public opinion against them grew stronger and stronger. The *Chronicle* published regular inflammatory editorials against the IWW in general and the defendants in particular.[45] The rhetoric cooled only after the issue of prejudice was raised in the motions for a change of venue. Without access to the local newspapers, the IWW Northwest District Defense Committee could only issue a series of fundraising letters and propaganda leaflets to tell its side.

Smith's family did what little it could to comfort Elmer and help in his defense. Jim and Harry Smith began tracking down witnesses who had seen Smith on the day of the raid. On December 20, Laura saw her husband for the first time since the raid. It was an emotional meeting for both of them, as they talked through a screen cage. Afterward, Laura begged the sheriff to lock her up in her husband's cell. Laura suffered when her friends turned away from her as they had against her husband. She stopped going to church, too embarrassed and ashamed to face the cold stares and silence of the congregation. She did not want to speak to anyone on the street, afraid that someone might refuse to speak to her. Smith was more used to this kind of behavior than Laura, but he was still surprised at the hostile reaction of his church community. The minister never called on him or his family, and no church members visited. As Smith sat in his cell day after day, his warmth for the church turned to bitterness.[46]

Deserted by many of his friends, Smith was also an object of curiosity and apprehension to many others. "Thank God the law finally got him," was the sentiment of more than one. "Centralians looked upon his actions as a case of 'biting the hand that fed him,'" the *Chronicle* reported.[47] He was unique among the eleven men facing a charge of murder, because he was a lawyer, a "professional" among the Wobbly working stiffs. Unaccustomed to seeing a local lawyer side with such a radical organization, many people were suspicious. The *Chehalis Bee-Nugget* reported:

> Most of the membership of the IWW was found to be ignorant and alien, but as always the case there is a set of brains leading them. Who this leader is cannot be definitely stated, but the officials are inclined to give a large share of this credit to Elmer S. Smith.[48]

The *Montesano Vidette*, under the headline "Elmer S. Smith Persecuted— 'Surely' " wrote:

> But Elmer S. Smith, brother lawyer of Vanderveer, man of money, man of education and man of egotism—he didn't do any shooting you know. At least the state doesn't say he did. It accuses him of concocting, inspiring, urging murder and the like. Well, pure unadulterated innocence will be the nicest role for him it is expected.[49]

Smith was particularly unhappy with this kind of personal attack. He objected to the insinuation that those who had opposed the war or who were sympathetic to the IWW were un-American and a threat to society. By exercising his lawful right to associate with and defend whomever he wanted, Smith saw himself as exemplifying the best of the American ideals. The *Nugget* saw it differently: "Smith may find himself enmeshed in a web from which he cannot extricate himself. He has been under suspicion for some time as a prominent IWW member."[50] This inaccurate linking of Smith with the IWW actually drew him closer to the organization than he had ever been before. His earlier legal work had led him to defend Wobblies as individuals, but he knew fewer than half of the other prisoners before the raid. He now found himself closely tied to the organization, and it would not be long before he would take a leadership role.

Most of the imprisoned Wobblies did not know each other very well. The men kept to themselves, leery that someone might be a stool pigeon. At Vanderveer's advice, they did not discuss the events of November 11.[51] The poor lighting made it hard to read, and the two cells the men were in were damp and cold. December was particularly bitter, with temperatures dropping to twelve degrees below zero. The men complained about the meager, overcooked meals of potatoes, thin soup, and cold coffee. To protest, Smith organized a silence strike, which lasted two days before the sheriff added bread to their diet.[52]

Smith was outwardly optimistic during those trying days. He tried to cheer up the others by reading aloud newspaper cartoons and by telling funny stories. He spoke with confidence to the newspaper reporters who interviewed him in jail. "There is not the slightest doubt in my mind regarding the outcome of the case," he said. "I know that every one of the eleven will be cleared. As for myself, I was in no way connected with the affair."[53] His confidence was not shared by the others.

For all of Smith's public optimism he had a tremendous amount of tension and anxiety. Smith had never had many friends to whom he confided his feelings, and he had turned his emotions inward. He behaved no differently in jail. His stomach hurt every morning when he woke up, and his gnawing hunger was never satisfied. He drank potfuls of coffee every day and paced the floor of his small cell when his stomach pains made it hard to sit still. It was the first sign of the ulcers he would later develop.[54]

Smith realized that his status as a lawyer would be an advantage to him in the courtroom. He knew that the jury would identify more with him than with the loggers, and he may have felt somewhat guilty about holding that advantage. The Wobblies, who were aware of Smith's more privileged position, could not share his positive attitude. They kept their thoughts to themselves and waited in silence and apprehension.

On the Prisoners' Bench

"Elmer Smith"—Anna Louise Strong, 1920

... He is more HATED
Than all the others
By the business men of
   Centralia
For he was the educated man
Of their OWN CLASS, ...
For he was one
Of those old-time Americans
Born on a HOMESTEAD
in North Dakota,
Working his way up
Through college and law
   school
Taking and improving
A NEW homestead
For himself in Washington,
Starting a little family,
Keeping alive
The plain and sturdy
   traditions
Of our REPUBLIC
And finding himself at last
On the PRISONERS' bench. [1]

The trial opened January 26, 1920, at the Grays Harbor County Courthouse in the lumbering town of Montesano, thirty-five miles west of Centralia. Montesano rested in a shallow valley along the Chehalis River just fifteen miles from the Pacific Ocean. Outside the windows of their timber-built houses, the twenty-five hundred inhabitants could see the bald tops of the surrounding hills covered with a thousand and more tree stumps.

A murder trial involving members of the notorious IWW promised to be the biggest event the area's residents had ever witnessed. The crowd that gathered was so large that it could not be accommodated in the town's few wooden boardinghouses, so many drove ten miles to hotels in the more populous town of Aberdeen. By the time the trial opened, every hardware store in Aberdeen and nearby Hoquiam was sold out of guns and ammunition. A special telegraph office was set up in the courthouse.

The Associated Press, United Press International, and International News Service sent writers to cover the trial, and extra seats had to be provided for the reporters in the courtroom. Several reporters for labor newspapers were also present, including John Nicholas Beffel of the *New York Call* and Ivar Vapaa of the Finnish paper *Industrialisti*, located in Duluth, Minnesota. On the eve of the trial, the *Chronicle* observed that the average citizen of Centralia "probably manifests more interest in the name of Elmer S. Smith than any other. Scores of Centralians will attend the trial . . . and many of them will go purely because Smith is one of the defendants."[2]

On the first day of the trial the courtroom was packed, and the spectators strained to get a good view of the eleven accused men. Judge Wilson sat in his black silken robes in a high-backed cushioned chair immediately to the left of the witness stand. The defendants sat on a long oak bench in front of the witness stand, facing the judge. Deputy sheriffs, looking younger than some of the defendants, sat behind them with guns on their hips and their belts lined with bullets. George Vanderveer, with Smith at his side for much of the trial, sat at a table directly in front of the judge at the right end of the defendants' bench. To Vanderveer's right was the prosecutor's table. To the judge's left stood the jury box.

Fifty of the two hundred courtroom seats were taken by uniformed veterans, recruited by the American Legion from the surrounding area and paid four dollars a day to watch the trial. The money came from public donations and contributions from the West Coast Lumbermen's Association, the Centralia Elks Club, and the Eastern Railway and Lumber Company. The Legionnaires slept in barracks set up above the largest garage in town and ate in a special mess hall in City Hall. When not at the trial, they patrolled the streets and met incoming trains, turning back anyone suspected of being a Wobbly.[3] In a front-page editorial, the *Montesano Vidette* summed up the anti-IWW atmosphere: "The men guilty of the murders at Centralia should be hanged."[4]

The job of defending the Wobblies rested on the broad shoulders of George Vanderveer, whose quick mind matched his temper. With degrees from Stanford and Columbia University Law School, he had served two terms as county prosecutor in Seattle. When he gave up that post to defend the city's derelicts and underdogs, he had earned his reputation as "Counsel for the Damned."[5] Since then, Vanderveer had become nationally known for his defense of IWW members. He admired the Wobblies for their willingness to stand up and take a punch as well as to give one, regardless of the odds, but he was not an advocate of their radical ideology.

As the trial opened in Montesano, Vanderveer was at a low point in his career. His last case had been in Chicago, where he had defended 101 Wobbly leaders charged with sedition. The trial had lasted five months, but it had taken the jury less than an hour to convict the defendants, many of whom were sentenced to twenty years in prison. Vanderveer had been confident of an acquittal, and the sweeping convictions had been a heart-breaking loss for him. Despite promises, he had received little money for his efforts. The IWW General Defense Committee in Chicago had made new promises of payment for his services for the Centralia case, promises that were never kept. To compound his worries, Vanderveer's home had been repossessed and his relationship with his wife, never strong, was deteriorating.[6]

Vanderveer was usually a well-organized and fully rehearsed lawyer, but he was uncharacteristically ill-prepared as the trial opened in Montesano. Last minute legal work for the Chicago case had kept him away from Centralia, so that he had only seven weeks to construct the case for the defense. Without funds, he found it difficult to hire defense investigators. Vanderveer had hoped to make use of Elmer Smith's legal training during the trial, but his efforts to have the judge dismiss the charges against Smith or to have him released on bail were unsuccessful.[7] Smith did consult with Vanderveer for most of the trial, but as a young, inexperienced trial lawyer, he was of little help.

To complicate things further, Vanderveer's law partner, Ralph Pierce, was unavailable for much of the trial because he had to work on two other cases involving members of the IWW. The first trial, which began in Tacoma on January 31, involved thirty-six Wobblies charged with criminal syndicalism following the Centralia outbreak. Vanderveer had asked the Tacoma judge, without success, for an extension until after the Montesano trial was over. After giving his closing argument in Tacoma, Pierce hurried back to Montesano without waiting for the verdict. All of the defendants were found guilty.[8] Pierce's second case came three weeks later in the Montesano courtroom, right across the hall from where the Centralia trial was being heard. Thirteen Wobblies had been arrested in southwestern Washington after November 11 and charged with criminal syndicalism. On February 20, eleven of them were found guilty.[9] So, Vanderveer confronted his court challenge in the Centralia case with little legal assistance.

Facing off against Vanderveer was a confident team of six attorneys for the prosecution. The leading counsel, special prosecutor Clifford D. Cunningham, had been an attorney for the Eastern Railway and Lumber Company and other lumber owners. Two years earlier, at the age of thirty-eight, he had enlisted in the army, but the war had ended before he finished basic training. Cunningham also had a personal involvement in the Centralia case. He was a member of the Grant Hodge Post of the American Legion and was a close friend of Warren Grimm. He had watched the November 11 parade and had seen McElfresh killed. He had also joined with the group of former servicemen who had led Wesley Everest to jail after the shootings. Later that evening, Cunningham had visited Everest in jail to interrogate him, but Everest had refused to talk. Cunningham had been present at the Elks Club meeting that evening, and he had watched from the sidelines when the mob broke into the jail to get Everest. It was rumored that he had been at the lynching as well.[10] If Cunningham had not been one of the prosecutors, he probably would have testified as a witness for the prosecution. So, as Cunningham built the case against the Wobblies, he was also shielding himself from any potential legal action for his role in the raid and lynching.

The other attorneys acting for the prosecution included W. H. Abel, the counsel for F. B. Hubbard and former prosecuting attorney for Grays Harbor County. Abel had worked closely with timber and mill owners to send striking workers to jail during the 1917–18 lumber strike. The rest of the team was composed of Herman Allen, prosecuting attorney for Lewis County; Frank Christensen, Washington state assistant attorney general; John Dunbar, assistant in the office of the attorney general; and J. H. Jahnke, an attorney from Centralia. Assisting the state in its investigation was Luke May of the Revelare International Secret Service, a private detective agency paid for by five Lewis County lumber companies. May's undercover agents were charged with infiltrating IWW circles to find out if the organization might cause trouble during the trial.[11]

Just as the families and friends of the dead Legionnaires gathered in the courtroom to watch the trial, so did the mothers and wives of all but two of the accused Wobblies. Five of the defendants—Britt Smith, Eugene Barnett, O.C. Bland, Bert Bland, and John Lamb—were permanent residents of either Centralia or Kopiah and knew each other.

Eugene Barnett, twenty-eight, was just eight years old when he went to work in the coal mines in the Blue Ridge Mountains for fifty cents a day. He became a member of the Socialist Party and left home at thirteen. After working at a series of jobs—pitching hay, mining, and working for the railroad—he moved to Idaho, married, and had a son. In December 1917, he spoke out against conscription, labeling it as unconstitutional, and was arrested for "seditious utterances." His jailors tried to convince him not to read or circulate IWW literature, but he refused. After eighteen days in jail, he was released and no charges were filed. He moved his family to

Kopiah, where he met Elmer Smith. After the war ended and the demand for coal dropped, he worked in the lumber camps. Returning to the mines, he was elected secretary of the United Mine Workers Local at Kopiah. He had been an IWW member since March 1919. On the day of the raid he was in town visiting friends during a nationwide coal strike.[12]

O.C. Bland, also known as "Commodore," was thirty-six years old and had lived in Centralia with his wife and seven children for two years. A Wobbly since 1917, Bland was a logger who also spent some time working in the sawmills. Twenty-four-year-old Bert Bland, Commodore's brother, had been a logger since he was sixteen. He had lived in Centralia for two years and had worked in the saw mills and nearby logging camps.

Logger John Lamb, forty, had a wife and five children and was a ten-year resident of Centralia. The tips of two fingers on his right hand had been cut off during an accident in the woods, and he had injured his back in another mishap. He had joined the IWW during the 1917 lumber strike.

Bert Faulkner, thirty-one years old, had served in the army for four months and worked as a logger. He had been a Wobbly for three years. His left middle finger had been torn off while he was on the job in the woods.

At sixty years of age, Irishman Mike Sheehan had a thick, white mustache that turned down over his mouth. A union man for more than forty years, he had served in the navy during the Spanish American War. His son Bill sat behind him in the courtroom.

James McInerney, twenty-five, was born in Ireland and immigrated to the United States in 1908. Six feet tall and 180 pounds, he was an outstanding boxer and gave boxing lessons to some of the Wobblies in the IWW hall. He worked as a logger and joined the IWW in 1916, the year that he was wounded on the steamer *Verona* during the free speech fight at Everett, Washington. He was one of the seventy-four Wobblies who were tried for murder, but he went free when all charges were dropped after the first acquittal. A quiet man, McInerney had not yet fully recovered from the beating he took in jail the night of Everest's lynching.

Loren Roberts at twenty-one was the youngest defendant. A Wobbly since early 1919, he worked in the woods to support his mother and three younger siblings after his father, a sawyer in the mill, died of tuberculosis.[13]

Twenty-six-year-old Ralph Burgdorf, the son of a Chicago preacher, stood only five and a half feet tall, but he was tough. Before going to work in the woods of Wisconsin, Illinois, and Minnesota, he had spent four years studying for the ministry. In 1917, he joined the IWW in Washington. Later, after escaping from a jail in Bellingham, where he was serving a year's time for trying to evade the draft, he changed his name to Ray Becker. In 1918, he was arrested in Spokane for failing to show his draft card to a police officer. A friend described Becker as honest "almost to the point of fanaticism," but to the deputy sheriff in Bellingham he was "just a damn ornery cuss."[14]

Despite the differences in occupation that separated Smith from his fellow defendants, he identified more closely with them than he did with George Vanderveer. Thirteen years older than Smith, Vanderveer was an experienced, big-city lawyer with an excellent command of courtroom theatrics. His tailored suits and stylish hat complemented his aggressive and, at times, flamboyant personality. He had arrived at Montesano with his secretary, who, it was rumored, was also his mistress. Fond of steak and expensive whiskey, Vanderveer drank heavily and openly carried a gun in town. In contrast, Smith was a courtroom novice. His legal skill lay more in arguing the rightness of his clients' position than in scoring technical legal points. Although certainly outspoken, Smith was much less abrasive than Vanderveer and he had more of the common touch with people. Smith admired Vanderveer, but he never tried to imitate him.

From the beginning of the trial, Vanderveer realized that the odds were against him, but he was comfortable with the role of the underdog. IWW trials were not merely a battleground over the legal question of an individual's guilt or innocence; they also became a stage where the economic rights of the working class were presented to the broader audience of public opinion. Even though the fate of the defendants would turn on the legal questions raised in the Montesano courtroom, the IWW considered it just as important to use the trial to wage a public education campaign. Sometimes this tactic was employed at the expense of the individual defendants. As the *Industrial Worker*, the largest Wobbly newspaper, explained:

> Legal defense can be valuable to the IWW only as it serves the purpose of providing publicity and propaganda. In a big case like the Centralia trial at Montesano a lawyer got results for the organization. The daily battle over legal technicalities and other lawyers' piffle served to give to the masses some knowledge of the fact that the victims of the class struggle were real and not fiction. We realized that the Centralia victims were our own vanguard, and this realization was not borne in upon us because Vanderveer made this or that objection, but because of the publicity that the legal battle received.[15]

Although this strategy might seem cold-blooded, it was a tactic born as much of necessity as principle. Few lawyers offered their services to defend the IWW, and the General Defense Committee had exhausted its funds on the Chicago trial. As a result, it urged Vanderveer to defend the men as a group, since a mass acquittal would generate more publicity and cash than would several smaller trials. Vanderveer did try—unsuccessfully—to separate two of the defendants, Loren Roberts and Elmer Smith, from the group, but he still conducted his defense primarily on the theory that the IWW was on trial. Although this approach helped spread the IWW name, it also put the individual defendants at greater risk, particularly those who were not so deeply implicated in the Centralia shootings. Smith and the others understood Vanderveer's approach and agreed that it was their best course of action. They were willing to stake some of their chances for acquittal in the courtroom on the hope that Vanderveer could convince the jury of the just cause of the IWW.

Vanderveer used a variety of tactics. The Labor Jury fit into his plans as a way for the Wobblies and their allies to educate both the public and the members of the jury. Vanderveer undoubtedly also knew what he was doing when he carried a handgun into the courtroom one day during jury selection. He had received several anonymous threats against his life, and he told the judge that he was carrying a weapon for his own protection. But his actions also emphasized the underlying anti-labor violence against which the Wobblies had reacted, a central defense position. The judge ordered Vanderveer to leave his gun in his hotel room.[16]

It took an unusually long time—eleven days—to choose the all-male jury of four farmers, one telephone employee, two construction laborers, and five other wage-earners. During the selection, Vanderveer questioned prospective jurors at length about their views of the IWW, but Judge Wilson ruled that "hatred" of the IWW, as long as it was not directed against the defendants, was not grounds for disqualification. Under the circumstances, Vanderveer probably got as favorable a jury as was possible.

On Friday, February 7, prosecutor Allen delivered the opening statement for the state:

> This gentlemen is the most important case that was ever tried in the whole country. . . . The evidence in this case will show that this shooting was premeditated by these defendants. . . . That they had picked out places or had stationed the different men and concealed themselves and made all arrangements to fire on this parade and kill these boys.[17]

Allen outlined the case, charging the eleven defendants with the vicious and premeditated first-degree murder of Warren Grimm. As he read off the charge against Smith—advising the other defendants in their unlawful conspiracy—the accused leaned forward, listening studiously, and occasionally made a mark in his notebook.

After Allen sat down, Vanderveer jumped to his feet and asked him whether there was an attack on the hall before the shooting. Allen replied:

> Our position is that the boys were standing in the street in military formation under the charge of their Commander, paying attention to him when he gave the command to halt and close up the ranks and they were marking time when they were fired upon.

Vanderveer quickly rejoined:

> In other words, it is equivalent to a statement that there was no attack on the hall and the doors were not smashed in before there was any shooting, and be judged by it hereafter?
> "Surely will!" Abel flashed back.[18]

The battle lines were drawn. The prosecution charged that the IWW had planned and carried out an ambush on the parade. The defense insisted that they had merely defended their hall from attack. Vanderveer waived giving his opening argument because he was not yet prepared, and Judge Wilson adjourned the court until Monday.

On Monday morning, Vanderveer announced that he would give his opening argument. "The big question in this case," he asked, "is, who was the aggressor, who started the battle?" Vanderveer declared that the IWW was on trial. He described its organization and purpose in an effort to educate the jury about the serious intent of its members to improve working conditions and create a better life for laborers. He recounted the 1918 raid on the Wobbly hall and the events leading up to the 1919 raid and shootings. Vanderveer asserted that only a dozen or so shots were fired from inside the IWW hall and that none was fired from either the Avalon or Arnold hotels (a position he would later abandon). The defendants, he said, decided to protect themselves after the law refused to intervene. Placed in the situation that the Wobblies were in, he asked the jurors, "What would you do? . . . From the beginning to end it has been a struggle on the one side for ideals and on the other side to suppress those ideals." Vanderveer placed the guilt for the tragedy in the hands of the commercial interests and exonerated the Legionnaires as being their "catspaws." He concluded: "I don't know what the verdict will be today, but the verdict 10 years hence will be . . . that these men were within their rights and that they fought for cause, that these men fought for liberty."[19]

The prosecution introduced a parade of witnesses who testified to the number, location, and angle of the bullets fired on November 11. Shell casings had been found on Seminary Hill. Witnesses disagreed on the number of shots fired; some said first three shots had rung out, followed by a volley from the street and then from Seminary Hill. Describing the wound that killed Warren Grimm, a doctor said that a single bullet had entered near his left nipple and had exited one and a half inches lower out his back. The police chief displayed the weapons owned by the defendants. Britt Smith had carried a .32-20 Special Colt pistol; Ray Becker a .38 Iver-Johnson pistol; Loren Roberts a .22 Savage rifle; Eugene Barnett a .30 Remington rifle; Bert Bland a .32-20 Winchester rifle; and O. C. Bland a .25-35 rifle and a .32 Iver-Johnson pistol.[20] The other defendants had carried no guns.

The first direct evidence against any of the defendants was the confession by one of their own, Loren Roberts. Cunningham had first interrogated Roberts on November 17 in the waiting room of the Centralia jail in the presence of his mother, sister, and five other witnesses. The next day, Roberts had made another statement from the Olympia jail, where he had been transferred. One week later, he had made a third statement, making minor corrections to the first two statements. When the prosecution attempted to read Roberts' November 17 statement into the court record, Vanderveer objected, saying that Roberts was pleading insanity and his confession was thus incompetent evidence. Judge Wilson ruled that the confession could be entered as evidence against Roberts but not the other defendants.[21] A later determination would be made as to whether or not Roberts was legally insane. By that time, however, the damage of the confession to the other defendants had already been done.

The confession was read into the record. On the morning of the parade, the statement said, Roberts was in the IWW hall during a discussion about protecting the hall from attack. He said Britt Smith told the men that the building across the street would be a good place for some of the boys to be.[22] Roberts said he did not want to be caught in any building when the shooting started, so he went up to Seminary Hill with Bert Bland and Ole Hanson, where the three of them opened fire on the parade after hearing shots from below.

Although Cunningham asked several leading questions in an attempt to get Roberts to admit that he did not see any soldiers move against the IWW until after he heard shots being fired, Roberts said he was not certain whether the shooting below began before or after the attack on the hall. Roberts said that he fired about five shots from his rifle and that the bullets went high, missing everything. He said that Bland and Hanson fired fifteen to twenty shots between them. Bland later admitted on the witness stand that he fired his rifle at the parade after hearing shooting from below. Vanderveer decided not to call Roberts to the witness stand because of his claim that he was insane.[23]

Tom Morgan, who quit the IWW in 1917, took the stand to give the second confession. He was in the IWW hall on November 11, he said, when Elmer Smith came over to talk to Britt Smith about the parade. He said that Britt pointed toward the Arnold and Avalon hotels while talking to Elmer. After Elmer left, Morgan testified, "I heard Britt Smith, I would not say for sure, make the remark it was kind of nice for an attorney to come in and tell you to do your duty." Morgan said the other men in the hall at the time were Roberts, Sheehan, Becker, Everest, and McInerney. He said Britt told the men to go to the front rooms of the Arnold, Avalon, Queen, and Roderick hotels. Morgan saw no one carrying guns, and he later refused to take one when it was offered. Morgan testified that the first shots came from one of the hotel buildings while the soldiers were still peacefully marching in line.[24] The prosecution wanted to use Morgan's testimony to establish a conspiracy among the defendants to fire on the parade. Morgan received immunity for turning state's evidence, and he was released following the trial.

There were a few differences between Morgan's trial testimony and his statement to Cunningham on November 24. In his statement he did not mention Britt's remark after Elmer left the IWW hall. He also said that Britt did not mention the names of any hotels. He told Cunningham that the Wobblies thought the raid would come after the parade was over and that they made no arrangements to fire on the parade. Vanderveer requested a copy of Morgan's pretrial statement. Cunningham said the statement had been lost, but there is some evidence suggesting that he deliberately withheld the statement at the trial.[25]

Laura Smith faithfully attended the trial proceedings with her daughter, Virginia, usually sitting behind the defendants' bench. One morning she was unable to find a seat where she could see her husband. She tried to catch his attention, but it was only when Virginia began crying that Elmer, recognizing her voice, turned around and saw them both.

Laura held Virginia up above her head and waved, while Elmer smiled and waved back. For a brief moment the serious courtroom drama became a warm family reunion.[26] Across the courtroom from Laura Smith sat Mrs. Warren Grimm with her baby, who was about the same age as Virginia. Mrs. Grimm was the town librarian and for a time was the Smiths' friendly next-door neighbor. But the women's marriages had separated them, and now they sat each day on either side of the room without acknowledging the other's presence.[27]

The trial put a great strain on Laura, although she received comfort from the railroad family that had put her up after the raid. A sympathetic Montesano widow and her daughter also welcomed Laura and Virginia into their home during the trial. Laura's family was not as supportive; her father insisted that she return home to Tacoma until the trial was over. He was shocked at Smith's connection with the murderers and felt that his arrest was a disgrace for Laura. But she flatly refused to leave her husband's side. "I admire your loyalty," her brother told her, "but I think it's misplaced."[28]

In contrast, Elmer Smith's relatives rallied solidly behind him, and on several occasions Isabelle brought Willard and Dorothy to the courtroom. During one recess, Isabelle spoke confidently to a newspaper reporter that her son had done no wrong. Under Vanderveer's directions, Jim, Harry, and Glen Smith hunted down witnesses while their wives ran the farms and kept their children fed. By the end of the trial, Jim had worn out his Model T Ford on the dirt roads between Centralia and Montesano. Harry spent some time at the trial, but as the weeks wore on he became more and more discouraged about the defendants' chances.[29]

A number of witnesses testified that Warren Grimm had been shot while standing in the street away from the IWW hall, and expert testimony strongly implied that the bullet that killed him had come from the Avalon Hotel. Many witnesses also placed Eugene Barnett in the Avalon at the time of the shooting, but the bullet that had killed Grimm was never tied to Barnett's gun or to any of the other defendants' guns. The confessions of Roberts and Morgan tended to establish that a number of defendants had planned an armed defense of the hall and had taken up several positions to do so. With the evidence presented, the prosecution's case came to a close.

When Vanderveer took the floor, he moved that the charges against Mike Sheehan, Bert Faulkner, and Elmer Smith be dropped because no evidence had been introduced to implicate them in the shooting. Sheehan and Faulkner had been in the hall but had carried no guns, and Smith had only visited the hall before the raid. Judge Wilson agreed to dismiss the charges against Faulkner, but not those against Sheehan or Smith. Sheehan had handled a gun earlier that day in the hall, and Morgan's testimony linked Smith to a conspiracy.[30] Suddenly a free man, Faulkner sat next to his mother in the courtroom and watched the proceedings.

On February 26, during the fourth week of the trial, a hundred soldiers from the 35th Infantry set up camp on the courthouse lawn, where the jury and everyone inside the courtroom could see them through the windows. Prosecutor Allen had asked the governor to send the troops without notifying either the judge or the sheriff. He announced that his detective agency had picked up rumors that armed Wobblies were gathering in the nearby hills, preparing to spring the defendants. The prosecution wanted to take no chances. One Wobbly was arrested on the streets of Montesano for wearing a lumberjack blazer. He was given thirty days and joined eight other Wobblies in the local jail. No hard evidence of any armed Wobbly group was ever uncovered, and the likelihood that it ever existed is remote.[31]

When Vanderveer arrived at the courtroom and saw the troops, he angrily demanded that they be withdrawn. They gave the trial a military mood that was prejudicial to the defendants, he told Judge Wilson. "Today I fear prejudice more than I fear the evidence," he said.[32] The troops did influence the jury, which had heard the rumors that Wobblies were hiding in the hills and might attack. After the troops arrived, the jurors grew increasingly concerned for their own safety, and two jurors secretly armed themselves.[33] Judge Wilson said that although he did not see the need for the troops, he did not have the authority to remove them because they had been sent in by the governor. The troops remained on the courthouse lawn for the rest of the trial. Elmer Smith followed the courtroom dramatics with concern, yet he still managed to strike an upbeat note with reporters who interviewed him during the trial:

> This sending for troops is, of course a theatrical performance.
> It is a bold play by the prosecution to influence both jury and
> public. If it were not that 10 men's lives are at stake here, this
> spectacle of military display would be amusing.[34]

Vanderveer began the case for the defense with his strongest evidence. He called numerous witnesses who testified that Barnett had not been in the Avalon Hotel and could not have fired the shots that killed Grimm. Barnett testified that he had been in the Roderick Hotel, next door to the IWW hall, when the shooting started. He reported that the shooting had begun from inside the IWW hall after the front door was broken in. Then Mr. and Mrs. McAllister testified that they had been with Barnett in the Roderick during the parade.[35]

Other witnesses said that Barnett had not been carrying a gun, and they contradicted the prosecution's witnesses who had identified Barnett in the Avalon. In his cross-examination of prosecution eyewitnesses, Vanderveer let the jury discover that one had been shown a photograph of Barnett before the trial and another had been taken to jail and shown who Barnett was. After several prosecution witnesses had identified Barnett on the prisoners' bench, Vanderveer called a recess. When the defendants came back into the courtroom, they took different seats. Interestingly, the next witness identified Barnett as the defendant who now sat in Barnett's seat.[36] There were reports that John Doe Davis was the man in the Avalon and had probably fired on the parade and killed Grimm. Davis had escaped and was never found. All in all, the case against Barnett was very weak.

To counter Roberts' confession, Vanderveer brought in a number of psychiatrists to testify that Roberts suffered from systematic hallucinations, had a fear of conspiracies, and was unable to recognize who people really were. Roberts was convinced that his bed was wired and that electricity was being passed through it each night. He thought Vanderveer was Colonel Disque, the organizer of the 4L's.[37] His behavior in the courtroom was erratic. At one point, he suddenly rushed to the front of the courtroom and sat in the witness stand. Roberts was never called to testify.[38]

Britt Smith testified that on the day of the parade he had told Roberts that "if some of the boys were in the buildings across the street and those hoodlums or a mob attacked the hall, they would be in a bad place." He said that there had been a general understanding among the Wobblies that they would defend the hall, but there had been no plan to fire on the parade in ambush. He contradicted Morgan's testimony, saying that he had not pointed to any hotels while talking to Elmer Smith in the hall. He also denied saying that Smith had told him to "do our duty." Britt said that the soldiers had kicked open the front door of the hall before any firing had begun and that he then fled to the back of the hall without firing his gun.[39] Mike Sheehan testified that he had been in the IWW hall but had carried no gun. Everest had fired three shots at the soldiers, he remembered. James McInerney testified that he had had a gun in the hall but he had not fired it.[40]

Commodore Bland and John Lamb had been in the Arnold Hotel, but their testimony showed that they could not have killed Grimm. Bland testified that he had seen soldiers break for the hall and bash down the door.

He had pushed his rifle through the window pane but in the process had cut his hand so badly that he had not been able to hold his gun. Bland and Lamb were both rooming at the Arnold on November 11. Bland had decided to go from the IWW hall back to the Arnold when the parade started in order to help defend the hall and have a better chance of escape. Lamb had gone along. He testified that they had not talked about defending the hall while they were together. Lamb had heard the IWW door being crashed in and then heard shots. He had carried no gun. The prosecution never seriously challenged the testimony of these two men.[41]

Dr. Frank Bickford, a major witness for the defense, remembered that as the parade began he had heard someone talk about raiding the hall. While standing in line near the hall, he had offered to lead the charge if enough men would follow, and he had joined six or eight men who had moved against the hall and were shoving against the door when the first bullets were fired. On cross-examination, however, Bickford admitted that he was somewhat deaf and that there could have been a shot fired before his charge. Further undermining Bickford's testimony, several rebuttal witnesses for the prosecution said Bickford had not charged the hall before shots were fired.[42]

Several defense witnesses came forward to say that the veterans had charged the hall before the firing began, but on cross-examination many admitted that they could not be sure. One witness thought he had seen Grimm in front of the hall before the shooting started, but he did not claim that Grimm had attacked the hall. Another witness placed someone who might have been Grimm near the front of the IWW hall. After their testimony and in full view of the jury, the police arrested both witnesses on charges of perjury, for contradicting the prosecution witnesses that Grimm had not been in front of the hall when he was shot. Vanderveer protested the harassment, but the judge did nothing.[43] Mort Barger, a Legionnaire, testified that he had heard someone in the parade say "Let's go get them" and then had seen soldiers of the second platoon kicking in the front door of the Wobbly hall. He had heard the first shots, he said, after the door had been broken in.[44]

Vanderveer's defense strategy was to claim justifiable homicide based on self-defense. In court, he asserted that the defendants had lawfully used self-defense in the face of a conspiracy to destroy the IWW hall. To prove the conspiracy, Vanderveer hoped to introduce testimony about the 1918 raid, the Elks Club meeting where threats had been made against the hall, and other evidence that showed the townspeople's hostility toward the Wobblies. But when Vanderveer asked the defendants about why they had feared an imminent attack against their hall, the prosecution objected. The judge agreed that no such evidence would be admitted unless it could be shown that Warren Grimm had been a conspirator. Because the defendants were only charged with Grimm's murder, the judge ruled that if Grimm had not been part of a conspiracy to attack the hall then testimony about the actions of others was irrelevant. Vanderveer was in a serious bind. None of the defendants had ever claimed that Grimm had been part of the attack on the hall, and defense witnesses had been unable to shake the prosecution's claim that Grimm had not been in front of the hall when he was shot. The best Vanderveer could do was to convey to the jury some of the atmosphere of fear in Centralia by repeatedly asking questions about the threatening incidents, even if the witnesses were not permitted to answer.

Vanderveer pressed ahead, trying to show that an atmosphere of fear had existed on November 11. Ten witnesses testified that two of the marchers in the parade had been carrying ropes, presumably to use on the Wobblies in the hall. Five witnesses testified that T. H. McCleary, the postmaster, had been carrying a rope about eight feet long. Three witnesses identified the other man as Reverend H. W. Thompson, the former mayor of Centralia. McCleary took the stand and admitted carrying a rope, but he said he had found it in the street at the start of the parade. He said he had no intention of hanging anyone. Thompson said he had been watching the parade and had not carried any rope. Another prosecution witness admitted having carried a rope in the parade with McCleary. He too said he had found it in the street.[45] While the rope may have been additional evidence that some of the paraders had anticipated a raid on the IWW hall, the testimony added little to the defendants' case.

Vanderveer wanted to call as a witness Earl Craft, the electrician in charge of the city lights. Outside the jury's hearing, Vanderveer said that Craft would testify that at seven-fifteen on the night of November 11 he had left the power station and locked the door behind him. The city's lights had been turned off after he left. When Craft had returned fifteen minutes later, he had found the mayor, the chief electrician, and the first assistant electrician in the power station and the lights were back on. The prosecution objected that the testimony was incompetent as a defense to Grimm's killing. The judge agreed, and Craft was not called to the stand.[46]

Throughout the trial, Vanderveer's defense efforts were undermined outside the courtroom. Legionnaires threatened potential witnesses who then refused to testify for the defense. Several defense investigators were arrested for allegedly harassing witnesses, but the charges were dropped after the trial. Mail addressed to Vanderveer was redirected to the prosecution, and prosecution detectives followed Vanderveer wherever he went and listened in on conversations in the jail between the defendants and their families.[47] Smith was also harassed while in jail. W. G. Graham, the high school principal, came to see him, only to call Smith a "traitor."[48]

Smith was concerned about the public's reaction to the trial. He read the daily papers and worried that their coverage was making it impossible for the public to understand the reasons behind the defendants' actions. Although outwardly confident, Smith was apprehensive about the progress of the trial, but he carefully hid his feelings from the others. His painful stomach cramps continued to bother him. Smith's stomach trouble was not helped by the miserable food the defendants received in jail. Prisoner complaints about the steady diet of cabbage, rutabaga, parsnips, macaroni, and potatoes got nowhere until Smith organized a hunger strike. The strike began in early March when the men threw their noon meal onto the floor. After two days, they won some concessions and occasionally got meat and green vegetables added to their plates.[49]

It was with a feeling of physical and mental relief that Smith took the witness stand on March 5. He described how he had gone to the hall on the morning of November 11 and told Britt Smith about the latest rumors of a raid. "Do you read the papers?" asked Vanderveer. "I do," said Smith. "Had you seen matters with reference to running the IWW out of town?" Vanderveer asked. Prosecutor Abel interrupted: "Object to that as incompetent." "Objection sustained," ruled Judge Wilson.[50] Smith continued: "My sole object in going down there was to tell [Britt] that the hall was to be raided. I thought the hall would be torn to pieces, and some of the members of the IWW taken out of town, at least, tarred and feathered." "What reason have you for thinking that?" Vanderveer asked. Abel objected and again the court sustained him.

Vanderveer tried to ask Smith about conversations he had had with Warren Grimm about the Lassiter kidnapping to show that Grimm had approved of such violent tactics. The court again prevented Smith from answering. If Vanderveer could not show that Grimm had acted directly and overtly against the hall, the court ruled, then he would not be able to introduce testimony about Grimm's views on violence against the IWW. The court refused to allow Smith to answer questions about the 1918 raid, the physical destruction of the IWW hall, and his appeal to the governor for protection after the Lassiter kidnapping.[51]

In cross-examining Smith, Abel was most interested in his advice to the defendants about the use of guns. Smith said that he had not known the Wobblies had guns. He denied telling any of them to position themselves in the Arnold and Avalon hotels, although he believed that they had a right to be there to defend their hall. Smith said he had not warned Britt against using guns, because "I certainly thought a man had a right to use a gun to defend his life and property." Although Smith did not advocate that the Wobblies use violence, he could not condemn them when they did. In Smith's mind, the fault for the tragedy lay with those townspeople in Centralia who had used threats, a kidnapping, and two raids to try and drive the Wobblies out. "I don't think you can kill ideas with a bayonet," he said at the end of his testimony.[52]

By the end of the case for the defense, the trial was into its seventh week and 271 witnesses had been called. Smith and Vanderveer were discouraged, and for good reason. Despite conflicting testimony, the weight of the trial testimony indicated that Grimm had not been attacking the hall when he was shot on Tower Avenue more than a hundred feet from the hall. Vanderveer had failed to show a conspiracy to raid the IWW hall. A number of the veterans in the parade had been from out of town and knew of no plan to raid the hall, and none of the marchers had been armed, although several had carried ropes. Six of the defendants had carried guns that day, but only Roberts and Bert Bland admitted firing on the parade; the prosecution did not offer any evidence that any other defendant had fired a gun. Ole Hanson, J. D. Davis, and Wesley Everest had also fired their guns, but they had disappeared or were dead.[53] The most reasonable conclusion to be drawn from the trial records is that J. D. Davis had killed Grimm while firing from the Avalon Hotel. Because the trial did not address who had killed the other two Legionnaires, the best reading of the evidence is that McElfresh had been shot by someone firing from inside the IWW hall, either Everest or one of the several men who escaped in the confusion. Cassagranda had been killed while running west on Second Avenue by a revolver probably fired by J. D. Davis from the Avalon Hotel.

At the same time, an analysis of the conflicting evidence tends to support the IWW position that the hall had been attacked before any Wobblies opened fire; no credible evidence was introduced to explain why the defendants, without provocation, would open fire on the parade. Although it can never be conclusively established that the attack had preceded the firing, it seems most likely that the Wobblies had fired in the sincere belief that their hall was under attack. They had expected an attack and believed they were legally justified in placing men outside the hall. But the Wobblies certainly had no coordinated plan to ambush the parade. Some of the defendants had not even known that others were in the hotels with guns, and not all of them had guns. There had been no arranged signal for firing on the parade and no escape route had been planned. The evidence supports Barnett's position that he was not in the Avalon Hotel and had not fired on the parade. It seems clear that some of the veterans, but not all, had been ready to rush the IWW hall that day. Had the Wobblies not armed themselves, a raid would have taken place and those in the hall would have likely been beaten and thrown out of town. Some of the defendants may have wondered whether they would have been better off if they had taken that beating.

In his closing statement, Abel asked the jury to convict all of the defendants of first-degree murder. Cunningham went over the case against each of the defendants and concluded:

> If these defendants are freed as guiltless, such action will mean that good government in the United States is at an end. It will mean anarchy and red murder, such as I saw on the streets of Centralia.[54]

Vanderveer then tried one last time to convince the jury that Grimm had been killed in front of the IWW hall while taking part in an unlawful raid and that the defendants had been justifiably afraid for their own safety. He concluded with words that he might well have used at his other Wobbly trials:

> They [the prosecution] have told you this was a murder trial, and not a labor trial. But vastly more than the lives of ten men are the stakes in the big gamble here; for the right of workers to organize for the bettering of their own condition is on trial; the right of free assemblage is on trial; democracy and Americanism are on trial.[55]

The jury received the judge's instructions on Friday, March 12, and retired for the night. They deliberated all the next day and just before dinner announced that they had come to a decision. The courtroom filled quickly, and the verdict was read. Elmer Smith and Sheehan were acquitted; Roberts was found insane; Barnett and Lamb were found guilty of third-degree murder; and the rest of the men were found guilty of second-degree murder. The jury had not believed the prosecution's claim that Barnett had fired the fatal bullet from the Avalon and that the Wobblies conspired to murder Grimm. But the judge refused to accept the jury's verdict because there was no legal charge of third-degree murder. He had given the jurors instructions on the charges of first-degree murder, which is premeditated; second-degree murder, which is unpremeditated; and acquittal. He sent them back to reconsider. The jury returned two hours later. Elmer Smith and Sheehan were again found not guilty, and Roberts was judged not guilty because of insanity. Barnett, Lamb, Commodore and Bert Bland, Britt Smith, Becker, and McInerney were found guilty of second-degree murder.[56]

The verdict represented a compromise between those jurors who wanted a first-degree conviction and those who wanted an acquittal. The jury believed that the hall had been attacked before the shooting had begun, and they found the defendants guilty of conspiring to commit unpremeditated murder—a somewhat illogical conclusion. The judge had instructed the jury that in a conspiracy each person is equally liable for the acts of the others. If only those in the hall (Britt Smith, Becker, and McInerney) had fired, then they probably would have been acquitted on grounds of self-defense. But because the others had fired from outside the hall, they were all found guilty of conspiracy, even though those on trial did not fire the bullet that had killed Grimm. Vanderveer failed to ask for a jury instruction on the lesser crime of manslaughter, because it would appear that he was admitting that his clients were partly guilty. Had he done so, the jury might have convicted the defendants of manslaughter and they would have served only a few years in jail. The Wobbly principle of putting the IWW's interests before individual safety most likely influenced Vanderveer's decision.

Although Vanderveer placed great emphasis on whether or not the firing had begun before the hall was raided, that issue was not critical to the final verdict. Under Washington law, armed self-defense of another person was lawful only when it occurred in the "presence" of the person being defended.[57] Vanderveer tried to argue that all the defendants did not have to be present in the hall to be able to use the plea of self-defense. But the prosecution persuaded the judge to read an instruction to the jury that said that the right of self-defense did not extend to those outside the hall. Thus, if Grimm had been shot from the Avalon Hotel, as the prosecution contended—and the defense never seriously challenged this point—then it did not matter if the raid had been in progress before the shootings.

This legal point was pivotal to the final verdict. Although the law was clearly against him, Vanderveer continued to argue about the right of self-defense. Elmer Smith also maintained throughout the trial that it had been justifiable to place men outside the IWW hall, long after the prosecution made it clear that the law did not support this view. Perhaps both men realized their indefensible legal position as they tried to argue that what the defendants did *should* have been considered self-defense. But Vanderveer's appeal to the jury and to public opinion went beyond legal justification. He wanted everyone to understand that the Wobblies had to fight for their right to join a union, to rent a hall, and to organize to improve conditions. They did this against determined opposition from a group that had used illegal means time and time again: the 1918 Red Cross raid, the harassment of Lassiter, the 1919 raid, and the lynching of Everest. The Wobblies had known their hall was going to be attacked, Vanderveer argued, and the attack had been supported, or at least tolerated, by the local legal community. The Wobblies who had been placed in such a position had had a moral right to defend themselves. Smith endorsed this view in his public speeches for the rest of his life.

Years later, several jurors admitted that they had agreed to the verdict because they had feared that if they held out for an acquittal, causing a hung jury, the next jury would convict the defendants of first-degree murder. Fear for their own safety probably also affected their verdict. And they anticipated that Smith and Sheehan, once freed, could work for the release of the other men.[58] Immediately after reaching their verdict, the jurors asked Judge Wilson to be lenient in his sentencing decision. Some jurors expected the defendants to be sentenced to two to five years in jail; but Judge Wilson gave the convicted Wobblies twenty-five to forty years, a sentence that shocked both the jury and the prisoners. Vanderveer filed a motion for a new trial, based on evidence that before the trial began juror Harry Sellars had threatened to "hang every goddamned one of them [the defendants]." Sellars denied the statement, and Wilson rejected the motion. Vanderveer appealed the decision to the Washington State Supreme Court, but in April 1921 the court upheld the verdict.[59]

No one was happy with the jury's decision. A reporter overheard one defendant say, "I think it was a bonehead jury, if ever there was one." Prosecutor Herman Allen complained, "The verdict is a travesty on justice." The headline in the *American Legion Weekly* read "Centralia Misses a Hanging Holiday," and the *Montesano Vidette* declared that

> America and American principles are positively endangered. . . .
> The acquittal of Elmer Smith, whose advice was followed in preparing to do murder; the acquittal of him who was the educated advisor of the crime, though he actually shirked the danger of participation, that is not understandable.

The Labor Jury concluded that the defendants were not guilty, that there had been a conspiracy to raid the hall, and that the defendants did not get a fair trial because so much evidence was excluded. Of course, the Labor Jury was as biased as the American Legion was. One member spent most of the trial searching for defense witnesses, and most of the men did not hear all of the evidence. The IWW press predictably called the verdict a judicial outrage, and it widely published the Labor Jury's findings.[60]

Smith shared a few brief moments of joy after the trial as he hugged Laura and his mother in the courtroom. He shook hands with Vanderveer and with the other defendants. Years later, Bert Bland recalled that emotion-packed scene:

> Elmer looks at us gathered around him and trying to be of some aid—the jailor yells, 'Come on, get a move on. We can't wait forever for you'—Elmer sticks out a huge hand to us and his voice trembles as he says, 'Boys, I will never forget you, and as long as there is a breath in my body I will work for your release.' I look into his eyes as I grasp his hand and see tears flowing down his cheek and I had to turn my head to keep from doing likewise.[61]

The eight convicted prisoners were then led back to jail.

Smith was packing up his belongings in his cell when a sheriff entered and arrested him and Mike Sheehan on a charge of conspiring to kill Arthur McElfresh. The prosecutors hoped that a new jury would find them guilty. Both men pleaded not guilty and remained in jail.[62]

Two days later, the *Portland Oregonian* attacked both the Montesano verdict and Smith. A Montesano newspaper reprinted the editorial, which is probably where Smith read it:

> The Montesano verdict violates both justice and common sense. . . . That there was a conspiracy to kill was plainly established in the minds of the jury, yet it acquitted the lawyer, Elmer Smith. If there was a conspiracy, here was the most culpable one of the lot. . . . But it was Lawyer Smith who instilled fear into the guilty consciences of those who later went forth armed on the day of a peaceful celebration of an anniversary of peace. He was the legal advisor, the presumably man of brains in a group of men associated to promote unlawful and disloyal doctrines and practices. To these prejudiced, and apprehensive and guilty souls he peddled the yarn that the supporters of loyalty and decency in

Centralia were to raid their hall and drive them from the town.

It is not difficult to arouse fear in a bad conscience. "Suspicion always haunts the guilty mind." Smith did it well. Once their fears were aroused he pretended to advise them as to their rights, knowing full well the probable consequences. And then while these stupid men, inflamed by his pernicious gossip, went out to slay, their lawyer and advisor went elsewhere. He possessed not even the mistaken courage of his fellow conspirators. Having, as one is justified in believing, inspired the deed, he thought of his own precious life but not one instant of that of his dupes or of that of the soldiers who were about to celebrate innocently their return to home and civil life. The acquittal of this slinking coward, when men of lesser intellect are found guilty of murder through conspiracy is an outstanding travesty on reason and justice.[63]

The harsh words no doubt greatly disturbed Smith. It was important to have public opinion on their side if the convicted men were to be set free. Also, Smith's arrest and the long months of the trial had drawn him into a close identification with the cause of the IWW organization. But his acquittal accentuated the differences between him and the other men. Smith found it difficult to accept the jury's verdict, since he believed that all of the defendants were equally innocent. But because most of the men were declared guilty, Smith thought that he deserved to share a measure of that guilt.

Smith was also hurt by the sharp words that accused him of being a coward. After the trial, he turned his frustration at not being able to act into determination that he would perform with courage once released. Partly driven by guilt after his acquittal, Smith prepared himself to show the public that he could face danger and take whatever personal consequences might follow. Once he gained his freedom, he would blossom into a fearless IWW leader who always took on risks himself and never again counseled others to use violence.

Smith and Sheehan had to sit in jail until May, when several of Smith's friends managed to raise the $5,000 bond that released them. But the possibility of a new trial hung over both men for another year. Finally, after hearing Smith's argument that he and Sheehan had already been tried and acquitted on the same charge, a judge granted Smith's motion to dismiss all charges. The prosecution did little to object after considering the expense (over $51,000 for the first trial) and time involved in a new trial.[64]

The *Industrial Worker* saluted Smith's freedom: "Great things may be looked for with Elmer Smith out of jail."[65] On the day he rejoined his family in Centralia, a friend in town, J. M. Eubanks, heard rumors from several of his leather shop customers that there were plans to lynch Smith that night.[66] When Eubanks learned of Smith's intention to attend a Triple Alliance meeting in Chehalis that night, he decided to go along and bring two friends. Keeping a careful eye on Smith from the back of the audience, the three men kept fingering the guns they had stashed in their pockets. Before the main speaker was introduced, the chairperson announced that "brother" Smith was present. Smith rose from his seat to the sounds of enthusiastic applause and smiled in acknowledgment. His popularity in labor circles had grown since his arrest. After the meeting, Eubanks and his friends escorted Smith back to his home and stayed to patrol the grounds until morning. There were no incidents that night or during the week that Eubanks kept his vigil.[67] Smith was grateful for friends like Eubanks, and he had no plans to leave town. Centralia was going to remain his home.

Lest We Forget

"The Centralia Horror—Up and in Action"
                                        —Henry C. Peterson, 1927

Up ye toilers hark! A voice a plea, despair, a call.
From men a sighing, and slowly dying,
Behind the slimy prison wall;
Help ope the portal, rouse, fear no mortal,
Like a flood, welling up,
Naught can stem your mass'd mighty forces. . . .
Then up and in action, fall in line, work and they will be free.[1]

The tragic events of the Centralia case marked the end of a violent period in America that had seen prolonged strikes, frequent bomb scares, and a hysterical reaction to "bolshevism." When the wartime boom was over and economic hard times arrived, many workers felt uncertain about the future. The end of the war meant a shrinking market for the once-thriving shipyards of Seattle and the lumber industry throughout Washington and Oregon. After the war, fifteen thousand loggers and sawmill workers were laid off in Washington, and the recession deepened. The ranks of organized labor began to thin. After 1919 there was a sharp drop in union membership and in the number of strikes in the state. The 1920s would prove to be a decade of economic decline and social conservatism in Washington. The era of progressivism was over, as popular interest in economic and social reform ebbed.[2]

But even as labor strikes and radical activism began to wane, public fears about dissent did not. The wartime strikes, dramatic trials, and violence in the streets were not quickly forgotten. In January 1920, the Bureau of Investigation conducted a series of raids against the homes and meeting halls of radicals and their supporters. Over five thousand people were arrested. The state of Washington had seen more than its share of radical activity, and frenzied patriotic fervor still held a strong grip on public sentiment. Many people still believed that something needed to be done about the "Wobbly threat." In May 1920, an American Legion committee, with C. D. Cunningham as a member, met in Spokane to recommend ways to combat the IWW. The committee's report called on the Legion to send out speakers and propaganda to expose the "vices and fallacies" of the IWW, assist in the prosecution of radicals, and report all radical activities to authorities. Although some Legion members had reservations about the report, the organization took a leading role in opposing the IWW and any efforts to free the Centralia prisoners. And to keep the memory of that day alive, Legion conventions around the nation showed the Legion flag carried in the 1919 parade.[3]

The Montesano verdict signaled the beginning, not the end, of the controversy over who was to blame for what had happened on Centralia's Tower Avenue. The IWW and its sympathizers began issuing a steady stream of newspaper articles, magazine stories, and pamphlets to counter public opinion that the Centralia Wobblies had committed cold-blooded murder. To raise defense funds during the trial, the ACLU published "The Issues in the Centralia Murder Trial," which put the Armistice Day events in the context of the industrial warfare in the lumber industry. The Legion commissioned an early anti-IWW booklet, *Centralia, Tragedy and Trial*, by Ben Hur Lampman, a reporter for the *Portland Oregonian*.

Ralph Chaplin wrote the first complete IWW account of the Centralia case in *The Centralia Conspiracy*, published by the IWW in May 1920. It sold forty thousand copies within a month and became the standard IWW interpretation of the events.[4] Chaplin's colorful polemic was responsible for creating a number of myths about the case, the most outrageous being that a Centralia businessman had castrated Wesley Everest while he was being taken to be lynched.[5] The IWW propaganda campaign seized on the unsupported story and spread it in countless pamphlets and speeches over the years. Smith repeated the castration story in his own speeches, although he had no first-hand knowledge of the deed, having been transferred from the Centralia jail before Everest's body was brought back.

In fact, there appears to be little evidence that the castration ever occurred. Chaplin's story, appearing six months after Everest's lynching, was the first published account of the castration. No contemporary report of those who saw the body mentioned castration, including the dozens of men at the lynching, the deputies who brought the body back to the jail, the IWW prisoners, the jailers, the coroner's jury, and those who placed the body in the coffin. During the trial, Vanderveer described Everest's death at length but did not mention castration when it might have done his clients some good. Neither did the Labor Jury. A police report on Everest, filled out the day his body was returned to jail, includes a set of fingerprints and a description of the body. No mention is made of castration. Nevertheless, most historians have uncritically accepted Chaplin's story.[6]

The Armistice Day events of 1919 spurred widespread prosecution of IWW members under Washington's new criminal syndicalism law, which had become effective in March of that year. Washington's law was virtually identical to those previously passed in Idaho, Oregon, California, and other states. The first Washington state criminal syndicalism bill was introduced in the House in February 1917 while the trial of the Wobblies arrested following the violence of the Everett free speech fight was in progress. Sponsored by legislators with close ties to the state's lumber industry, the bill was clearly directed against the IWW. Governor Ernest Lister vetoed the bill because he believed it would jeopardize the liberties of many loyal citizens and would only give added force to the organizing appeal of radicals.

Three weeks after Lister's veto, the United States was at war. When the legislature reconvened in 1919, it had two years of bitter industrial strife to look back on, including the great lumber strike and the Seattle General Strike. Governor Lister vetoed the new syndicalism bill that had been passed, but the legislature overrode it. By then, Lister had become ill and power had passed to the new governor, Republican Louis Hart.[7] Washington's new law said that "whoever shall advocate, advise, teach or justify crime, sedition, violence, intimidation or injury as a means or way of effecting or resisting any industrial, economic, social or political change" was guilty of a felony, with a sentence of up to ten years in prison. Anyone who printed or distributed handbills or books advocating such doctrines and anyone who was a member of or aided a member of an organization formed to advocate such doctrines could also be guilty under the law.[8]

Laws to safeguard the public from violent attack against the government and property already existed, and this new law added no new protection. The law was directed at radicals who spoke out against existing laws but who otherwise obeyed them. It was not directed against those who professed a belief in law and order but who resorted to lawless practices to enforce their beliefs.

The danger in the law, from the IWW point of view, lay in the notion that one need only advocate violence to have broken a law. Someone could be guilty of criminal syndicalism if he or she advocated a strike to improve intolerable conditions and violence happened to break out. Furthermore, the law allowed the authorities to declare an *organization* guilty of advocating violence; that is, all members could be convicted even if they individually opposed violence. Although the law would also be used later against members of the American Communist Party (formed in 1919), the IWW was the main target. Between 1917 and 1920, twenty-three states passed criminal syndicalism laws, with the common aim to destroy the IWW.[9]

The first major use of Washington's criminal syndicalism law came in January 1920 when police arrested sixty-seven Wobblies in Spokane. Two days of testimony by the prosecution purported to demonstrate that the IWW was a "menace to society and that if allowed to continue its activities in this country, it would lead to violence and bloodshed." The defendants had no attorney—Vanderveer and Pierce were tied up with other cases—so one of the arrested Wobblies handled the defense. The Superior Court judge convicted all sixty-seven, but on appeal by Vanderveer the state Supreme Court reversed the convictions because the judge had not disqualified himself after the defense filed an affidavit of prejudice against him. The men went free. But fifteen criminal syndicalism case convictions arising from arrests in police raids following the Centralia case reached the state supreme court in Washington, Oregon, and Idaho, where most were upheld.[10]

Less than a month after Smith's release from jail, he became involved in a criminal syndicalism case. Five men, including the blind news vendor Tom Lassiter (recently released from prison for selling Wobbly newspapers), had been arrested in Chehalis in the Wobbly roundup on November 11 and charged with criminal syndicalism. Vanderveer had originally represented the defendants, but he turned the case over to law partner J. F. Emigh and called in Smith to help out. Herman Allen, one of the prosecutors at Montesano, handled the case for the prosecution. On June 8, Allen began by calling eight witnesses who testified that the IWW advocated sabotage and violence. Allen read aloud from IWW literature, written before the war, which urged members to use direct action. He closed by introducing other evidence identifying the defendants as members of the IWW.

Smith attempted unsuccessfully to have the court disregard all IWW publications written before Washington's criminal syndicalism law went into effect. He tried to counter the violent image of the IWW by arguing that, wartime Wobbly rhetoric notwithstanding, the IWW was intent on pursuing peaceful methods of change. He read a resolution passed in

1918 by the General Executive Board of the IWW: "said organization does not now, and never had believed in or advocated either destruction or violence as a means of accomplishing industrial reform." When organized labor had attempted to improve working conditions during the war, Smith pointed out, it had been met with violence from government officials. In the closing arguments for the defense, Emigh described IWW doctrine as being fundamentally peaceful, and Smith appealed to the sympathies of the jury and pleaded for the defendants' freedom.

After eight hours—a long time for a Wobbly case—the jury found four of the defendants guilty. Each was sentenced to six months to ten years in prison. One of the four later had his sentence suspended because he was only nineteen years old. The fifth defendant was freed because of a lack of clear proof that he was a Wobbly. Smith and Emigh unsuccessfully appealed the convictions to the state Supreme Court.[11]

The criminal syndicalism law was proving to be a very efficient way of disposing of the Wobbly threat. The U.S. Army recruiting station in Seattle reported that the American Legion was influential in molding public opinion:

> The rigor with which the Criminal Syndicalism cases were waged in this state after the Centralia Massacre of the last year can probably be attributed to public sentiment, backed by the American Legion in the numerous county seats. Every sheriff and officer of the law finds it easy to do his duty in order that public sentiment may approve his actions.[12]

The Employers Association of Washington reported that as of May 1, 1920, there had been seventy-four cases of criminal syndicalism, resulting in fifty-two convictions and four acquittals of those cases that had been decided. In Lewis County, there had been eight cases with four convictions and four still pending. Smith and Emigh could claim a small victory in the case they defended; in nearly all of the others, those found guilty were sentenced to five to ten years in prison.[13]

Smith's active efforts to defend the Wobblies, coming so soon after his own trial, attracted a good deal of local attention. His popularity among the working class had grown after his ordeal in Montesano, which may have accounted for the less severe sentence. His credentials as a teacher and church member brought a measure of credibility to his defense work that was not normally associated with IWW trials. The day after the Chehalis verdict, Smith spoke to a large, enthusiastic gathering at a labor picnic in town.[14] But later that month, when Smith traveled to Bellingham, a port city north of Seattle, he ran into stiff opposition, an experience that would become common during the years ahead. After hearing an appeal from the local American Legion post to block his appearance, Chief of Police Powell summoned Smith to the police station and warned him that there would be no meeting and that Smith should take the next train out of town. Smith insisted that he would speak, and at eight o'clock that Sunday night he sat on the Labor Temple stage before a packed crowd of loggers and shipyard workers.

Before the proceedings could begin, Chief Powell announced that there would be no meeting about the Centralia affair and that Smith would not be allowed to speak. But after several other orators had talked about general labor conditions and the Triple Alliance, Powell relented and said that Smith could speak on Americanism. After a few minutes, Smith turned and pointed to the large American flag hanging behind him. He said that he respected the flag and the principles that it stands for but that he had no use for the business profiteers who hide their crimes behind it in the name of patriotism. In a steady, clear voice, he continued: "I do not believe in overthrowing the government by force or violence, but neither do I believe in maintaining it by force and violence." Chief Powell jumped to his feet and shouted, "All of your remarks are inflammatory!" The crowd yelled for Smith to continue, but Powell closed the meeting. Smith had reason to be content with the outcome, for his aborted speech drew sympathy for the IWW and increased interest in the case.[15]

The *Bellingham American Reveille* had harsh words for Smith:

> The constitutional rights of citizens do not extend to such curs as the promoter of the dastardly affair at Centralia. He is a murderer even if he was too smooth for the officers charged with bringing the Centralia assassins to the halter. He should be denied habitation in any decent community.[16]

After Bellingham, Smith embarked on a series of public speaking engagements in Seattle and Everett on behalf of the IWW Northwest District Defense Committee. The committee hired Smith at five dollars a day, the usual Wobbly wage, plus traveling expenses to give talks and raise money for the families of the Wobbly prisoners. Because the committee had paid Vanderveer for his defense work in Montesano, Smith felt obliged to them and he agreed to pay most of his own way for several years. He spoke before IWW locals, the annual Finnish Socialist picnic, the Metal Trades

Council, and other labor groups. Smith told his listeners that repression used against the IWW would next be used against other militant and liberal labor organizations, and he urged these groups to embrace the Centralia cause as their own.[17]

Smith's speeches in Seattle were meant to attract publicity, but he did not know that they also attracted undercover agents from the detective agency the prosecution had used in Montesano. State officials and local police were still uneasy after the conviction of the Centralia Wobblies, and their spies searched for signs of another general strike or of plans to use force to spring the prisoners from jail. Although Smith's speeches indicated no such incitements to violence, local law enforcement officials closely monitored labor gatherings and Smith's speeches.[18]

The Bureau of Investigation of the Department of Justice was also attracted to Smith's activities. Bureau agents and undercover informants regularly attended his public speeches and sent reports, often with a complete stenographic transcription, to J. Edgar Hoover. The Bureau kept close watch on all IWW activities in the Pacific Northwest, but Smith received particular attention because of his numerous public appearances and his outspoken views. As the years passed, Smith's personal file in the Bureau grew to several hundred pages.[19]

When he returned home, Smith turned his attention to local political activity and the upcoming fall election. In July, members of the Triple Alliance and other progressive organizations met in Chehalis to endorse several resolutions that outlined their political program, including the repeal of the state's criminal syndicalism law, the release of all political prisoners, the nationalization of the mines and railroads, the right of labor to organize, and progressive taxation on land and timber held for speculative purposes.[20] The Triple Alliance was experiencing difficulty attracting support, as personal and organizational rivalries weakened the organization and prevented unified action. Deep divisions over whether the Alliance should support a third-party movement or remain nonpartisan continued to divide its members until August 1920, when the Alliance disbanded after throwing its support behind the newly formed Farmer-Labor Party. The national independent party sought support from progressive farmers and workers who were dissatisfied with the pro-business stances of the two major parties.[21]

Smith was enthusiastic about the potential of the Farmer-Labor Party to have a broader appeal. He and two other former Alliance members organized a county convention to nominate candidates to run on the party's ticket in Lewis County. The convention drew a hundred people to elect delegates to the state convention in Seattle. Not surprisingly, the convention chose Smith as one of its three delegates and nominated him to run for prosecuting attorney in Lewis County. Smith announced that his main goal was to bring to trial those men responsible for the lynching of Wesley Everest.[22]

Smith was a popular figure among the delegates at the Seattle Farmer-Labor convention, and he was urged to be the party's candidate for state attorney general. But his attention could not be drawn away from his hometown case, and he withdrew his name from nomination.[23] This would not be the last time Smith would put the cause of the prisoners above his own career.

Major newspapers in Washington lost no time in labeling the Farmer-Labor Party as radical and un-American. For six weeks, the Tacoma American Legion ran a series of full-page ads against the IWW. Democratic and Republican candidates, playing on widespread anti-Wobbly prejudice, declared that a vote for the Farmer-Labor Party was a vote for the IWW. In August, vice-presidential candidate Franklin Roosevelt spoke in Centralia and eulogized the American Legionnaires, describing his visit as a "pilgrimage to the very graves of the martyred members of the American Legion who here gave their lives in the sacred cause of Americanism."[24]

The anti-IWW propaganda used by Republicans and Democrats alike was designed to scare middle-of-the-road supporters away from the third party. The actual number of Communists and Wobblies in Washington was very small—only a few thousand—so the Farmer-Labor Party's only hope for success was in attracting moderates. It was good strategy for the two established parties to brand all progressive social movements with the IWW label.

In principle, the Wobblies were opposed to any political party. They believed in industrial unionism and economic direct action to effect change. They did not trust politicians of any kind and left political decisions up to each member. The IWW had no official relationship to the Farmer-Labor Party, although many workers gave their support to both organizations. Nevertheless, in the minds of most people the two organizations were working hand in glove.

The anti-IWW policy of most newspapers did not go unnoticed by Smith, and in the early fall he took the offensive. When he sued one paper for libel—it had called him a "murderer"—the paper apologized and Smith dropped the suit. He also sued the *Raymond Herald* for printing a story that said he had been convicted at Montesano. The suit was settled when the *Herald* printed three front-page retractions saying that it had confused Elmer with Britt Smith.[25]

Criticizing newspaper reporting and initiating libel suits were only defensive actions, so to counter the newspapers' opposition to the Farmer-Labor Party, Smith made plans to establish a paper in Centralia that would print the views and ideas of Farmer-Labor candidates. He went to Seattle to seek the help of Harry Ault, the editor and publisher of the *Seattle Union Record*. Ault singled out his youngest staff member, Harvey O'Connor, to be the paper's editor. O'Connor, Smith, and a few friends drove a truck to Toledo, Washington, to pick up a linotype flatbed press and type from the defunct *Toledo Messenger*. They set up the equipment in the back of Smith's office on Tower Avenue and christened the paper the *Farmer-Labor Call*.[26]

Lewis County's working-class community financed the paper by purchasing two thousand shares of stock at five dollars each. The weekly paper sold for a penny an issue, was eight pages long, and reached several thousand readers. The *Call* primarily carried news about the state and county Farmer-Labor campaign, although it occasionally reprinted articles from socialist and Wobbly newspapers around the country. The advertising came from local businesses in Centralia and Chehalis, such as the furniture store, tailor, bar, car repair shop, co-op grocery, and clothing store. This support was a good sign that local retailers recognized that many of the *Call*'s working-class readers had families and participated in the day-to-day life of the small towns in the county. This fact was often lost in the hostile anti-labor fumings of the newspapers dominated by the middle and upper classes.[27]

Smith's opponents in the campaign for prosecuting attorney were Republican Herman Allen, the incumbent, and Democrat Albert Buxton. The Republicans, with close ties to the business community, claimed the mantle of leadership in the fight against radicalism. Several times during the campaign, Smith challenged Allen to a debate over Allen's failure to prosecute Tom Lassiter's kidnappers and his participation in the prosecution of the Montesano defendants. Not surprisingly, Allen refused the invitations.[28] Buxton, a conservative judge, gave a few speeches, but his campaign consisted mostly of newspaper advertisements attacking radicalism and the IWW.

Smith propelled himself into the campaign with tremendous energy and enthusiasm. He was "overflowing with animal spirits and joviality, but in dead earnest on the IWW matter," remembered O'Connor. His style was much more enterprising than that of his opponents, and he ran a hard, untiring campaign. To gain recognition as a third-party candidate, he planned speaking tours that reached every town in the county at least once and went to many places two and three times. Friends and relatives traveled in advance to the next town, distributing literature advertising Smith's appearance. Smith followed in a car caravan, enlisting Connor Harmon, who would soon be the husband of his sister Dorothy, to drive. Harmon also acted as Smith's bodyguard and carried a gun underneath his jacket.[29]

Smith's aggressiveness and leadership made the Farmer-Labor Party a vigorous force in Lewis County politics. The main issue in the campaign for prosecuting attorney was the Centralia case. Smith told a hometown audience that if he were elected, "the criminals in this town who were responsible for the Centralia tragedy—and I don't mean the little fellows—are going to Walla Walla [the state prison]." He was running "to fight hard for my rights and your rights as American citizens," he continued. "If you don't get into the fight to preserve your rights in this campaign, you may never have the opportunity to do it again."[30]

Although supportive of the Farmer-Labor Party's progressive platform, Smith's singleminded concern was bringing to justice those men responsible for the lynching of Wesley Everest. His chances of accomplishing this, even if elected, appeared to be remote. Few people would have agreed to testify against any of the lynchers, and it was likely that a jury would refuse to convict, either out of sympathy for the fallen veterans or because they feared the town leaders who were rumored to be involved. But Smith would not let the matter drop.

Smith's public utterances made him an open target for those who hated the IWW and believed that the Centralia defendants had gotten off easy at Montesano. "A vote for candidates who represent the radical element, is a vote for the Elmer Smiths of the county, the man who openly excuses the I.W.W. murders in Centralia last Armistice Day," cried the *Chehalis Bee-Nugget*.[31] As Smith raised up his voice, the newspapers responded even more loudly, repeatedly stating that the veterans had been shot down in cold blood. To this Smith replied in one of his speeches:

> That lie is an outrage on Centralia and the effort to saddle it onto the Farmer-Labor party is a sample of what you may expect from the court house gang in Chehalis and the lawless elements in the American Legion and the Commercial Club here. The immediate cause of the deaths of Wesley Everest . . . [and the ex-servicemen] was the failure to prosecute guilty persons in this

county when they were known and the evidence against them was overwhelming.[32]

Smith was referring to Lassiter's kidnapping, believing that this failure to enforce the law had led to the vigilante mentality and the raid on the Wobbly hall. Smith boldly held Herman Allen responsible for the breakdown in law and order.

Smith was an effective campaigner, especially with his direct attacks on his opponents. Once he brandished a fake Farmer-Labor program that had been circulating around the county. The program called for atheism, free love, and common ownership of just about everything, including women. "They're whipped when they resort to cheap lies of this kind," Smith shouted. "Are you going to stand for these calumnies? Quit hugging the empty fantasy of hope to your breasts and Get In The Fight!" The crowd responded with loud applause.[33]

Opposition to Smith's candidacy sometimes took the form of petty harassment. After adopting a resolution forbidding anyone but "100 percent American[s]" to use its facilities, the Centralia school board refused to allow the Farmer-Labor Party to hold a meeting in its high school auditorium. On another occasion, when George Vanderveer came to Centralia to speak at the Rialto Theater on Smith's behalf, the theater manager changed his mind and the meeting place had to be moved.[34] Sometimes the opposition was more sinister. Smith received several anonymous threats from callers and letter writers. At the town of Dryad, where angry Legionnaires had spoken out against Smith, an armed mob waited by the side of the road leading into town. The mob stopped a car that they thought was his, but Smith was actually scheduled to speak elsewhere.[35]

In early October, Smith took his motorcade on a three-city tour south of Centralia. At the first stop in Doty he was unable to secure a hall, so he spoke on the street outside a sawmill where men leaving work were passing. Although most of the workers were curious and stopped to listen, a few began heckling. But Smith was not deterred, and his antagonists returned to the sawmill and blew the whistles of a steam engine to drown him out. That night his caravan stopped at Pe Ell for dinner. The men retired to a bar and the women went to the Collins House, a restaurant and hotel across the street. When the manager heard that Elmer Smith's party was present he announced, "I will feed you women but I won't feed Elmer Smith." Nora Dishong, Smith's secretary, was indignant. "Anybody that won't feed Elmer can't feed me!" she said. The rest of the party agreed and walked out. As a result of this incident, local railroad union workers began a boycott that later forced the hotel to close. The next day the motorcade reached Onalaska. Dishong was passing out some Farmer-Labor literature along with announcements of the evening meeting when three men carrying guns approached her. They ordered her to stop leafleting, but she refused to be intimidated. "I'm handing out more literature. Pull the trigger if you want to," she said. The men backed off.[36]

The meeting was held at a vacant lot, where Smith spoke in front of an American flag draped over his car. The audience appeared to be friendly, but many heads turned when several local sawmill owners and businessmen joined the crowd in the back. Smith had spoken for only a few minutes when a question was fired from the audience: "What were you in jail for?" "For speaking what I think," Smith shot back. He then launched into an account of the Centralia case, but hearing his defense of the Wobblies, some people in the audience grew angry and shouted insults. A dozen men tried to push their way through the crowd to get at Smith while those in front linked arms and stood fast. After a few minutes the men backed off, hooting and jeering while Smith finished his speech. The six deputy sheriffs present made no move to arrest anyone. Connor Harmon kept his gun on the front seat of the car as he drove Smith away.[37]

When Smith and his tired entourage returned to Centralia that night, they found that a vandal had painted a red "IWW" on the front window of a Chehalis store that displayed one of Smith's campaign posters. The store owner, a Farmer-Labor candidate for county treasurer, had refused to remove the poster when requested to do so by a wealthy landowner.[38] Despite such incidents, Smith and his campaign workers maintained a high morale, for they knew that a large number of voters in the rural areas were solidly behind him. The *Call* ran an article on Smith's campaign under the heading: "Smith Worst-Hated Best-Loved Citizen in All Lewis County."[39] It was an accurate reading.

On October 23, Smith and Vanderveer spoke at a Farmer-Labor rally in Centralia. Before the rally, a festive parade down Tower Avenue attracted two thousand supporters, including many of Smith's relatives. Harry's wife, Grace, pushed her baby along in a new carriage Elmer had bought. The rally was held outdoors because no meeting hall was open to them, but the crowd was appreciative and sang labor songs at its conclusion.[40] Three days later, Smith took his motorcade to Winlock, fifteen miles south of Centralia, where his campaign met its stiffest opposition.[41] A hundred Farmer-Labor supporters formed a parade and began to march up First Street, with Smith at the lead. Down a side street roared several cars and trucks, their drivers honking their horns and racing their engines.

After a few blocks, Smith climbed onto a soapbox and looked out over the thousand people who had gathered, while Governor Hart watched the scene from his hotel room. The noise from the vehicles continued and drowned out Smith's words, so that only the people in the first few rows could hear. Several Farmer-Labor women then tried to strike up a song, but the racket still did not subside. Smith put his hands to his mouth and tried calling out to Hart for assistance, but his words could not be heard. Moments later, the sound of the siren of the town's firehose cart silenced the din. Those closest to the soapbox backed away, fearing that they would be doused with water. "Let them turn the water on us if they want to," shouted Smith, coaxing everyone to stay. The fire cart drew closer and then dashed around the corner out of sight. A false alarm.

With the crowd largely distracted, Smith decided to end the meeting, and he led his supporters back down First Street, singing along the way. After the crowd had traveled a block, someone dragged a big wooden box into the street and set it on fire near the crowd. The fire engine appeared to put the fire out, but after a few seconds the firefighters turned their hose on the parade and the crowd scattered in confusion. In the midst of the chaos, a high school boy cut the water hose with his knife, and the evening's drama was over.[42]

Although news of such incidents always made the front pages of local newspapers, the Farmer-Labor Party had a harder time getting coverage of its message. Newspapers carried front-page accounts of the speeches of the Republican and Democratic candidates, but they ignored the Farmer-Labor Party, claiming that it lacked any voter support. One refrain in many articles criticized the third party for having Elmer Smith on its ticket. As November approached, the attack intensified. On October 26 and again on November 1, the day before the election, the *Chronicle* ran a half-page advertisement showing photographs of the four veterans who had been killed in Centralia the year before. Above the pictures was the heading "Lest We Forget." Below them, it read: "The Four Reasons Why Elmer Smith and the other Farmer-Labor Candidates Should Be Defeated at the Polls November 2nd."[43]

Throughout the campaign Smith was outwardly optimistic about his chances of winning. Although he had more than a few private moments of discouragement, he looked positively to the dozens of large, mostly friendly crowds that came to hear him speak. O'Connor distributed ten thousand copies of a special election issue of the *Call*. Clearly, Smith had created more attention and enthusiasm than any other candidate in Lewis County. But he called off a large rally and parade on election eve in Centralia for fear that there would be violence. He wanted to avoid any conflict that would be used to further discredit the party. Instead, he attended an indoor meeting on election eve in Chehalis, defusing a potentially dangerous confrontation.[44] Smith had learned a lesson from the Centralia tragedy.

Election day was quiet. That night, Smith gathered with his supporters in his office to await the results. They heard rumors that county officials had tampered with the ballot counting. Smith believed that a thousand votes were stolen in this manner, but no evidence of this ever surfaced. The final results showed that Allen won with 6,100 votes; Smith had 3,400 and Buxton 1,300.[45]

Although Smith was deeply disappointed by his loss, his opponents were shocked by his strong showing. Smith carried most of the county's rural precincts, losing heavily only in the strong Republican precincts of Centralia and Chehalis.[46] Several factors accounted for his defeat. The anti-IWW propaganda campaign directed specifically against Smith and his pledges to bring Wesley Everest's lynchers to justice may have scared away some moderate voters. In addition, election laws prevented migratory workers (including the itinerant loggers) from voting, and many of them would have voted for Smith.

In fact, Smith and the Farmer-Labor Party made an impressive showing in their first statewide campaign. Smith received one of the highest percentages of the total vote of any Washington Farmer-Labor candidate. Across the state, Farmer-Laborites averaged half the vote of the Republicans, who won the major state offices. The leader of the Seattle General Strike of 1919 ran for mayor of Seattle on the third-party ticket, received thirty-five thousand votes, and lost by sixteen thousand. The Farmer-Labor Party in Washington produced far more votes for its presidential candidate than in any other state in the nation.[47]

The failure of the Farmer-Labor Party to win more votes was largely due to worsening economic conditions and the effective suppression of radical labor activity. By the middle of 1920 the price of agricultural goods had dropped sharply, and it stayed low for another two years. The postwar depression had thrown thousands of workers out of work, which also hurt the party's chances. Employers everywhere opposed the new third party for being too radical, and they had convinced many workers, anxious about their jobs, to steer clear of the "troublemakers."

Much of Smith's support could be attributed to his personal appeal and effective campaign style. The IWW believed that workers could best effect change by striking for economic and social benefits, but Smith was also willing to work on the political front. He understood that many of the more conservative people he knew from church, school, and work could more easily show support for IWW principles by voting than by going out on strike.

Smith was a prominent figure at the December convention of county Farmer-Labor members in Centralia. In discussing post-election strategy, he urged members to strengthen their economic base by building up farmer and labor unions. He continued to stress the importance of economic as well as political power. He was also elected as a delegate to the party's state convention in Tacoma, where he took an active role in formulating the party platform.[48]

After the excitement of the election was over, Centralia and Lewis County began to quiet down. Businessmen were happy to see the end of the labor disturbances that had discouraged people from shopping in town. The sober memories of Armistice Day 1919 had dampened the town's spirit, and many shopkeepers looked forward to the day when Centralia would no longer be associated in the public mind with violence and community unrest. The working-class community feared that the Armistice Day parade of 1920, held only a few weeks after the election, might bring more violence. Smith was concerned that the town's businessmen might use the occasion to destroy the *Call*'s press, but the day of the parade passed without incident.[49] The Wobblies no longer had a hall, and those who were not in prison were laying low. It was not the day to make a stand or to teach the radicals a lesson.

The Kicking Jackass

"The Prison"—Ernest Crosby

And I saw within the jail them that give liberty to the slave,
And them that unbounded the mind of man,
And them that led onward to Freedom and Justice and Love.
Woe to the cause that hath not passed through a prison![1]

Following his election defeat, Smith faced a decision about his career. To Laura's distress, shortly after the Montesano trial he sold his homestead for $18,000 and turned over $12,000 of that money to the IWW to help pay defense bills.[2] Smith knew that making a living in Centralia as a labor lawyer who was so closely identified with the IWW would be extremely difficult. He had struggled to pay his bills even before the 1919 tragedy, and resuming his legal career after the trial did not look promising. But he did not despair about his financial condition. In fact, he took little notice of how his decisions affected his family; he was much more interested in speaking out about the Centralia case and doing what he could to help release the prisoners. Somehow he had to change the anti IWW sentiment that was prevalent in the state.

Before the Centralia violence, Smith had known little about the organizational activities of the IWW, its goals, or its general economic philosophy. But once he found himself sharing a jail cell with Wobblies, he began reading Wobbly publications and listening to the personal experiences of Vanderveer and the other prisoners. Smith would later say that his jail experience was his third college education, after Macalester and law school.[3] After he was freed from jail, Smith began studying labor history, political theory, and economics. The 1916 Industrial Relations Commission Report also helped shape his thinking. Formed by President Wilson to look into growing industrial unrest before World War I, the commission had gathered a wealth of statistics and testimony about working conditions across the country. And Smith began to compile a file of newspaper clippings on the concentration of wealth in America and the role of labor unions in creating economic justice.[4]

By his own estimate, Smith made two hundred and fifty speeches from 1921 to 1924.[5] City newspapers rarely covered labor's positions, and labor newspapers generally reached only a handful of supporters. A union meeting was a special opportunity for working people to hear labor's side of local and national events, and many workers looked forward with great anticipation to seeing Elmer Smith. In July 1921, the IWW General Defense Committee sent Smith on a nationwide speaking tour to raise money for its badly depleted accounts. By train, he visited eighteen cities in seven weeks, speaking to crowds that ranged in size from fifty to nearly a thousand. Beginning in San Francisco, Smith spoke in most major midwestern cities, including Minneapolis, where some of his old college and law school classmates came to hear him.

As might be expected, Smith encountered trouble during his tour. In Cloquet, Minnesota, where a bitter paper mill strike was in its fourth month, other IWW speakers had been tarred and feathered. A group of businessmen and Legionnaires pressured the sheriff to stop Smith from speaking, but Smith ignored the warnings. He spoke to a packed opera house, denouncing the "millionaire dictators" of the lumber industry and the superpatriots who were destroying free speech with their attacks on the IWW. He charged Legionnaires and businessmen with being unwitting "lackeys" for powerful lumber interests. When the commander of the local Legion post interrupted and asked whether the Wobblies were armed in Centralia, Smith launched into a description of the background that had created a climate of violence. He silenced the commander by arguing that he would be justified in being armed in Cloquet after having been threatened with violence.[6]

From Cloquet, Smith traveled east and finished his tour in New York in September. The Bureau of Investigation continued its surveillance of Smith and recorded his speeches, watching for such strong statements as "When a government becomes destructive it is time for a change."[7] While in New York, Smith stopped at the office of the American Civil Liberties Union, organized just a year earlier, to talk with its founder and director, Roger Baldwin. Baldwin had been a member of the IWW and had served time in prison for his opposition to the war. Under Baldwin's talented and aggressive leadership, the ACLU had aided many jailed Wobblies. Smith told Baldwin about his frequent run-ins with the law, and Baldwin promised that the ACLU would help him in the future.[8] It was a promise that would be kept many times.

Most of Smith's speeches were organized by local IWW contacts who passed out handbills in advance. Friends traveling with Smith sold IWW newspapers, songbooks, and pamphlets before and after his speeches. Traveling labor singers often began the program with a popular song, and the audience usually sang several songs from the *IWW Little Red Songbook*. On several occasions Laura accompanied Smith on his trips, driving their beat-up Model T Ford and staying in inexpensive hotel rooms. Smith was no mechanic, and when his car got a flat, which was often, they limped into the next town to find someone who could fix it.[9]

Introduced as "the well-known fighting red-headed lawyer of Centralia," Smith was a dynamic speaker with a forceful, optimistic message. He spoke about the concentration of wealth, the repeal of the criminal syndicalism laws, the right of free speech, and support for a local strike. Using Marxist economic analysis, Smith often warned about the unequal distribution of resources in which two percent of the people owned over seventy percent of the wealth, while the producers of this wealth, sixty-five percent of the people, owned less than three percent of what they produced. He argued that capitalists must find foreign markets for the goods produced by underpaid American workers and described how U.S. armies often had to be called in to protect the capitalist investments. Smith pointed to military interventions in Hawaii and the Philippines and to World War I as examples of foreign policy driven by corporate greed. Industrial unionism, he argued, where workers produced things for use, not for profit, would reduce the threat of another world war.[10]

Although Smith spoke on a variety of topics, most of his talks were on behalf of the Centralia prisoners. He urged his audience to support their release through political and economic pressure. Their support made a difference, he said. "Organize the lumber industry in the state of Washington and you can free the Centralia victims in 48 hours," he pleaded with more than one audience.[11] Smith so closely identified with the cause of the prisoners and the IWW that he began one lecture with an apology for being a lawyer and for not being in jail. "There is only one thing I have against the Wobblies," he said. "I have applied for a card on two or three occasions and they won't give me one, and it makes me awful sore." Only wage-earners could join the union, and Smith did not qualify. He also waxed, "I am with the Wobblies because they would make a heaven out of this capitalistic hell." Smith's speeches fully championed the IWW cause, describing the teachings of the IWW as self-evident truths. No matter how much denunciation was heaped on their heads, he said, or how many of them were slain, the ideas and spirit of the IWW would not be destroyed.[12]

Such statements endeared him to the workers, who loved to hear him speak and often stood patiently outdoors for hours regardless of the weather. One Wobbly writer compared Smith favorably to other national orators in his ability to awaken enthusiasm in his audiences. A spectator once observed that Smith's "own passions were so stirred that his voice broke, and he trembled. Then he seemed to use his will power to effect a control on his emotions." Even the Bureau of Investigation noted the effectiveness of Smith's speeches: "His listeners were very much interested, as they never budged all through his speech, although there were two showers—enough to drive any crowd away from anyone but an interesting speaker."[13]

Smith regularly used biblical stories to illustrate his message. In Everett, his speech was entitled, "The Feast of Belshazzar," taken from the Old Testament story of Daniel, who castigated the king for worshiping the false gods of gold and silver. Using the story as a parable on the greed of mill owners, Smith concluded, "The great kings of Capitalism have seen the handwriting on the wall, 'Capitalism, thy days are numbered. Thou hast been weighed in the balance and found wanting.'"[14] He saw himself as an American idealist, and he often quoted Abraham Lincoln and Thomas Jefferson, whom he greatly admired. In describing the IWW theory of industrial unionism, Smith quoted Lincoln: "Inasmuch as labor produces all of the good things of life, it follows that all such things of right belong to those who have produced them." He once said that he was not half as radical as Lincoln or Jefferson, the author of that "radical" document, the Declaration of Independence.[15]

Despite the serious message of his speeches, Smith maintained a healthy sense of humor. He could laugh at length about the time his mother and a neighbor went out to pick strawberries and inadvertently found themselves part of a scab outfit.[16] He loved to tell stories that poked fun at greedy bosses, apolitical workers, and hypocritical ministers. A favorite story was about Maud, the hard-working mule. It seems that Maud's boss thought he could feed her less and she would do the same amount of work. But Maud would have none of it, and she knocked her boss down. He complained, "Your father was a good slave and he worked for me for many years and he never kicked me; what is the trouble?" Maud replied, "Boss, you seem to have forgotten that my father was a jackass." Smith then concluded:

> Fellow workers, that is what our fathers were and that's what most of the working stiffs are right now—just ordinary jack-asses who never kick no matter how abusive the bosses are. If you could realize even as much as Maud did how much power you have, you would organize and kick the rotten capitalists, who are now forcing you to keep them living in luxury, clean off the earth.[17]

Smith made an impact on his audiences chiefly because he had an ability to communicate in a convincing, personal way to even the largest crowd. He talked freely about his own involvement in labor cases, and he appealed directly to his audiences to become personally involved. Using a blackboard and easy-to-understand metaphors, he made sure his points got across. Referring to the coming change in the social order, he told one audience, "You can't stop a storm by breaking a thermometer."[18] He complimented his listeners for not being drunk and scolded those who held back their support. He talked of his own sacrifices and tried to spur the crowd on to action by making them feel guilty. One of Smith's favorite poems was "The Prison":

> And the hosts within held up their arms,
> And the marks of their shackles were upon them.
> But I hid my hands behind me, for there was no mark on my wrist.
> Woe to the cause that hath not passed through a prison.[19]

The poem may have reminded Smith of his own lack of punishment for his role in the Centralia killings. In many of his speeches, he urged workers to take action that would free the men, perhaps in the belief that if they acted at his direction his own culpability would be lessened.

Behind his positive public image, Smith was troubled by guilt and was unsure of himself. He was never comfortable in his role as the primary spokesman for the IWW prisoners. He told one Wobbly that he hated appearing in public and would rather speak briefly and then take questions from the audience. Nervous before making a speech, he often took a handful of aspirin to calm himself. Although his audiences saw a persuasive, confident man, Smith occasionally wrote out his speeches six or eight times, afraid that he would otherwise forget what he wanted to say.[20] But Smith hid his private fears and concerns from all but a very few close friends. Before a crowd, he had no time for self-doubt. His fiery rhetoric and controversial message brought him constant harassment from the American Legion and local officials, and he needed to maintain a clear head to stand up to the intimidation.[21]

But sometimes he could not overcome the powers directed against him. In Aberdeen, Washington, Smith reserved the Eagles Hall for the evening of Abraham Lincoln's birthday. But at the urging of local businessmen, Aberdeen Mayor Bailey issued a proclamation stating that Smith's appearance was "a menace to the peace and quietude of the city and safety of our citizens, and renders acts of violence imminent." He prohibited Smith from speaking at or attending any public meeting in the city.[22] When Smith stepped off the train, the Aberdeen police asked him to accompany them to the police station. "Where is your warrant?" Smith asked. "I have the only warrant I need right here on my belt!" the officer replied. At the station, Smith was shown the mayor's proclamation and told that he would not be allowed to speak. But Smith was determined to deliver his speech. Five policemen barred the door to the Eagles Hall, where over a thousand people were standing out front waiting to hear Smith speak. An attempt to secure another hall failed; the owners feared that they would be arrested and their hall wrecked. While Smith stood in the street arguing with the owners and several police officers, a bystander walked up. He wanted to hear what Smith had to say and he asked the deputy sheriff, "Wasn't America a free country?" "I should say not!" the sheriff replied. "If it were, I would shoot Elmer Smith down this second." Undaunted, Smith announced that he would give his speech in a nearby vacant lot. As Smith stepped onto a soap box and began to speak, he was arrested. Charged with violating the mayor's proclamation, he was held overnight in jail and released the next day.[23]

The *Industrial Worker* ran a front-page story about the Aberdeen incident and reprinted the proclamation in large type. The paper's editorial drew a clear line:

> Either a citizen of the United States has a right to speak in pub-
> lic, or he has not. If he has not, then all public speaking should
> be prohibited. If he has, then it should be the duty of those in
> charge of the public peace and safety to see that violence does
> not result from such speaking. . . . Is the question of the con-

stitutional rights of American citizens to be left to any village
mayor or village clown, or is it to be decided by the majority of
American citizens? . . . We'd like to know.[24]

Eugene Barnett wrote to the *Industrial Worker* shortly after the Aberdeen
incident:

> The arrest of Elmer Smith in Aberdeen shows clearly the need
> of support. Elmer Smith is as honest as the day is long, and
> will put the truth before the people if he gets the support he is
> entitled to.[25]

At the court hearing a week afterward, an Aberdeen judge found Smith
guilty and fined him five dollars. Smith paid the fine because the cost of an
appeal was too high.[26]

Smith's most dangerous encounter on his speaking tours occurred
in Eureka, California, in March 1922. Labor-management disputes flared
frequently in Humboldt County, a major lumbering center for the northern part of the state. To discourage such activity and cripple IWW organizing activity, local prosecutors stepped up their arrests of Wobblies on
criminal syndicalism charges. The county boasted the highest number of
syndicalism arrests in the state outside of San Francisco, Los Angeles, and
Sacramento.[27] The Eureka Wobblies announced Smith's lecture with handbills sporting a bright red headline, "Noted Labor Lawyer to Speak." The
local American Legion post responded by passing a resolution opposing
"the un-American doctrines advocated by Elmer Smith" and described him
as "a menace to the peace and security of this Nation and to this community." Smith had intended to speak about the significance of criminal
syndicalism laws, but he changed his subject to "The Centralia Conspiracy"
after hearing about the resolution. Because of pressure from the Legion,
the local Wobblies were forced to find a hall on the outskirts of town,
and the forty drunken Legionnaires in town convinced one Wobbly, Herb
Edwards, to arm himself so that he could protect Smith. About two hundred people showed up to hear Smith speak, including two police officers
and three county sheriffs.[28]

Smith began by countering the statement in the Legion resolution that he advocated un-American doctrines. "Free speech, free press
and peaceable assemblage are the very essence of Americanism," he said,
quoting excerpts from the United States and California constitutions. He
continued: "Abraham Lincoln, one of the greatest presidents we have ever

had, said, 'If a majority should deprive a minority of any clearly written constitutional right, it would, from a moral standpoint, justify revolution.'"[29] George Cloney, commander of the local Legion post, interrupted from the rear of the hall: "We don't recognize the right of Elmer Smith to quote Abraham Lincoln." "By what authority do you censor or interfere with my address?" asked Smith. "By this authority! Isn't that right, boys?" With shouts of "Yes!" about fifty Legionnaires rushed the platform. Police officers stepped in and escorted Smith off to jail.[30]

The chief of police and the mayor, while acknowledging Smith's right to speak, worried that they could not control the angry townspeople. They advised Smith that the best course would be for him to leave town. The Legion insisted that he leave on the morning train, but Smith said that he would leave town when he was ready. That night he stayed in the home of a Finnish woman sympathetic to the IWW, guarded by Edwards and several other Wobblies. Outside, Legionnaires circled the block all night in their cars, horns blaring. Edwards, with his gun at hand, marveled at how calm and unruffled Smith seemed to be, but neither man slept soundly.[31]

Smith left town the next morning in a two-car motorcade with Edwards and several other Wobblies, the Legionnaires following in their own car caravan. When Smith's party reached Scotia, headquarters of the Pacific Lumber Company, the local marshal stopped them and ordered Smith out of his car. Smith refused to get out without a warrant. When the Legionnaires arrived, they seized Smith, Edwards, and another man and sent the rest of the Wobblies back to Eureka. They drove the kidnapped men to the local Legion hall. During the drive, a marshal in the front seat turned around and said: "Where I come from we used to string up fellows like you every week." Smith replied evenly: "From what I have heard about you and your kind, that doesn't surprise me any."[32] Some fifty Legionnaires, armed with rifles and drinking heavily, kept their three captives hostage for hours as they discussed what to do with them. Some cursed the three men and threatened to lynch them. They rifled Smith's briefcase and destroyed his file of newspaper clippings. Edwards grew angry as time wore on and was ready for a fight, but Smith calmed him down, assuring him that it was best to keep still.[33]

With darkness approaching and tempers cooling, an armed guard took Edwards and the other Wobbly to the depot and put them aboard the train to San Francisco. A convoy led by Legion commander Cloney drove Smith back to Eureka, where the police took him into custody and charged him with disturbing the peace at the meeting. Smith spent a day and a half in jail until the charges were dismissed and he was put on a train to San

Francisco. The police considered charging him with criminal syndicalism, but feelings were running so high that they feared Smith would be harmed if he was released on bail before a trial.[34]

The majority of Eureka's citizens rejoiced at how the Legion had handled Smith and the Wobblies. The Chamber of Commerce, the Elks Lodge, and the Knights of Columbus all passed resolutions praising the Legion. The *Humboldt Times* wrote triumphantly:

> The law-abiding and self-respecting citizens of Humboldt county [*sic*] do not want to hear speeches by the Elmer Smiths, the Edwardsons [*sic*] and other off-scourings representative of communism, IWWism, sovietism and the like, and they do not want the appearance of such people tolerated in their county. In this respect at least, the American Legion members are reflecting accurately the concensus [*sic*] of public opinion.[35]

Smith met up with Edwards at the IWW defense office in San Francisco, where they were interviewed by the *San Francisco Call*. "American Legion boys were not all against us," said Smith. "I learned that at least two members tore up their cards and took off their buttons as a result of the affair. The lumber interests are using the legion [*sic*] as their catspaw just as they did in Centralia."[36] He was echoing the Wobbly view that the Eureka Legionnaires had done the dirty work for local anti-union lumber operators who stood to gain economically from the destruction of the IWW.

In a letter to his parents, Smith wrote calmly about his experience in Eureka:

> I had a little conflict with the American Legion. . . . There [in jail] I had lots of time to think and my mind went back to all the dear folks at home. I have been terribly lonely for you all, especially mother and Dad. . . . the little trouble has enabled us to get out more publicity in connection with the Centralia Case and the Criminal Syndicalism Law than we could have gotten out in a year with our papers. . . . I am enjoying my fight here and I believe I am doing considerable good.[37]

When Smith returned to Centralia in between his many speaking tours, it was not easy to carry on a normal family life. After their Presbyterian church turned its back on Elmer and Laura, the Smiths never returned there to worship.[38] Elmer Smith's friends came mostly from the Logan district of Centralia, also known as "IWW town," where railroad men, loggers, and miners lived. When the landlord did not renew their lease, Elmer and Laura moved across the railroad tracks to the Logan district, where they rented a large, two-story house with a wooden front porch and a garden. To bring in a little income, Laura gave piano lessons to neighborhood children. She also joined the local bridge club and the Card and Label League, a group of women who promoted using the union label on clothing and other items. Through these activities Laura drew closer to Smith's working-class world and gained some valuable friends. The day the Smiths moved into the new house, twenty people appeared after supper to welcome them to the neighborhood. They moved the tables and rugs from the livingroom, and everyone danced to a lively fiddler. Smith loved to dance, and he was on his feet until the party broke up hours later.[39] The family's second child, Stuart Ross, was born in their new home in late 1921.

The Smiths spent their best times together during the summers when Elmer managed to relax on family picnic vacations. Nearly every Fourth of July, the family enjoyed a weekend at Deep Lake, a favorite spot near their old home in Mendota. Elmer and Laura loaded up their car with tents, swimming gear, and a large bucket of ice cream. The rest of the family always knew when Elmer had arrived because he would shout a loud "Yahoo!" as he reached the lakeside and dived into the water. After a long day of swimming and fishing, Elmer joined his brothers for card games of Hearts and Five Hundred. Elmer played cards recklessly, taking long chances to bring a quick end to the game. He usually lost, but he loved the excitement.[40]

The Smiths were a tightly knit family. Outsiders often noticed the short tempers and loud shouting matches, but the family remained fiercely loyal to and protective of each other. Elmer's notoriety made family members turn to each other even more. His youngest brother, Bill, who was cautious about making outside friends, waited a month after becoming engaged before telling his fiancée about his famous brother. She was shocked because of all the terrible things she had heard about the IWW.[41]

Only Laura did not share in the family closeness. She and Elmer were the only highly educated members of the Smith clan, which had attracted them to each other but which isolated Laura from the rest of the family. When Dorothy became engaged to logger Connor Harmon, for example, Laura told her she was foolish to marry a man with no education.[42] Also, Laura was not reconciled to Elmer's involvement with the IWW. She wanted him to settle down and establish a more conventional law practice in town. She was never comfortable with Elmer's traveling, his odd work

Elmer Smith, high school graduation picture

Elmer with his sister Dorothy and mother Isabelle

Elmer Smith, c. 1920 (*courtesy of Virginia Smith Waddell*)

The Smith family: (*from left*) Thomas, Harry, Dorothy, Isabelle, Bill, Elmer, Jim

Elmer in his Centralia law office (*courtesy Virginia Smith Waddell*)

Elmer with his daughter Virginia and son Stuart, late 1920s or early 1930s
(*courtesy Virginia Smith Waddell*)

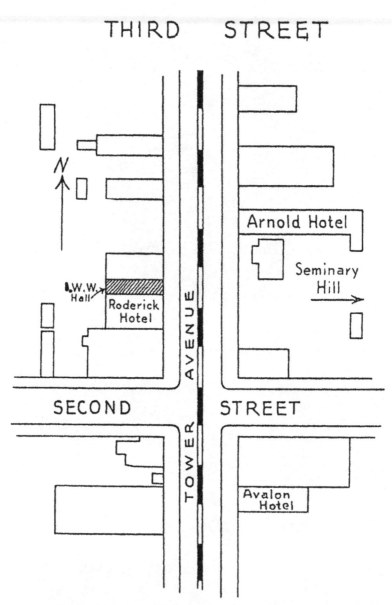

DIAGRAM SHOWING THE LOCATION OF THE I. W. W. HALL.

Map of downtown Centralia, showing the location of the IWW Hall
(from Federal Council of Churches, *The Centralia Case*)

Centralia IWW office, 1920s

FREE LECTURE

ON THE

Famous Centralia Case
of 1919

The True Story of the Event That Has Become the
Grave Problem That Each Conscientious
Citizen Must Now Help Solve.

Told by 3 Speakers

ELMER SMITH
Lawyer and one of the Original Defendants.

CAPT. EDWARD P. COLL
Legionnaire and Investigator of Case.

REV. J. HERBERT GEOGHEGAN
Preacher.

Att. George F. Vanderveer
Defense Attorney at the Trial, Chairman.

EAGLES AUDITORIUM
Cor. 7th Ave. and Union Street   Seattle, Wash.

Sunday February 10th, 3 pm
Everybody Come - - Admission FREE

(OVER

Flyer for the February 1929 Seattle meeting, with a note from Ed Coll

DON'T FAIL TO HEAR

Elmer Smith   George Vanderveer
Capt. Edward P. Coll, Rev. J. H. Geoghegan

On the True Story of the

Famous Centralia Case
of 1919

and the

Eight Men Now Buried Alive

An Original Defendant, Lawyer, Preacher and Legionnaire will give you the True Facts of this case that has become a serious problem of every conscientious citizen of the State of Washington.

EAGLES AUDITORIUM
Cor. 7th Ave. and Union Street   Seattle, Wash.

Sunday February 10th, 3 p.m.

Everybody Come - - Admission FREE

 28

(OVER)

Mass meeting on the Centralia case, Eagles Hall, Seattle, February 10, 1929 (*courtesy University of Washington Libraries*)

hours, and his uncertain financial prospects, but she did manage to keep the household running and care for the two small children. Although there was never any doubt about her commitment to the relationship, Laura was not able to share her daily joys and sorrows with Elmer, an unspoken frustration for her. Smith's first commitment was to freeing the Centralia Wobblies, and he showed no signs of making fewer family sacrifices to do it.

Although many of Smith's speaking engagements turned into free speech battles, they did generate publicity, and he was able to raise money for the Centralia prisoners and their families. One year, he organized a fundraising effort to give the families a Christmas dinner. Mrs. Commodore Bland and her six children, Mrs. John Lamb and her two children, and Mrs. Eugene Barnett and her son were all happily reunited with their husbands over the special meal. The hardship for the prisoners and their families had increased in June 1921 when the prisoners were transferred in chains and handcuffs and under heavy guard to the state prison in Walla Walla, 275 miles east of Centralia. Groups such as the Womens' Prison Comfort Club of Seattle helped raise money to send the wives and children on visits to the prison, but it was a long way to Walla Walla.[43]

To further the campaign to release the men from prison, Smith established a Centralia Publicity Committee (CPC) in 1921. He donated space in his office, and C. S. Smith, a local Wobbly and no relation to Elmer, volunteered to be secretary. "Smitty," as he was known, had once been severely beaten by a prison guard while he was serving time, and he was always ready to fight.[44]

When Smith and Smitty talked to the Montesano jurors, they found to their surprise that some of them were willing to help in the release campaign. Five of the jurors signed affidavits saying that the Wobblies had not gotten a fair trial and that the soldiers in front of the courthouse had intimidated them and influenced their decision. Many of the jurors believed the defendants were innocent, and they had voted for a second degree guilty verdict for fear that if the jury could not reach agreement then a new jury would hang the men.[45] The affidavits received wide publicity in the Washington newspapers. Shortly after their release, police in Aberdeen arrested nearly twenty men and women in a raid on the IWW hall and charged them with criminal syndicalism. Some labor sympathizers said the raid was an act of retaliation because of the affidavits.[46]

The jurors' statements lent support to the release campaign and garnered more sympathy for the prisoners. As the affidavits piled up, Smith visited with the families of the prisoners to offer them encouragement. But not everyone was won over. For example, the *Daily Washingtonian* in Hoquiam editorialized:

> If . . . the jurors believed the defendants innocent, it was their duty to hold steadfastly for acquittal. If they did not they violated their oaths. But they voted for conviction. If they committed a lie in rendering the verdict, their word . . . is no better now.[47]

Although encouraging to Smith and other IWW supporters, the affidavits had no legal value and had limited influence on the governor.

Shortly after the CPC published the affidavits, Smith's landlord tripled the rent on his law office and gave him notice. Unable to find space in any of the commercial buildings downtown, Smith was forced to move his office into his home. At odds with much of the Centralia business community since he had moved to town, Smith was surprised when he received a letter from the Chamber of Commerce in early 1922 urging him to join: "Knowing that you are interested in the growth and development of our city, and that you want a part in its up-building—we want you with us." But Smith was in no mood for a reconciliation with his professional colleagues. He accused members of the Chamber of conspiring with others to raid the Wobbly hall in 1919 and with railroading other Wobblies to jail under the criminal syndicalism law. "There will be no industrial peace in this state or in this city until this great wrong has been righted," he predicted. Urging the Chamber to demand the release of all IWW prisoners, Smith concluded: "Until this is done you need not expect the city of Centralia to occupy its proper position among the cities of the state of Washington." The Chamber did not reply to this brash letter, which Smith probably wrote to gain publicity for the cause.[48]

Smith continued to be a thorn in the side of the town's business interests when he ran once more for county prosecuting attorney on the Farmer-Labor Party ticket in the fall of 1922. He campaigned on a platform calling for the release of the Centralia prisoners, the abolition of the criminal syndicalism law, and an end to the harassment of Wobblies in Lewis County:

> If I am elected prosecuting attorney of Lewis county I will bring back the right of free speech and peaceful assemblage. To date

Lewis county had been the stamping ground of mob rule. A place for these persons will be found in Walla Walla.[49]

Smith's outspoken rhetoric and strong showing during the earlier campaign worried his opposition, but the incumbent Republican, Herman Allen, need not have been concerned. Times had changed since 1920. A general economic depression in Washington had hit the shipping and lumbering industries hard during the previous two years, and a major fire had destroyed a large sawmill in Centralia, affecting one hundred workers and their families.[50] The Farmer-Labor Party had been weakened by the decline of the moderate and radical union organizations and had split on the question of political versus nonpartisan action to achieve its goals. And for an increasing number of workers, even near Centralia, the Armistice Day raid was not the vital issue it once had been.

Although Smith's campaign drew some harassment from local authorities, it was much milder and his speeches drew fewer people than before. He was aware that the election lacked the drama and excitement of the previous campaign, but he still believed it was important to generate publicity for the IWW and the Farmer-Labor Party. In the end, Smith finished third. He received fewer votes than he had in 1920, even though he was the leading vote-getter on the Farmer-Labor ticket.[51] It was Smith's last personal political campaign.

Acid in a Wobbly Shoe

"Hold the Fort"—*IWW Songbook*, 1880

We meet today in Freedom's cause
    And raise our voices high;
We'll join our hands in union strong,
    To battle or to die.

Hold the fort for we are coming—
    Union men, be strong.
Side by side we battle onward,
    Victory will come.

The effort to release the Centralia Wobblies in 1920–21 was overshadowed by the amnesty campaign for the many Wobblies who had been convicted of violating the Espionage Act during World War I. The IWW General Defense Committee in Chicago and the ACLU organized support among labor groups and liberals concerned about civil liberties. In late 1921, pressure from these groups persuaded President Harding to release the most famous of the wartime prisoners, Socialist leader Eugene Debs, who had been jailed in 1918 for encouraging opposition to World War I. In releasing Debs, Harding was able to at least partly deflate the growing sentiment for amnesty. The American Federation of Labor officially called off its campaign to free the remaining political prisoners, although some AFL locals still supported the amnesty movement. But Harding considered political prisoners, such as the Wobblies, to be more of a menace "to all we hold dear" than ordinary criminals were.[1] Over seventy Wobblies remained in Leavenworth Prison, insisting that they had done no wrong and demanding a group pardon.

For the most part, the national amnesty campaign ignored the victims of criminal syndicalism laws and criminal cases such as the one in Centralia. While many of the federal prisoners were national IWW leaders and public figures, those in state prisons were the rank and file. And although the president had the power to release federal prisoners, many different state officials determined the fate of state prisoners.

Smith supported the general amnesty movement in his speeches, but he was disappointed that the national campaign was not focusing more on the Centralia case. So when the IWW's General Defense Committee sent speakers, Smith welcomed them. In early 1921, Ralph Chaplin came to Centralia. Chaplin was a national IWW organizer and poet, out on bail during an appeal of his conviction for violating the Espionage Act. He spoke before the first open IWW meeting held in town since 1919, where he recruited new members and urged his listeners to join in the amnesty fight. The meeting closed with the singing of "Solidarity Forever," the unofficial anthem of the IWW, which Chaplin had written.[2]

Chaplin's visit coincided with a resurgence of local IWW organizing efforts and kicked off a flurry of activity. The Wobblies put up recruitment placards in the town's residential districts and openly distributed literature at nearby lumber camps and mills. They also sold the *Industrial Worker* on the streets in downtown Centralia. It was not long before local authorities moved in to stop them, and in early April 1921 police arrested Wobbly Tom Nash and charged him with criminal syndicalism for distributing the IWW paper. Smith raised the five thousand dollar bond and Nash was released.[3]

Other arrests soon followed, but the IWW did not consider going to jail to be a setback. For years, Wobbly organizing campaigns had been built around packing the jails in a community. Because the IWW was a small organization, it had focused on one town at a time and put out a call for all "footloose" Wobblies to come into town and get arrested. The strategy was more than just a stunt. Speaking in the streets and hawking their newspapers were often the only ways the Wobblies had to reach other workers and organize their union. The publicity from the confrontations and arrests resulted in new members and eventually forced the authorities to release the men from jail. Shortly after Nash was released, he was arrested again for selling newspapers. This time the bond was set at ten thousand dollars, and Nash had to stay in jail. Each week a few more Wobblies were arrested until there were more than a dozen in the small cells.[4]

In late May, while chairing an IWW-sponsored meeting, Smith asked if anyone had seen any strange faces in town recently. When several shouted "Yes!" Smith boasted that there would be two thousand Wobblies coming to town within three weeks if the boys in jail were not released.

It was an obvious exaggeration, but the audience roared with approval. Food collected at the meeting was given to the families of the jailed men. Many in town who had been afraid to talk openly about the Armistice Day tragedy began to appear at IWW meetings. The arrests of Wobblies were generating broader support for the cause.[5]

On Memorial Day, Centralia again witnessed two different celebrations that emphasized the town's divided loyalties. The official military parade, held downtown, was complete with six war tanks, army trucks, and armed soldiers marching to honor the men who had died in the nation's wars. At the same time, several of Smith's brothers, his mother, and a few dozen union families drove in a caravan out of Centralia to one of the town's cemeteries. They gathered under the shade of the spruce trees and placed American flags and flowers on the spot where Wesley Everest had been buried. At dusk, other workers arrived to stand at the spot and pay their respects.[6]

On June 13, the trial for four of the Wobblies charged with criminal syndicalism for distributing union newspapers—Tom Nash, W. F. Moudy, Charles Beavers, and Glen Smith (Elmer's brother)—began in the county courthouse in Chehalis.[7] Elmer Smith and Ralph Pierce defended the men. The trial created a lot of interest because of Smith's involvement, and the courtroom was packed with people every day. Smith first moved to have Judge Reynolds removed from the case because of his prejudice against the IWW, and a new judge was seated.[8]

Prosecutor J. H. Jahnke made his opening statement: "I am going to state to you frankly that I am deeply prejudiced against the IWW organization."[9] He asked the defense counsel to state in court whether they approved of all IWW actions, saying that if they refused to answer then they were not entitled to be taken seriously by the jury. Smith, unafraid to identify himself with the IWW, replied in his opening statement that he had believed strongly in IWW principles since 1919:

To win its case, the prosecution needed only to show that the IWW advocated violence and that the defendants were members. The prosecution opened by introducing an old IWW pamphlet that had a black cat on the cover, the IWW symbol for sabotage. The defense countered with Wobbly Hiney Heathcote, who testified that the black cat did not stand for violence and destruction, but rather for the establishment of a new economic system controlled by the working class. He explained that sabotage simply involved workers using the peaceful means of a strike to fight for better conditions. Noticing that Heathcote wore a Wobbly button on his lapel, the prosecutor picked up the Wobbly button the police had seized from Tom Nash and stepped closer to compare the two. Pierce jumped up and shouted, "Turn that lapel over! Don't let him see it." Heathcote did so and probably saved himself from arrest.[10]

An undercover agent, who had been hired by the Luke May Detective Agency to investigate criminal activities and report to local authorities, was posing as a Wobbly when he testified for the defense. The agent passed on defense strategy, reporting that there were no plans by the Wobblies to use violence either at the trial or during the educational campaign in Centralia. The agent's reports were also turned over to the Bureau of Investigation in Washington, D.C. Enjoying the unsuspecting confidence of Smith and the rest of the defense team, the agent rode to the trial with Smith's brother Jim. Smith, always the soft touch, took up a collection among his friends to pay the agent's way home.[11]

After a long deliberation, the jury found Tom Nash and W. F. Moudy guilty and Charles Beavers and Glen Smith innocent. Nash and Moudy were sentenced to Walla Walla prison for two to fifteen years at hard labor. It was hard to explain the jury's verdict, since all four men had admitted on the witness stand that they were members and organizers of the IWW. The only difference among them was that those convicted were single and from out of town and those acquitted were married and from Centralia. Moudy had been tried earlier in Seattle for criminal syndicalism, but that jury had acquitted him, holding that the IWW organization was legal. Now he found himself convicted on the same charge in the same state by a jury that held that the IWW was an unlawful organization. Several of the jurors later said that they had been divided in their vote and had decided to avoid a hung jury by splitting the verdict. One juror believed that all the men were innocent, but she was afraid that a new jury would convict all four. Smith unsuccessfully appealed the convictions.[12]

In less than two weeks, the courts, citing insufficient evidence, released nine other Wobblies arrested in Centralia. In dropping the charges, it is likely that the authorities considered both the favorable publicity the IWW would gain from more trials and the high costs of prosecuting such a minor matter. The Centralia Wobblies celebrated the news by parading up the street to hear Smith speak at an outdoor meeting in front of IWW headquarters.[13]

Because of Smith's legal experience, the California District IWW Defense Committee hired him to help defend Wobblies charged with criminal syndicalism in that state. California's version of the law, passed in 1919, was almost identical to Washington's. The hysteria of the postwar years, stories of IWW terrorism and plots, the nationwide federal raids on the IWW, and pressure from employers of migrant laborers combined to create an atmosphere conducive to the restrictive language of California's law. By early 1922, twenty-seven men were serving time in San Quentin state prison simply for being members of the IWW. California was particularly active in prosecuting Wobblies (and occasionally members of the Communist Party of California). Between 1919 and 1924, over five hundred people were arrested under the anti-syndicalism law, and most of them were convicted (although an unusually high number of the convictions were reversed by state appellate courts).[14]

In late April 1922, Smith went to Sacramento to defend J. Casdorf and Earl Firey on charges of criminal syndicalism. Both had freely admitted their membership in the IWW, so the only issue was whether the organization advocated crime, sabotage, and violence. To prove his case, the prosecutor introduced two star witnesses, former Wobblies Elbert Coutts and John Dymond. Both had testified in 1918 in a highly publicized trial in Sacramento, in which fifty-five Wobblies were convicted of sabotage on the flimsiest of evidence.[15] The men were now making a living as professional witnesses, traveling around the state to testify. So far, their testimony had sent more than twenty Wobblies to prison.

Dymond testified first in the 1922 trial. He admitted to having destroyed property in North Dakota while he was a Wobbly and said that someone had told him that a Wobbly had burned some haystacks in Modesto, California, in 1917. Another prosecution witness, Joe Arata, claimed that a Wobbly had put acid in his shoe. But on cross-examination, Smith had Arata show his scar, which clearly had not been caused by a burn. Elbert Coutts, an admitted arsonist who had also served time for a burglary conviction, testified in support of Arata's story. The prosecution called no other witnesses. The only other evidence introduced was IWW newspapers and pamphlets, which the prosecution claimed advocated sedition and violence.[16] By themselves, the haystack and acid stories were insignificant, even laughable. There was no direct evidence that members of the IWW were involved in these incidents, only testimony by someone who heard that Wobblies were involved. And both of the alleged crimes had been committed between 1915 and 1917, well before the state's criminal syndicalism law went into effect. Both defendants had become Wobblies after the law was passed, and neither was implicated in the incidents.

Despite the lack of direct evidence against the defendants, Smith had to contend with the violent reputation that the Wobblies had acquired. Some Wobblies had set fires, ruined lumber, and spoiled crops, but those acts were a product of individual grievances or revenge and were never part of IWW policy. The violence that erupted in the midst of labor-management clashes was the result of working conditions and political pressures that could not be blamed on any one company or labor union, but the IWW still took the brunt of the blame. Smith attempted to show that the IWW did not advocate sabotage or violence. He tried to read from current IWW literature that had modified earlier, more militant positions, but the judge ruled that such evidence was irrelevant. The prosecution claimed that the IWW was trying to overthrow the U.S. government, and Smith countered by arguing that if this was so then why had not the federal government outlawed the IWW or revoked its newspaper's second class mailing privileges? But the judge interrupted: "We are not concerned with the United States government; this is the state of California."[17]

The judge refused to allow one of Smith's witnesses to testify about the IWW because she was not a member and her information was necessarily acquired second-hand. He ruled that only Wobblies could testify to the philosophy of their organization, so Smith brought in ten Wobblies—including Herb Edwards and Walker Smith, a member of the IWW General Executive Board—to describe the union's official, nonviolent nature. But as each witness stepped from the witness stand, he was arrested outside the jury's view and charged with criminal syndicalism for admitting IWW membership. Despite the seriousness of the situation, Smith enjoyed a moment of fun with the judge when he asked Edwards to recite the Declaration of Independence. "He'll do no such thing!" shouted the judge. Edwards was relieved; he could not recite it and Smith knew it.[18]

The trial was almost two weeks old when Smith rose to give his closing argument. By this time, he had become an accomplished courtroom orator. Using humorous stories and a common language, he spoke directly to the jury about values and principles that had improved society for everyone. It was warm inside the courtroom, and many of the spectators fanned themselves to keep cool. For two hours, Smith's voice carried well enough so that those lining the hall corridors could hear him. Smith described how workers often had to strike to obtain a dollar's worth of pay for a dollar's worth of work. He accused employers of committing sabotage when they created shoddy goods and charged high prices for them. "All we are trying to stop is the exploitation of one man by another man," he said.[19] He ridiculed the testimony of Coutts and Dymond. Comparing their role in the trial to that of a Judas steer leading cattle to the slaughter pen, he expressed amazement that their stories had been taken seriously.

Probably the most effective part of Smith's argument came when he challenged the prosecution's tactic of reading selectively from Wobbly literature to prove that the IWW advocated criminal syndicalism. That is the same, he said, as charging a member of the Presbyterian church with criminal syndicalism and using the Bible as evidence against him. He read excerpts from the Bible, including "Put every man his sword by his side, and go in and out from gate to gate throughout the camp, and slay every man his brother, and every man his companion, and every man his neighbor." "Is there any one here," he asked, "that would say such tactics as that would be fair? Does that give you a fair idea of that Bible? Why of course not."[20] Smith sat down feeling optimistic about his clients' chances. But the jury found both Casdorf and Firey guilty, and the judge sentenced them to one to fourteen years in San Quentin.

The verdict shocked the *Sacramento Star*: "Their case presents an instance of flagrant abuse of traditional American justice, of extravagant disregard for the right of anybody to a fair trial." The *Industrial Worker* called it "one of the most flagrantly unfair trials that ever disgraced the American courts." The *Nation* denounced the arrest of defense witnesses during the trial: "Such procedure is unparalleled in criminal law and amounts to intimidation of witnesses. It would make defense impossible in criminal syndicalism cases. . . . The issue quite transcends State lines in its importance."[21] In an article for the *Industrial Worker*, Smith wrote:

> If you happen to be an American and come into California you are very apt to be prosecuted for belonging to that organization of citizens known as the United States because a long while ago some Americans dumped some tea into the harbor at Boston.[22]

The IWW General Defense Committee announced that it would fight to repeal California's criminal syndicalism law. Most of the trials involving Wobblies in California had gone just like the one in Sacramento, and rarely had the defendants been charged with a specific crime. California authorities were clearly using the law to suppress the union.

After promising to defend Herb Edwards and the nine other Wobbly witnesses who had been arrested, at the trial scheduled to begin in two months, Smith left Sacramento for El Centro to handle another criminal syndicalism case. At El Centro he managed to get a hung jury, and a new trial was ordered for a later date.[23] Smith returned to Eureka for a similar case, where the highly charged atmosphere had not subsided much since his visit three months earlier. Timber owners remained nervous about increased Wobbly recruiting activity and the spread of Wobbly literature in the county. The *Humboldt Times* reported that the Legionnaires bitterly opposed Smith's return, which was "regarded locally as simply a test that the authorities fear may lead to serious results."[24]

Smith's client was Omar Eaton, an organizer for the Lumber Workers Industrial Union. Eaton and his principal defense attorney, A. U. Monroe, had asked for Smith's assistance. The prosecuting attorney was State Senator H. C. Nelson, who had been appointed to block Smith's appearance, probably at the request of the timber owners. Smith had tried cases in California under a rule that permitted out-of-state attorneys to practice at the discretion of the local judge and district attorney. Thousands of out-of-state lawyers regularly practiced in California under this rule. Nelson moved to have Smith excluded, stating that the Eureka Bar Association had asked that Smith be kept from practicing law in Eureka and in the state of California. The judge, a former lumber company attorney, ruled against Smith and ordered him to sit with the spectators in the courtroom.[25]

Upon hearing the ruling, J. Kennedy, secretary of the California District Defense Committee, sent the judge a telegram: "Does the fact that this is an IWW case explain your honor's discrimination?" The judge fined Kennedy five hundred dollars for contempt of court. To prevent the fine from being collected, Smith advised his friends not to raise any bail money, and Kennedy spent 250 days in jail.[26]

The prosecution brought out Elbert Coutts and John Dymond to retell their stories about burning haystacks and acid shoes. Arthur Ward, secretary of the Eureka branch of the IWW, testified by reading from some IWW literature, but he was later arrested while talking with Smith out in the hall. After deliberating for twenty-four hours, the jury announced that it could not reach a verdict and the judge declared a mistrial. At his second trial, Eaton was found guilty in fifteen minutes and sentenced to one to fourteen years in prison. On appeal, the California Supreme Court upheld his conviction.[27]

After working on several other criminal syndicalism cases for the Defense Committee in California, Smith returned to Sacramento in June to defend the ten witnesses who had testified at the Casdorf-Firey trial. As the prosecution began to present its case, Smith could see that it was going to be a repetition of the first trial. Joe Arata returned to tell his acid shoe story again, and Coutts and Dymond repeated once more that the Wobblies started fires in 1917. The former deputy sheriff of Modesto, California, testified that a great many fires were set in his district in 1917, but he could not say who started them. Smith unsuccessfully tried to have his testimony stricken from the record as irrelevant. But he was able to get an investigator of radical activities from the San Joaquin Protective Association to admit that he had not uncovered one act of sabotage or violence since the passage of the state's criminal syndicalism law.[28]

Smith brought to the stand defendant Walker Smith, who outlined the principles of the IWW and revealed that the IWW Executive Board had adopted resolutions against violence at its latest annual convention. He asked a Wobbly witness, who was not a defendant, if the IWW believed in violence as a means of accomplishing industrial change. The prosecution rose to object that the witness was not qualified to answer the question unless he was an IWW member. Exasperated, Smith asked the judge if his witness would be arrested after he left the stand if he admitted such membership. Irritated by the question, the judge said no immunity would be granted. Rather than have any more Wobblies arrested, Smith decided to call no more witnesses. In his closing speech to the jury, he gave a stirring account of current labor conditions and of the IWW's efforts to improve them.

After six hours of deliberation, the jury announced that they were nine for acquittal and three for a conviction. All but one of the jurors said they thought they could reach a verdict. Over Smith's protests, the judge declared a hung jury and ordered a new trial. Smith was certain that, had further deliberations been permitted, his clients would have been acquitted.[29]

Shortly after the trial, the district attorney's office in Sacramento brought a motion before a district court of appeals to prevent Smith from practicing law in California. In late June, the court held that Smith had no right to practice in the state, basing its decision on a recent state law that barred out-of-state attorneys who were not of good moral character.[30] The *Industrial Worker* commented:

> Because Elmer Smith, a man who stayed a man in spite of his profession, put up a great defense in the Sacramento courts, the courts of California have barred him from practicing in their "fair" state. When they did that they drove another nail in the coffin of the law. No one will be able to respect a law or judiciary that does things like that.[31]

For their next trial, Edwards and several other defendants suggested putting up a silent defense. Wobblies had used this tactic before. The defendants, without an attorney, folded their arms in the courtroom, remained silent throughout the trial, and refused to present defense. The strategy was designed to dramatize their contempt for the trial proceedings and to save the IWW defense expenses. But Edwards was unable to convince enough of his fellow defendants to try the approach. With a new lawyer at their next trial, all of them were convicted and sentenced to one to fourteen years in prison.[32]

In the fall of 1922 Smith handled another criminal syndicalism trial that became a watershed case for the IWW. Police had arrested two Wobblies during a free speech fight in Hoquiam. Several months earlier seventeen others had been arrested in a raid on the IWW hall. The trial was held in Montesano, in the same courtroom that had been used to try the Centralia Wobblies. This time, Smith was determined to take a more aggressive role for the defense. With the help of an associate counsel, J. M. Phillips, a former mayor of Aberdeen, Smith decided to use this case to argue that the state's criminal syndicalism law was unconstitutional. It was a sound legal move. Having used all other defense strategies with mixed results, this time he introduced a novel objection. He argued that because of the prosecution's tactic of reading from old IWW literature, written by authors who were either dead or unavailable at trial, the defendants never had the opportunity to face their accuser. The procedure did not permit the defense to cross-examine the author, Smith insisted, and thus it was unconstitutional under Article VI of the Bill of Rights.

The judge granted Smith's motion, ruling that the prosecutor could only introduce current IWW literature to prove his case. It was a major victory for Smith. The prosecutor did read from literature seized during the Hoquiam raid, but it was not nearly as inflammatory as the older IWW materials and his case was severely weakened. For the defense, Smith called Robert Whitaker, pastor of the Congregational Church in Seattle, who had served three months in a county jail for his opposition to the war. Whitaker testified that three-fourths of the prosecution's evidence could be found in the state's major libraries and could hardly be considered dangerous.

At the end of the trial, Smith moved that not enough evidence had been presented against his clients for the case to go to the jury and that the case should be dismissed. The judge granted the motion, and with the ruling the cases against the other accused Wobblies also collapsed. It was a significant triumph for Smith and the IWW. The case also sounded the death knell for the state's criminal syndicalism law, which was eventually repealed in 1937.[33] Smith took a special pride in leaving this courtroom victorious. It was his greatest legal victory.

During his career, Smith assisted in approximately twenty criminal syndicalism cases, probably more than any other defense attorney except Vanderveer and his law partners, and he had lost less than his share in the bleak atmosphere of public persecution against the IWW.[34] As a leading trial defense attorney for the IWW, his professional reputation was at its peak. The IWW officially had a cool attitude toward lawyers, but the union's members sang Smith's praises. He had a special relationship with his working-class clients, and he consulted with them freely for advice about trial strategy. The Wobblies trusted him as they trusted no other defense attorney.[35]

Smith enjoyed the theatrics of the courtroom, and he effectively used humor and sarcasm to attack the absurdities of the criminal syndicalism law. His closing arguments were wide-ranging discussions of free speech, IWW history, and philosophy, and he always described the working conditions that had given rise to IWW grievances. In an attempt to change anti-IWW sentiment, his comments were addressed as much to the general public as they were to the jury. His next battleground would be in his own hometown.

Get Thomas Jefferson

"The Popular Wobbly"—T-Bone Slim, *IWW Songbook*, 1920

I'm as mild manner'd man as can be
And I've never done them harm that I can see,
Still on me they put a ban and they threw me in the can,
They go wild, simply wild over me.

Then the judge, he went wild over me,
And I plainly saw we never could agree,
So I let the man obey what his conscience had to say,
He went wild, simply wild over me.

In early February 1923, Wobbly organizers initiated a publicity campaign in and around Centralia that turned into a major free speech battle. It would also be the town's last significant IWW organizing effort. The Wobblies were trying to recruit loggers and other workers to their cause by distributing circulars door-to-door in the residential parts of town; they then moved downtown to sell IWW newspapers and literature along Tower Avenue. After only two weeks, they had sold two hundred and fifty copies of the *Industrial Worker* in Centralia and Chehalis. Several businessmen complained to Centralia Mayor George Barner, who warned that if the Wobblies were arrested then hundreds more would arrive to pack the jails, causing further trouble. Barner did not want a repeat of Centralia's free speech fight of 1921.[1]

The police department showed less reluctance to act, and police arrested two Wobblies for selling the *Industrial Worker*. Both were quickly convicted under a city ordinance patterned after the state criminal syndicalism law, which made distributing IWW literature punishable by thirty days in jail or a fine of ninety-nine dollars or both. Two days after the first arrest, the police raided the Wobbly office; seized piles of pamphlets, books, and office supplies; and nabbed two more organizers. When Smith heard about the raid, he volunteered to give a speech on the coming Sunday in support of the Wobblies' campaign. Workers immediately distributed handbills announcing that Smith would speak on "The Road to Freedom."[2] When Centralia's chief of police, James Compton, saw one of the handbills, he went to the Bureau of Investigation office in Tacoma. Mayor Barner believed that public sentiment against Smith speaking was "growing very warm," Compton told the Bureau, and he wanted to prevent the address on the grounds that it would incite a riot.[3]

The day before Smith's scheduled speech, Compton and Barner called on Smith at his home. They asked him not to make his speech and told him he would be arrested if he did. Although they were willing to allow an outside speaker to take his place, Smith said that he intended to stand on his constitutional right of free speech. The only way they could stop him from speaking, he said, was to arrest him. Later that night, Smith met with the organizers of the meeting, who agreed to send for a backup speaker, Floyd Hyde from Portland. Smith saw his speech as an opportunity to test the constitutionality of the city ordinance.[4]

Compton and Barner were also preparing for a confrontation. Compton sent a letter to the Tacoma Bureau office:

> I do not know how we will come out in this matter. I suppose they will send ten men here for every one we pick up but we will do the best we know how to handle the situation. We feel that we have got to stop them now or throw the city open to them.[5]

A crowd of two hundred fifty people nearly filled the Labor Temple on Sunday afternoon. Floyd Hyde opened the meeting with a reading of the First Amendment. When he introduced Smith, the crowd greeted him with several minutes of rousing applause. Smith announced that he intended to conduct a peaceful meeting and that anyone who interfered was not worthy of being called an American citizen. After only a few words, Chief Compton stepped up to the platform and placed Smith under arrest. The chief let him tell the crowd the meeting could go on in his absence, and then Mayor Barner took the platform. Perhaps feeling a bit embarrassed, Barner explained somewhat apologetically that the arrest "was not an attempt to interfere with free speech or assemblage." The police were acting under a city ordinance designed to prevent meetings that would "tend to create or incite trouble." It would be up to the courts, he said, to decide whether the actions of the police were proper.[6]

Years later, both Barner and Compton stated that they had arrested Smith for his own protection because they were afraid that Centralia citizens would attack him. But they also acknowledged that Smith had said nothing objectionable and that the meeting had posed no danger of a riot. Obviously, Smith could not win in a situation where the city officials thought that upholding free speech meant arresting the speaker instead of those who threatened to disrupt the speech. A few days later, the Centralia police allowed a Ku Klux Klan meeting to proceed undisturbed in a local auditorium. It was clear that the police had been more interested in preventing Smith from speaking than in protecting public safety.[7] As Smith was led off to jail, Floyd Hyde took over the meeting and spoke uninterrupted for two hours about the aims of the IWW. He challenged anyone in the audience, especially city officials, to debate him. No one volunteered.

The following evening Smith appeared in court to face charges of violating the city ordinance that made it a misdemeanor to speak at an IWW meeting that advocated violence. Two hundred spectators, nearly all supporters of Smith, assembled in the courtroom. The judge was Lloyd Dysart, who was rumored to have been involved in planning the Armistice Day raid and the lynching of Wesley Everest. Pleading "not guilty" to the charges, Smith asked the court to appoint an attorney to represent him because he had no money, an unusual appeal for an attorney. Dysart appointed Albert Buxton, the Democratic candidate who had finished behind Smith in the 1920 election for prosecuting attorney. Buxton was also well known for his strong anti-IWW views.

When Dysart told Buxton that he would have to get his fee from Smith rather than the court, Smith protested that a court-appointed attorney must be paid by the court. A number of spectators applauded in approval. The judge angrily rapped his gavel and asked everyone who had applauded to stand up. When no one moved, he ordered the courtroom cleared. After a short trial in the now almost empty courtroom, Dysart found Smith guilty and sentenced him to five days in jail and a twenty-dollar fine. Smith filed a notice of appeal and remained in jail for a day and a half until he was released on a reduced bail.[8]

Hearing of Smith's arrest and conviction, Roger Baldwin of the ACLU wired a telegram of protest to Mayor Barner: "The suppression of free speech as a purely practical matter defeats its own ends. From a legal standpoint it is indefensible."[9] Barner sent a telegram back:

Free speech has nothing to do with Elmer Smith arrest. Great feeling here against him due to his connection with Armistice Day outrage of 1919. City authorities felt it detrimental to peace of community if he made speech as advertised under the auspices of IWW whose members were convicted of murder of exservicemen here.[10]

In his reply, Baldwin vowed that the ACLU would take the case to the Supreme Court, if necessary. He also sent a telegram to Smith with an offer of legal help.[11]

Two days after his release, Smith returned to the police court to defend two Wobblies who had been charged with vagrancy while they were trying to sell IWW literature. Again the judge was Dysart, and again things did not go well for Smith. At one point Smith rose to make an argument, and the judge ordered him to shut up and sit down. Smith remained standing in silence while Dysart commanded him three times to sit down. When Smith remained fixed in his position, Dysart directed Chief Compton to take him off to jail, where he was found in contempt of court and fined one dollar. Smith, still angry and stubborn, refused to pay. But with his legal work piling up, the Wobbly defense committee could not wait for Smith to cool off, so they paid his fine and he was released. Dysart found the two Wobblies guilty and gave them a choice of leaving town within an hour or serving ten days in jail. They chose jail.[12]

While the Wobbly-organized free speech fight was in full swing, Smith spent many afternoons at the Olympia Cafe on Tower Avenue near the railroad depot. Smith's brother Glen and other Wobblies gathered at the cafe to talk over their strategy of hawking their newspapers, being arrested, and packing the jail. They hoped to repeat the success of their free speech campaign of two years earlier. They also wanted to have as much fun as possible with their opponents, even when it involved a potentially explosive test of wills. Smith shared in the general laughter when he heard about the latest Wobbly tactic. After bumming a ride into town on the train, itinerant Wobblies would come to the Olympia Cafe and pick up several copies of the *Industrial Worker* to sell on Tower Avenue. The men expected to be arrested; in fact, they were given a description of Chief Compton and told to try to sell him a paper. When Compton made his rounds, he would make the arrest and walk the Wobbly back to jail, several blocks away. After a few days of marching prisoners to jail only to have another take his place on the street, Compton was overheard complaining, "These guys are wearing my feet out!"[13]

Compton was determined to rid the city of the impertinent radicals, despite complaints from businessmen about the large amount of money it was costing to hold the Wobblies in jail. Hoping to capitalize on these concerns, local Wobblies called for reinforcements from throughout the Pacific Northwest. Wild rumors circulated that five hundred Wobblies from Seattle and Portland were heading for Centralia. Deputized citizens stood guard on the roads leading into town and searched at gunpoint each car that passed. Compton kept the Tacoma Bureau of Investigation informed of the rumors, but he claimed that the situation was under control. Some Wobblies from out of town did make it to Centralia, but they numbered fewer than fifty.[14]

During the week following Smith's aborted speech, twenty-three Wobblies were arrested and found guilty of vagrancy. They were given the opportunity to leave town immediately, but all of them chose to serve their thirty-day sentences. Their routine in jail was five days on bread and water alternated with two days on regular rations.[15]

Compton swore in one hundred citizens as special officers, warning, "If 100 can't do it, we'll get another hundred." Mayor Barner became more and more impatient as the jails remained crowded. "We're going to run this town—not the IWW," he said. "They started this trouble, and we're going to finish it. We tried to get their co-operation in avoiding friction, but they apparently want friction." Barner weakly explained to the newspapers that no effort was being made to prevent free speech or assemblage but that the police were trying to make the sidewalks passable for law-abiding citizens.[16]

On February 26, eight days after the public meeting, seven more Wobblies were arrested for selling the *Industrial Worker*. When Judge Dysart heard the cases that evening, he left no doubt as to his feelings toward the IWW:

> In 1919 we lost four of our best young men, because we were not prepared. We are prepared today. We have a hundred sworn deputies who are instructed to have no mercy. . . . There will be no IWW papers sold here. I will see to it that Elmer Smith will not speak in this town as long as I am judge.

One defendant then spoke up, "Do constitutional rights count in Centralia at all?" "No, constitutional rights do not count at all," replied Dysart, who proceeded to find everyone guilty.[17]

To spread the news about the arrests and to win over public opinion, Smith wrote a circular entitled "A Message from the City Jail of Centralia, Wash." He described the recent arrests as "simply monuments to the ignorance and infamy of that criminal element in Centralia who are keeping Centralia back from taking its proper place among the advanced cities of the state." Those who tried to prevent the IWW from organizing lumber workers were "traitors" because they denied citizens their constitutional rights. He pointed out that not one criminal syndicalism case was pending in the state of Washington outside of Lewis County.[18]

By March 2 the free speech campaign appeared to have been successful. All but five Wobblies had been released from jail, and despite Dysart's prediction the police allowed the sale of the *Industrial Worker* on the streets again. Apparently, city officials gave in when it became clear that the arrests only stiffened the Wobblies' resistance. Many of the town's residents had complained about the warlike atmosphere in Centralia, and local businesses had been hurt by the general upheaval. The mounting costs of the multiple prosecutions and outside pressure from the ACLU also contributed to the change of heart. Arresting Wobblies had become more trouble than it was worth.[19]

Roger Baldwin wanted to test this newly won freedom by holding a public meeting under the auspices of the ACLU and the IWW. Smith would be the main speaker, and Baldwin suggested that Robert Whitaker, the Seattle minister, be the backup speaker. Smith and local Wobbly leaders readily agreed.[20] On March 17, the day before the meeting, Mayor Barner informed the Tacoma Bureau of Smith's speech and asked for advice. The city's attorney had counseled Barner and Compton to arrest Smith, to hold him long enough to prevent his speech, and then to release him without charging him. Barner and Compton opposed the plan, fearing that the Wobblies would easily label such action "capitalistic lawlessness." The Bureau agent agreed with them and suggested that Smith be arrested, charged with violating the city ordinance, and then prosecuted.[21]

The meeting began at two o'clock on Sunday afternoon. Between five hundred and a thousand people gathered on an empty lot just two blocks from the old Wobbly hall. Whitaker, hoping to persuade the police that Smith had a right to speak, began by stating that those who suppressed free speech showed their lack of confidence in Americans' ability to solve their own problems. The idea that the words of any one man could overturn the government, he said, was preposterous. The American people were able to decide for themselves what was rational, and they would reject any unsound doctrines. In the days to come, Whitaker said, Americans would be ashamed of the treatment inflicted on the Wobblies. He appealed to the audience to show its solidarity with the forces of labor on the side of free speech.

Smith stepped up to the makeshift wooden platform and removed several file cards from his pocket. "There's an old document which runs somewhat as follows: 'We hold these truths to be-'," he said, beginning to read the Declaration of Independence. But that was as far as he got. Chief Compton made his way to the front of the crowd and cried out, "For the peace and dignity of Centralia, I arrest you!" Smith stopped and looked over his file cards down at Compton. The crowd was quiet, straining to hear. Smith's voice was calm, but he could not completely disguise his angry tone: "Have you a warrant for my arrest?" Compton froze for a moment. Smith repeated his question. Compton threw back his overcoat with a flourish, revealing the officer's star pinned on his chest. Without further words or delay, he escorted Smith to the jail.[22]

The crowd watched without interfering and remained standing to sing "Solidarity Forever" and "Hold the Fort." They heard a few more words by Whitaker, placed a donation in the collection box, and went home. By acting peacefully and with a measure of courage, Smith and the IWW made a positive impression for their cause.

Smith was upset and a little surprised by his arrest, but he assumed that because the police had eased up on arresting Wobblies he would be treated in the same manner. On the way to jail, Smith asked Compton what position the police were taking. "I am running this town," said Compton, "and you're not going to speak as long as I am in charge here."[23] At the jail, Compton took Smith's file cards, quickly read them, and berated him for having written such radical and inflammatory words. "Thomas Jefferson wrote these words," said Smith. Compton shouted to his deputies, "I knew that there was someone else back of all this. Get Thomas Jefferson, he's the guy you want!" At the time, Smith was angry, but for years afterward he loved to make people laugh by retelling this story to audiences all over the Pacific Northwest.[24]

Released on one hundred dollars bail, Smith joined Whitaker for dinner and then drove out to the bridge where Wesley Everest had been lynched. Although Whitaker was content to rest there a moment, Smith could not relax and enjoy the sunset. He worried aloud about the men in Walla Walla and how their families were doing. Whitaker was touched by Smith's rare open display of his personal feelings. He was concerned that Smith was not getting enough legal and emotional support to sustain his labors, and he later wrote to Baldwin that although Smith was admired by many working people, he was isolated in Centralia from other sympathetic lawyers. He could use additional local legal backing.[25] The *Seattle Union Record* editorialized about Smith's arrest:

> What is it that the Centralia public authorities are afraid of, that
> they won't allow Elmer Smith to speak[?]. . . . Any one who
> knows Smith knows that he is no inciter to violence and person-
> ally is utterly opposed to the use of violence in any manner.[26]

Compton testified at the trial, but Smith refused to offer any defense. After both sides waived their closing arguments, the judge found
Smith guilty, fined him fifty dollars, and sentenced him to ten days in jail.
Roger Baldwin secured an attorney for Smith's appeal. Released on bail,
Smith got in touch with George Vanderveer, who agreed to speak with him
at a public meeting to be held April 1 under the joint auspices of the IWW
and the ACLU. Baldwin advised Smith's attorney to secure an injunction
to make sure the meeting would take place. He also issued a press release
promising that the ACLU would fight for liberty in Centralia, "until the
mayor and local business interests behind him are forced to recognize the
right of unrestricted speech."[27]

Public interest grew as the day of the meeting neared. Some nine
hundred copies of the *Industrial Worker* were being sold each week on the
streets. Smith wrote another four-page circular that quoted Voltaire, Wen-
dell Phillips, and Thomas Jefferson on the right of free speech. He urged
those who believed in that right to come to the meeting in a show of support.[28] Nearly four thousand people showed up, crowding into a vacant lot
and spilling out into the street. Excitement and anticipation ran through
the crowd; many had come to see what the police would do about Smith's
plan to speak.

George Vanderveer, the first to speak, was fully primed, and his
voice, filled with righteous indignation and defiance, carried easily to the
back rows of the standing audience. What would the audience think if their
vote was taken away from them, he asked. It is much more dangerous and
criminal to take away the right of free speech, he said, because only through
that right can people know how to vote intelligently. The minority of every
age has become the majority of the next age, he continued. Today the minority is wrong only because they do not have the power, but tomorrow
they will be in the right. If Elmer Smith is wrong, he added, he should be
permitted to speak so that the errors of his reasoning could be exposed.[29]
"Now this meeting wasn't called to hear me speak but to hear Elmer Smith,
and Elmer is going to speak!" Vanderveer shouted. "Woe be unto any man

who tries to prevent it!"[30] With that, Smith took the platform to enthusiastic applause and cheers. Then the crowd grew still as all eyes turned to the mayor and the chief of police. But the two men stood with their arms folded across their chests and showed no signs that they would arrest him.

Smith opened his speech, entitled "Relationship of the Job to War," with a quote from Abraham Lincoln: "I see in the near future a crisis approaching that unnerves me and causes me to tremble for the safety of my country." Smith then launched into his talk about how the concentration of wealth could lead a capitalist society to the verge of another world war.[31] After urging the audience to embrace industrial unionism as the answer to society's problems, Smith turned to the subject of the eight workers from Centralia who had been "railroaded" to the penitentiary. There is your fight, he told the crowd; they believe in you and they wait for you to act. After an hour and a half, Smith finished speaking amid cheers and sustained applause. Twenty-five men immediately lined up to join the IWW. In a telegram to Baldwin, he described the meeting as a "wonderful success" and expressed surprise that he had not been stopped and arrested. Compton had not arrested Smith because the Bureau agent in Tacoma, concerned about the ACLU protests, had told him not to interfere. There is little evidence that anything had changed since Smith's aborted second speech, but perhaps the authorities were influenced by the growing public interest. Five months later, an appeals judge dismissed Smith's two convictions.[32]

Even though no official action was taken, the police and the Bureau still considered Smith's speeches to be filled with dangerous ideas and they hired a stenographer to take down every word. Smith was soon to discover that there were other steps, besides being arrested, that could be taken against a lawyer with radical opinions and a large following of workers.

The Lumberjack and the Mule

"Christians At War"—*IWW Songbook*, 1913

Onward, Christian soldiers, rip and tear and smite!
Let the gentle Jesus, bless your dynamite,
Splinter skulls with shrapnel, fertilize the sod!
Folks who do not speak your tongue, deserve the curse of God,
Smash the doors of every home, pretty maidens seize;
Use your might and sacred right to treat them as you please.

On June 1, 1923, Smith was relaxing in his new office when the postman delivered a thick envelope. It contained a legal complaint charging Smith with "unprofessional conduct as an attorney," violation of his oath to support the state and the United States constitutions, and "acts involving moral turpitude."[1] Clifford Cunningham and Herman Allen, the former prosecutors against Smith at the Montesano trial, and Judge Lloyd Dysart had signed the complaint as members of a grievance committee of the Lewis County Bar Association. The complaint was endorsed by twenty-eight of the thirty-six attorneys in Lewis County, including every Centralia attorney except Smith.[2] The State Board of Law Examiners, which had authority to hear evidence and make recommendations to the state supreme court as to whether Smith should be disbarred, scheduled a hearing on the complaint for July 5 in the Superior County Court in Chehalis. The final decision would rest with the state Supreme Court, which usually acted favorably on the board's findings. The complaint, signed on the day before Smith's speech in Centralia, was clearly a reaction to his insistence on speaking out about the IWW in his hometown.

Most of the nine-page complaint focused on the IWW, with Smith mentioned only infrequently. The organization's purpose, the complaint charged, was the destruction of capitalism, "the overthrow of the orderly form of government," and the setting up of a communist state. It claimed that IWW publications incited members and others to "insurrection, violence, sedition, and the practice of sabotage" and advocated the general strike to overthrow "the existing order of government by force and violence." The complaint mentioned Smith's role in the Armistice Day tragedy and reported that many Wobblies had been convicted under the state criminal syndicalism law for advocating IWW principles. It specifically charged that Smith "advocated and approved the principles" of the IWW, made many public speeches under the union's auspices, and urged workers to become members.[3]

For some time, Smith had known that a move to disbar him would be made. Two years earlier, in his opening statement to the jury in the Chehalis criminal syndicalism trial, he had said:

> I have been informed for some time that I was to be teased into
> a position so that I could be disbarred by reason of my work
> and my beliefs, but I have nothing to camouflage. . . . I believe
> in the principles of the IWW. . . . and if this be treason and be a
> crime, make the most of it.[4]

Now that something *was* being made of it, Smith needed legal help. With no local attorney to turn to, he hired George Vanderveer and called on Roger Baldwin and the ACLU. In a letter to Robert Dunn, the associate director of the ACLU, Smith wrote that the grievance committee would try to prove that the IWW was an illegal organization and that he had defended its principles and urged men to join:

> This I have done, not once but many, many times, and especially
> have I advocated this as the only means of getting the Centralia
> Defendants out of Walla Walla, as all other methods have failed,
> and as organization in the timber industry so thoroughly as to
> enable the workers in that industry to call a general strike, seems
> to be the only method left. You will readily see, therefore, that in
> defending myself, I must defend the principles of the Industrial
> Workers of the World.[5]

Smith told Dunn that the charges against him were based primarily on his social views and on his attempts to release the Centralia prisoners and bring to justice the killers of Wesley Everest. The men who signed the complaint had been so closely involved in the Armistice Day events, he pointed out, that their petition to disbar him was made to protect themselves if the conspiracy to raid the IWW hall and lynch Everest was uncovered.[6] But Smith had misread the complainants' motivations. The chances of any legal action against the raiders of the hall or the lynchers of Everest were practically nonexistent. Smith was the only person who still spoke out about the two incidents, and he did not have enough popular support to force the case to court.

From the ACLU's point of view, Vanderveer was a poor choice to defend Smith because of his close connection to the IWW. Dunn wrote to a number of lawyers in the American Bar Association: "The Civil Liberties Union is eager to get into this fight to help Smith and to assist in securing a group of strong lawyers, one or two of them with fairly conservative connections." The ACLU asked lawyers to write letters of protest on behalf of Smith to the American Bar Association. Dunn told Smith that Baldwin was eager to "make a strong fight" and that the "ACLU will back you to the limit."[7] The ACLU began to generate some publicity for Smith, but it had trouble securing additional legal aid. Baldwin wrote to Washington Senator C. C. Dill, a supporter of the ACLU:

> This presents a clear issue of an attack upon a lawyer for defending his clients. Smith is one of those rugged, courageous chaps who has risked personal unpopularity and social ostracism by championing the rights of men so grossly misunderstood and so bitterly attacked.[8]

But Dill begged off. Despite a lot of effort, the ACLU was unable to find a single attorney to come to Smith's defense.[9]

In his communications with the ACLU, Smith was optimistic about his chances of beating back the attempt to disbar him. "I believe absolutely that I am right in the stand I have taken in this connection," he wrote Baldwin, "and would not back down one iota, disbarment or no disbarment." He believed that the large radical and liberal element in the state would be able to exert enough political pressure to prevent his disbarment. The *Nation* pointed out that if the charges against Smith were true, then he would be liable for prosecution under the criminal syndicalism law. "Why is that course not taken?" the article asked and reported that the case "gravely concerns everyone who is jealous for the traditions of the American bar."[10]

Smith was a target primarily because of his effective work on be-half of the IWW in criminal syndicalism cases, free speech fights, and the release campaign. All of these issues had a financial impact on the big business interests in Centralia. For years, Smith had urged workers to strike in order to put economic and political pressure on authorities to release the Centralia prisoners. In late April 1923, largely because of his speeches and organizing activities, a faction of the IWW staged a walkout in the logging camps from Canada to northern California; their first demand was freedom for the Centralia prisoners. The General Defense Committee in Chicago did not support the strike, and many Wobblies felt that, with a boom in the timber industry, the time for a strike was not right. Nevertheless, about three to four hundred Wobblies shut down thirty logging camps near Centralia, and nearly ten thousand men went out in Washington, about 10 percent of all loggers.[11]

On May Day, Smith told five thousand people in Seattle that because the lumber trust had sent the Centralia defendants to Walla Walla it could also release them. "All they would have to do is pick up the telephone and call up Governor Hart," he said. "Cutting off the log supply in this state will be notice to the lumber trust of our demand for the release of these men."[12] Warming to his subject, Smith pressed home his message:

> Now look here! Who owns the resources of this world? You do. You own these forests; you own these coal mines around here; you own the ships on yonder water; you own the facto-ries in the city over there. They are yours. You don't need to take them over—they are yours now. Those who now "own" them are thieves and robbers. What would you do if you would see some one wear your watch and who had stolen it? Why, you would take it away from him, of course. Do the same thing here. How they say to me—"Elmer, you are fanning the fire of discontent with your speeches!" Of course I am! Did ever any-thing worth while ever come to pass in the history of the world without fanning the fire of discontent? No!
>
> I will fan the fire of discontent until every political prisoner is out of jail, until the earth and its riches are taken out of the hands of the robbers and put into your hands. Was it in vain that we fanned the fire of discontent to do away with negro slavery? That we fanned the fire of discontent to give the women suf-frage in this country? No! By the Almighty I will fan the fire of discontent till I draw my last breath; until I see the world that Ingersoll saw; a world full of joy and peace where there is no

crime and no bloodshed, no sorrow and outstretched hands of
beggars, no parasites or robbers, no tyrants and no thrones, no
gallows to throw their shadows of horror over a sick world. This
is the world of the Industrial Workers of the World.[13]

Despite the best efforts of Smith and the strikers, the strike steadily lost
ground and never spread from the camps to the mills, where a shutdown
might have had a greater effect. By May 7 the loggers had tried to repeat the tactic used during the 1917–18 strike by transferring the strike back
to the job. The slowdown did not succeed, and the effort soon spent itself.
The strike ended a week later.[14]

The *Seattle Union Record* applauded the strikers' efforts but also
noted their faulty reasoning. The striking Wobblies had claimed that the
lumber trust, aided by big industry, controlled the government and that by
shutting down the lumber trust they could put pressure on the government
to release the prisoners. But as the *Union Record* pointed out, the government depends on a certain amount of popular approval for its survival and
it cannot be too crassly subservient to the interests of big business. The
Union Record called for a more direct approach to freeing the prisoners by
working through a political organization. Otherwise, the *Record* said, it is
"like using a saw to drive a nail."[15]

Smith strongly influenced the IWW strike strategy. He was not
averse to working through a political organization, but he was drawn more
to using the tactic of a strike because it involved the most direct use of
the workers' power. He believed that politicians rarely improved the lot of
working people and that strikes often did. With the decline of the Farmer-
Labor Party, political action offered little hope. Smith was also impatient
at the long intervals between elections. But the *Union Record* did have a
point. Although the powerful lumber interests did help put the Centralia
Wobblies in jail, the complex political and legal system could not easily respond to a call from the lumber interests to let them out. And as it stood,
neither the businessmen nor the politicians wanted the prisoners freed. A
strike would have to be extensive enough to generate widespread popular
support before it might indirectly affect the state's political balance.

For a year Smith had worked out of his home, unable to find a
landlord who would rent to him. Finally, he managed to obtain some land
by asking a friend to buy and then transfer to him an empty lot on Tower
Avenue, two blocks from the site of the 1919 Wobbly hall. In May, with the
help of some friends, he built a one-story building with two large windows

in front. Half the space was for his law office, and half was rented out to the local IWW chapter and the Centralia Publicity Committee.[16]

Even though his hearing was pending, Smith continued an active speaking schedule. On July 2 he spoke at Crystal Lake Park, just outside of Portland, Oregon. While a stenographer for the bar association took down every word, Smith told a story that would soon come back to haunt him. It was a tale similar to the one he told about Maud the mule, but this one had more bite:

> There are two animals in this world for which I have a profound admiration. One is the lumberjack and the other is a mule. As between the lumberjack and the mule I think more of the mule. (laughter and applause) Why? Because a mule is a profound animal, and when he is through with his eight hours of work he is through, and when you try to work him more than eight hours you have a battle. How many people ever saw a mule lie down in a fenced in yard where there was a fine haystack and a great big box of oats and starve to death? How many of you ever knew him to pull that? How many ever knew a lumberjack to come into Portland where there are millions of tons of food stored away and sleep in the street and go hungry? I am a profound admirer of the mule. I repeat it.[17]

The hearing before the State Board of Law Examiners opened in a crowded courtroom. Vanderveer and Smith sat next to each other at the defense table, facing the hearing officers: John Dunbar, state attorney general; R. G. Sharpe, assistant state attorney general; and Howard Findley, a lawyer and chairman of the state board. Dunbar had been on the prosecution team for the Montesano trial. After the charges against Smith were read, Vanderveer moved to have the complaint amended to be more precise in its definition of "sabotage" and "syndicalism," to specify instances of alleged criminal acts by Smith, and to give the exact language Smith allegedly used to advocate and approve IWW principles. The board granted his motion and promptly adjourned the hearing to give the complainants time to file an amended complaint.[18]

Smith wasted no time in going out on the road again, speaking in nearly twenty towns before the end of the month. In Everett, Washington, he talked about his hearing:

> Because I am telling the truth about the Armistice day tragedy in Centralia in 1919, they are trying to silence me by disbar-

ment proceedings, but I serve notice on whom it may concern
that, disbarment or no disbarment, I will not be silenced until
the truth has forced the release of my eight fellow workers
who were wrongfully convicted and who are wrongfully held at
Walla Walla.[19]

His speeches were well attended in both large and small towns. But many
came because they were curious to see the famous Elmer Smith, not because they supported the IWW or wanted the release of the prisoners.
Smith spoke with great feeling and conviction about the Centralia case,
and his tour raised money for the prisoners' defense work. In several towns
noisy cars raced up and down the streets where he was speaking, but there
were few such incidents and most people who heard Smith came away
feeling sympathetic to the IWW cause.

To relax from this grinding pace, Elmer and Laura went square
dancing on Saturday nights. They took Virginia and Stuart and laid them
on blankets with other sleeping children in the front room of the dance
hall. Smith was a popular partner, picking up his feet in quick steps to the
music. By the time the last dance was over, he was bone-tired and miles
away from his troubles.[20]

Smith was brought back to earth in early August when he received
the amended complaint against him. Much the same as the first, it more
clearly defined sabotage and syndicalism and specified the dates of several
of Smith's speeches that were judged to be offensive. The speeches included
his April 1 talk in Centralia, the May Day speech in Seattle, and more recent ones in Crystal Lake Park and Yakima. The complaint charged that
Smith had "cast aspersions upon the integrity of the judiciary of the State
of Washington and also publicly and wrongfully and unlawfully advocated
a general strike" to free the prisoners. A new hearing date was set for
October 1.[21]

Smith sent a copy of the amended complaint to Roger Baldwin,
who, though not optimistic about Smith's chances, asked several attorneys
in New York to examine the case and give their opinion. Albert De Silver,
former director of the National Civil Liberties Bureau (the forerunner of
the ACLU), responded that the Washington Supreme Court had already
ruled that membership in the IWW was enough for a conviction under the
state's criminal syndicalism law and that Smith's public speeches for the
IWW were likely to get him disbarred. "It looks to me," De Silver wrote,
"as if they could disbar him if they have the will to go thru [*sic*] with the
proceedings, and that if he is going to beat the proceeding he will have

to do it by public opinion."[22] Another attorney wrote the ACLU that the charges against Smith enlarge

> a trifling contempt of court amounting at most to a minor indiscretion such as resolute and peppery lawyers frequently commit, into an act of moral turpitude. . . . The issue is not whether he is guilty of a crime, but whether he is a fit person to be a lawyer.[23]

In late August, Smith took Laura and their two children with him on a speaking tour north of Seattle. The American Legion harassed him during appearances at Sedro Woolley and Mount Vernon; and the police arrested him for disturbing the peace. Officials later agreed that there might have been less trouble if Smith had been allowed to speak. The IWW was past its heyday and was no longer a serious threat to public order. Nevertheless, the Bureau of Investigation continued to monitor Smith, reporting that he

> uses well the cunning and the language of the lumberjack and this Agent believes that he is a menace and that if his speeches are carefully checked, it will be only a short time when he can be convicted of the Violation of the State Syndicalism Laws.

Smith knew he was being watched but he refused to be intimidated, challenging the "stoolpigeons" who attended his speeches to take down every word and report it back to their "Masters."[24]

During his speaking tours, Smith continued to push for another walkout, believing that the pressure created by strikes would eventually make a difference. On September 1, Wobblies working near Centralia took the lead in promoting a new strike call to release the prisoners. But the strike was hastily organized and not all IWW locals endorsed it. Many loggers did not even hear about it until an airplane pilot, hired by the IWW, dropped leaflets on their camps announcing that the strike had begun. After a few days, several thousand men left their jobs, but the strike never spread beyond that. It ended within two weeks in utter failure, demoralizing many Wobbly supporters.[25] With the membership and influence of the IWW waning in the lumber camps, the strike was becoming a weaker and weaker tactic to use in the release campaign.

A week after the strike ended, Assistant Attorney General Sharpe, who had served on the Board of Law Examiners in Chehalis, presented evidence against Smith in a special hearing. Smith listened as four men testified about his speech at a meeting of some five hundred people in Yakima on July 23, part of his summer tour. One witness, a reporter for the *Yakima Morning Herald,* said that Smith had referred to Judge Wilson, who had heard the Montesano trial, as "ever faithful to the lumber trust" and that Smith had called for a strike to release the Centralia prisoners. The mayor of Yakima testified that he went to the speech with his next-door neighbor, Thomas Grady, who was now serving as the hearing officer. After the evidence was taken, the *Yakima Daily Republic* reported: "Grady considers that Smith's remarks are the more offensive because, as an attorney, he knows quite well his charges are not true and that he is overstepping the bounds in making them."[26]

Smith's second disbarment hearing began in a Chehalis courtroom on the morning of October 1. Before hearing officers Findley, Thomas Grady, and Dix H. Rowland, Vanderveer made several unsuccessful motions to have the complaint dismissed because the charges were too vague. Vanderveer then moved that Smith be granted a trial by jury because the board members were clearly prejudiced against him. Grady was prejudiced by his statements to the Yakima paper, Vanderveer argued, and Findley had signed an affidavit stating that he believed the amended complaint against Smith was true. It was therefore impossible, the IWW lawyer charged, for Smith to receive a fair and impartial trial. Findley replied that the state Supreme Court had already ruled that the Board of Law Examiners could properly verify complaints against Smith as Grady had done in his special hearing. In dismissing Vanderveer's motion, Findley also announced that the board would not consider in their deliberation the special hearing testimony or the newspaper article about Grady, a strange compromise. Vanderveer protested that Findley's response did not answer the charges of prejudice against board members. But Findley ordered the formal hearing to begin.[27]

During the eight days of the hearing, nearly two dozen witnesses were called. The prosecution's general strategy was to introduce IWW publications to show that the organization advocated violence and then to introduce evidence of Smith's speeches to show that he did the same. The Wobbly literature consisted almost exclusively of material seized in 1919 and 1920 in police raids on Wobbly halls in Seattle and Portland. The pile of material included IWW membership cards and pins, pamphlets about unionism and the Centralia case, a book of poems by Ralph Chaplin, proceedings from the union's 1916 convention, financial statements, and songbooks.

It was pamphlets such as "The Revolutionary IWW" (which was not reprinted after 1917) that received the most attention. The pamphlet preached: "Labor produces all wealth. Labor is therefore entitled to all wealth. We are going to do away with capitalism by taking possession of the land and the machinery of production. We don't intend to buy them either."[28] The prosecution even introduced IWW songs, such as "Christians At War" to show the violent nature of the organization.[29] Prosecutor Sharpe called several former law enforcement officials who testified that such literature was produced by the IWW. These witnesses included a former inspector of the U.S. Immigration Service in Seattle, a former special agent for the Department of Justice in Portland, two former Seattle police officers on the Red Squad, and a former sergeant of inspectors for the Portland Police Department. Vanderveer protested strongly that the material was irrelevant, and he moved to suppress all such documents because many were seized without a search warrant. The board denied his motion.[30]

Vanderveer had more success when the prosecution called P. J. Welinder, the business manager for the *Industrial Worker* in Seattle, to identify old issues of his newspaper. Under Vanderveer's cross-examination, Welinder said that the *Industrial Worker* often published articles by authors who did not agree with each other. "The IWW is absolutely opposed to violence in any way, shape or form," Welinder said. "Violence means weakness; it is contrary to organized and orderly conduct and cannot accomplish anything."[31] Prosecutor Sharpe then called in several witnesses to testify on the speeches that Smith had made in Washington. The director of the Department of Justice in Washington allowed special agent R. E. Skelly to testify against Smith. The local Bureau office in Tacoma, which handled the request about Skelly, also gave Sharpe additional background information about the IWW and suggested the names of several other agents who might help. Skelly had been in the audience when Smith had spoken in Seattle on May Day earlier that year. Centralia's Mayor Barner and Chief of Police Compton testified about Smith's arrests the previous spring for speaking at an IWW meeting, and a transcript of Smith's April 1 speech was introduced. Other witnesses testified that they had heard Smith advocate a general strike and call Judge Wilson "ever faithful to the lumber trust." After four days of testimony, Sharpe rested his case.

Vanderveer unsuccessfully moved to have all charges against Smith dropped for lack of evidence. He spoke at length about the history of the IWW and its position on sabotage and violence. Since 1918, he said, the

IWW had modified its revolutionary language and had removed references to violence from many of its publications, including the song "Christians At War." Smith's description of Judge Wilson, Vanderveer said, fell within the right of a lawyer to engage in fair, honest criticism of any judge. "The courts enjoy no more immunity from criticism personally or officially than anybody else," he said. "It is the very essence of democracy, of free speech and of constitutional government that the utmost freedom shall be enjoyed in such matters, whether you be right or wrong." He asked the board to rule on whether he must prove that Smith's statement about Wilson was true or simply that Smith honestly believed it to be true, but the board never ruled on that point.[32]

On Friday morning, the fifth day of the hearing, Smith took the witness stand. He testified for two and a half days. Vanderveer led Smith through a detailed recital of his involvement with the IWW and the Centralia case. There were many things published by the IWW, he said, that he "radically disagreed with."[33] He described "Christians At War" as "just simply a picture of what war was," not an IWW call for murder.[34]

Much of Smith's cross-examination had to do with his views on IWW-led strikes and revolution. Smith said the IWW advocated strikes for "any and all legitimate and lawful purposes." Strikes called to release the Centralia prisoners were meant to attract people's attention to injustice and to influence the owners of industry so they would pressure the governor. Change would come by a revolution, he believed, as had all changes in history, but the IWW was trying to avoid the violence of such a revolution. "I am putting forth all of my energies to avoid [revolution] and try and bring it about otherwise," he testified, "but I believe it is perhaps going to come that way."[35]

Smith justified his description of Judge Wilson by citing the judge's actions in eulogizing the fallen Legionnaires and in denying a change of venue to the Montesano defendants. Smith argued that he had not meant that Wilson was in the employ of the lumber industry or that there was some arrangement or contract between them to send the prisoners to the penitentiary. But "the lumber trust certainly did try that case," said Smith, "and they certainly used Judge Wilson to good advantage." Vanderveer described several incidents during the Montesano trial where Wilson had shown prejudice against the IWW. On October 9, the board adjourned to deliberate. Sharpe was confident that the board would recommend disbarment, and he wrote to the Bureau in Tacoma: "I think that the record is as satisfactory as we could have hoped to have it."[36]

The board filed its recommendation that Smith be disbarred on January 24, 1924. The three men had ignored the significant moderating influences in IWW literature since 1919 and concluded that it incited members to violence, insurrection, and sedition in order to "paralyze the production and distribution of commodities and to revolutionize if possible, the present social, political and economic status."[37] The board justified its recommendation on three grounds. First, Smith's lumberjack and mule story that he had told at Crystal Lake Park was interpreted to mean that he "advised and counseled the commission of the crime of theft and holds up to ridicule the lumberjack because he will not steal the property of other people." Second, Smith had advocated in the same speech an "unlawful" general strike in the lumber industry, in violation of his oath to support the Constitution. The strike would "demoralize and disrupt" the entire Northwest lumber industry. The board clearly revealed its bias:

> It is an obvious fact of which we may take judicial notice that the larger number of employers of labor in the lumber industry treat their employees fairly and justly and are willing to treat with them on questions involving wages, hours of labor and general working conditions.[38]

Third, it was false and unjustifiable for Smith to label Judge Wilson "a tool of the lumber trust." "If Judge Wilson was a 'tool of the lumber trust,'" the board wrote,

> then the same charge could be made against the entire membership of the Supreme Court of the State of Washington where the case was reviewed. It is inconceivable that if the defendants did not have a fair and impartial trial, that the Supreme Court of this state would have permitted the verdict to stand.

The board concluded that the offenses proven against Smith are "unethical, unprofessional and involve moral turpitude."[39]

Smith never had a chance. Law officials and the Bureau of Investigation had been building the case against him for a long time, and there was little that he could have done differently to change the board's decision. For years his speeches and defense work had linked him inescapably with the union. Vanderveer and the few other attorneys who defended the IWW had managed to keep distance between themselves and their clients, but Smith had chosen not to follow their example.

Smith was deeply discouraged by the board's findings, and he and Vanderveer began preparing a response to the disbarment recommendation. They could only hope that Smith would have a better chance with the state Supreme Court, which was scheduled to hold a hearing on the matter in June.

The Spirit of Persecution

"Hallelujah I'm a Bum!"—*IWW Songbook*, 1908

O, why don't you work
Like other men do?
How in hell can I work
When there's no work to do?

Hallelujah, I'm a bum
Hallelujah, bum again,
Hallelujah, give us a handout—
To revive us again.[1]

By the end of 1923, President Calvin Coolidge had unconditionally commuted the sentences of the last of the federal IWW prisoners in Leavenworth. With their release, the general amnesty effort ground to a halt. For many people, the release of the prisoners signaled the final chapter of the nation's wartime preoccupation with radicalism and Americanism. The domestic war wounds had been sutured, even if they were not quite healed, and national attention moved away from the labor struggles of the past.

The IWW had been bitterly divided over the issue of the prisoners' release. In late 1922 President Harding had announced that he would consider individual pleas for clemency, but many Wobbly prisoners had greeted the offer with scorn. A majority had written Harding an open letter refusing to sign individual appeals. All of them had been arrested, they had written, simply because they were Wobblies. But several Wobblies, including Ralph Chaplin, had broken the solidarity by petitioning for individual pardons, and a few had trickled out of Leavenworth over the next year. By the time that all of the prisoners were out at the end of 1923, the memories of this division were still alive, and the newly released prisoners remained deeply resentful of those who had walked out earlier. The ideological debate over this issue raged within the IWW.[2]

The Centralia prisoners had been too proud to ask for individual clemency and had demanded to be released as a group under a general amnesty. In January 1924, Washington Governor Hart announced his steadfast opposition to any general parole, saying that the prisoners would have to lay aside their "role of martyrdom" or serve out their long sentences.[3] Four Wobblies who had been convicted of criminal syndicalism in Walla Walla joined the Centralia men in refusing to ask for pardons, which they saw as an admission of guilt. "We are merely living up to our motto: 'An injury to one is an injury to all, all for one and one for all,'" wrote Tom Nash, one of the Walla Walla men.[4] By late 1923 the parole board was willing to grant pardons to the criminal syndicalism prisoners, but the men would not accept freedom until everyone was released.[5]

By 1924, the clemency issue was only a symptom of a severe split within the IWW as a protracted internal debate boiled over organizational tactics. Some Wobblies favored a more autonomous industrial unionism, and others argued for a centralized structure, pointing to the Russian Revolution as a model. Declining organizational fortunes created an atmosphere of widespread frustration at the 1924 national IWW convention. Chaotic infighting splintered the union and drove away many members.[6]

Smith steered clear of any direct participation in the split and remained friends with leaders on both sides. Still, he was discouraged by the divisiveness and hoped that the factions could somehow reunite. Personally, he sided with the industrial unionists, still favoring the direct action of strikes over a lengthy political battle. He believed that the Bolsheviks had merely substituted "one set of dictators for another set of dictators."[7] But Smith welcomed any Wobbly leader who helped publicize the Centralia cause; and both Ralph Chaplin and James Rowan, leaders on opposite sides of the clemency argument, came to Centralia to work for the prisoners' release.

Smith was spending half of his time on the Centralia case, making speeches, raising money, and collecting resolutions from labor groups that demanded pardons for the prisoners. He also maintained a private correspondence with nearly all of the prisoners, keeping them informed of release efforts and strikes and offering personal encouragement and news from their families. When Eugene Barnett published a short book of draw-

ings of wild animals to raise money for his family, Smith wrote the introduction.[8] Most of the men felt close to him and were always glad to hear
that they had not been forgotten.

In early April 1924, Smith met with Vanderveer in his Seattle office
to discuss filing a petition to the Washington Supreme Court to reverse
the disbarment recommendation of the Board of Law Examiners. In the
petition, Vanderveer argued that no evidence had been presented to show
that Smith approved of sabotage or violence. The attorney insisted that the
board members were prejudiced against Smith and that they had "abandoned the methods of constitutional procedure and reverted to the methods of the inquisition where judge and accuser were one." The board had
ruled that it was not enough for Smith to believe Wilson to be a "tool of
the lumber trust" but that he must prove his statements to be true. Vanderveer argued that the requirement was improper because he had introduced
uncontradicted evidence to support Smith's statements and the board had
told the defense that it need not produce other witnesses to prove the point.
Finally, Vanderveer challenged the board's claim that employers treat their
workers fairly and chided them for being "devoid of a sense of humor" for
taking the lumberjack speech so seriously. After a hearing in June, the state
Supreme Court agreed to consider the disbarment recommendation. All
Smith could do was wait for the decision.[9]

While Smith was fighting to keep his license, he enjoyed few re-
wards from his profession. Emotions still ran high from the Centralia case,
making it hard for him to try his cases. In one case, while defending a man
charged with drunken driving, Smith made a motion to change the location of the trial because the local judge was prejudiced against him. After
his conviction, the client skipped bond without paying Smith's fee. Such
cases were not unusual. Laura relied more and more on her garden to raise
food for the family table. As she took responsibility for the family finances,
she scraped the bottom of her butter dish more than once to make it last.[10]

In the spring, Smith decided to turn his meager law practice over
to a friend, Alexander Mackel. Mackel had practiced law in Montana for
twenty years and had an undistinguished reputation as an attorney. But
Smith's publicity work gave him more satisfaction than his legal work,
and he wanted to devote more of his time to it. So he shared office space
with Mackel and became temporary secretary of the Centralia Publicity
Committee.[11]

A short time later, Mackel delivered the dedication address for the
new Labor Temple, which had been built with small donations and the free
labor of many loggers and sawmill workers. Smith had provided free legal

assistance to establish the worker-owned Temple, and he had loaned several hundred dollars to help pay construction costs, in foolish disregard of his own perilous financial condition. The local IWW and the Centralia Publicity Committee soon moved their offices into the new building. Smith thought that the Temple would also be an ideal place to house a Workers' College for the IWW, like the one in Duluth, Minnesota, that educated the children of working people. He hoped that the college would be a memorial to Wesley Everest, and he offered to be a teacher at the school. But because of a lack of money and interest, the idea never went anywhere.[12]

In early July, the state convention of the Farmer-Labor Party met in Seattle to adopt a platform and nominate candidates. High on the list of positions supported by the 110 delegates was the release of the Centralia prisoners and the repeal of the state criminal syndicalism law. A number of prominent party leaders expressed interest in nominating Smith for governor; they regarded him as one of the best-known men in the state and as the logical candidate to crystallize sentiment for the prisoners' pardon. The convention eventually decided not to endorse any candidate for governor, and the party's executive committee recommended that Smith be nominated for attorney general. But Smith was not interested in either office. He told friends that a political campaign would distract from his work for the prisoners, and he also did not want to appear to be taking political advantage of them by using their case as a steppingstone to personal power. Smith saw his life as inexorably tied up with the fate of the Centralia prisoners, and he would not pursue his own interests until they were released.[13]

Smith was pleased that the convention took a strong position in favor of release. He wrote to a friend:

> I believe that the Centralia Case will be one of the leading political issues the next gubernatorial election. . . . It is my firm belief that no man can now be elected governor of this state without declaring in favor of the release of the Centralia defendants. The disbarment case against me is helping the situation as the people of the state realize that it is simply an attempt to stop me from exposing their villany [*sic*].[14]

But it was wishful thinking. From a political standpoint, nominating Smith on the Farmer-Labor ticket would have been poor strategy because many voters were still opposed to the IWW. In any event, the Farmer-Labor Party had steadily declined in influence among the more moderate and progressive voters. Since 1920, poor economic conditions and the suppression of radical movements had contributed to a sixty-five percent drop in the membership of the Washington Federation of Labor, the state's largest labor union. A lack of effective leadership had reduced the party to more of an educational organization than a political power.[15]

As election day neared, Smith chose to speak on the release campaign rather than the Farmer-Labor ticket. News of his speeches still provoked local harassment. In Arlington and Ellensburg, he spoke only after local police had arrested and released him.[16] In Seattle, hundreds gathered outdoors to hear Smith speak on the now-familiar theme:

> We must organize the lumber industry so that no matter who
> is elected governor we can come out on strike and close every
> camp and every mill and keep them closed until our boys come
> home free men. . . . They can disbar me, and they may, but there
> is no power in heaven or hell, no power except death, is going
> to silence my voice until they are free.[17]

At the end of August, Smith visited the prisoners in Walla Walla, passing on news from their families and expressing his hope that the fall elections would improve the chances for their release. A couple of the prisoners were worried about Smith's disbarment case, but he reassured them that he would continue to work for their release, regardless of what happened. Always exhibiting confidence with the prisoners, he had some real doubts about the election and his own legal future. But because his main objective was to build public support for the prisoners, he wrote about his visit in dramatic fashion for the *Industrial Worker*:

> It is hard indeed for me to express the feeling and emotion which
> swept over me as I visited the victims of the lumber trust. After
> five years of prison hell they stand erect, invincible and uncon-
> querable, their spirits untamed, and still as much in the fight for
> a better world as the day they entered.[18]

In private, Smith spoke with less confidence. After his trip to Walla Walla, a close friend found Smith looking sad and depressed, and he confided to her that it looked like the prisoners would not get out in his lifetime. He rarely lost control of his emotions, and he always sounded full of hope. Only occasionally did he let down his barriers. One evening he made a rare admission to his sister-in-law: "Oh I just feel like doing something absolutely different! I do not want to have to think about struggle or people in prison or anything. I want to take in a good movie."[19]

By the time Smith returned to Centralia in early September he was exhausted. He had been on the road for four months, speaking to thousands of people in dozens of cities. He did not know it yet, but his touring days were over. During the coming years, Smith's financial worries and health problems, along with declining IWW support, would keep him at home.[20] Resuming a more normal family life was not easy. Sometimes Elmer would come home from work, throw his hat onto a bench, and walk into the bedroom, without a word of hello. Neither he nor Laura were demonstrative about their love for each other, and there was a persistent tension that expressed itself in regular bickering. Laura was a meticulous and orderly housekeeper who always kept herself and the children neatly dressed. She disliked Elmer's sloppy personal habits and his baggy, worn clothing. "I can't stand him and his proletarian habits," Laura once complained to a friend. But such matters were unimportant to Elmer, and despite Laura's pleas, he declined to change his ways. Elmer kept his own counsel and did not share with Laura his worries about personal or professional troubles. Although he loved his family, he did not apply himself to create a supportive home life.[21]

Smith now had more opportunity to share the hospitality of his home with others. Workers who stopped by his law office in the morning would get an invitation for lunch. "We've got ample," he would say, even though Laura often had only enough food to feed the family. Local union men told Wobblies who got off the train in Centralia to go over to see Smith, who was always glad to talk about working conditions and the Centralia case over a meal. As the men left, he shook their hands, gave them pamphlets on the Centralia case to distribute, and invited them to return any time.[22]

Smith also offered the men a place to spend the night. This was a source of great discomfort to Laura, who thought of the itinerant workers as "bums." But Elmer loved spending time and singing labor songs with the men, and they often stayed for several days. One Wobbly stayed on for nearly a week while looking for a job. Laura reluctantly agreed to put him up on the condition that he not eat meals with the family. But the man always managed to be hanging around just as dinner was being served, until Elmer would invite him to join in. Finally, Laura issued an ultimatum: If the "bum" did not leave, she would. Elmer argued that the Wobbly would soon be on his way, but Laura packed her bags and took the children with her to Jim and Mary's. Elmer soon got the Wobbly to leave and brought Laura and the children back home.²³

But the fight with Laura did nothing to change Elmer's blind compassion for the workers. On another occasion, one of Elmer's friends begged him to help his sick daughter. Smith brought her home and put her to bed in the guest room. When Laura went to change the girl's bed the next morning, to her shock she found the mattress soaked with blood. The man had neglected to say that his daughter had just had an abortion and needed a few days to hide out.²⁴ Elmer was also a soft touch for other members of the Smith clan. His brother Harry gambled excessively and sometimes asked Elmer's help to buy food for his family. Elmer always gave him a little, although he occasionally gave a few dollars to Harry's wife Grace to make sure Harry's family actually got the money.²⁵

With more time on his hands, Elmer enjoyed playing games with his children and telling jokes. As they grew older, Elmer called his children the "Katzenjammer Kids." The label fit, for they were a rambunctious pair and constantly fought with each other. Once Virginia stabbed Stuart between the eyes with a pair of scissors, but luckily no serious injury resulted. Laura was devoted to her children, but she grew anxious every time they climbed on a gate or played in the woods. One day she went next door to borrow some flour and her neighbor asked her to sit and rest. "Oh I can't," she said. "The children would kill each other."²⁶

Despite the strains, Elmer and Laura were committed to their children and to each other. During the summers, they often rented a cottage at Deep Lake, and they took weekend trips to the ocean where they camped, swam, and dug for clams. Those days away from Centralia may have been their happiest times together.²⁷

In the November elections, the Farmer-Labor Party finished a poor third in every state and county race. The party was finished; it was the last election in which it fielded any candidates. Republican Roland Hartley, a wealthy, conservative timber owner from Everett, won the governorship. He believed fiercely in "rugged, individualistic capitalism," and few industrialists hated organized labor more. His attitude toward the IWW was unambiguous: "I believe in raids on Wobbly halls if we can't get rid of the Wobblies any other way. They are a menace to civilization."²⁸

Smith realized that another avenue for the release of the Centralia prisoners had been closed. After the unsuccessful legal appeals of the Montesano decision, it was clear that working through the courts was ineffective. Now the hope of electing a sympathetic governor was gone as well.

What was left? For years Smith had advocated a general strike by the IWW to force a release of the prisoners, but by late 1924 even he was beginning to see that the idea was hopelessly unrealistic. Smith's only hope was to appeal directly to the parole board and the governor for clemency. He had collected affidavits of jurors in earlier years, and now he began gathering affidavits from witnesses who claimed that the raid against the IWW hall had been planned in advance and that the shooting had begun only after the attack was in progress.[29] The affidavits could not be used in court because all legal appeals had been exhausted, but Smith did use them to try to change the minds of the parole board and the governor.

On November 11, the American Legion held ceremonies in Centralia to dedicate a monument honoring the four Legionnaires who had been killed five years earlier. A parade down Tower Avenue to the city park passed by Smith's office, where he had hung a placard in his window showing photographs of the prisoners with a large caption reading, "Buried Alive by the Lumber Trust." A Legion drive to raise $250,000 for a memorial building had begun in early 1922, but the effort quickly bogged down as most of the money went for fundraising salaries and expenses. The Legion finally settled on a more modest statue of a World War I soldier. Underneath the statue, next to the plaques of the four Legionnaires, was an inscription: "To the memory of Ben Cassagranda, Warren O. Grimm, Earnest Dale Hubbard, Arthur McElfresh. Slain on the streets of Centralia, Washington, while on peaceful parade wearing the uniform of the country they loyally and faithfully served." Because of the slowly changing attitudes toward the IWW, the inscription did not say that the men were murdered or that the IWW murdered them. Governor Hart and C. D. Cunningham spoke at the dedication ceremony, and Cunningham read a congratulatory telegram from President Calvin Coolidge.[30] Smith did not publicly oppose the construction of the monument, saying that it would be generally recognized as a monument to Wesley Everest.

On February 24, 1925, Smith learned that the state Supreme Court had affirmed the Board of Examiners' recommendation and disbarred him. Associate Justice Kenneth Mackintosh wrote the majority (six to two) decision:

> The substance of the charge against him is that, in public addresses since 1919 he has advocated and approved sabotage, syndicalism, and general violation of the law as a means of social reform. . . . any person who advocates such general principles is unworthy of the office of attorney at law.

The court also cited Smith for calling for a general strike to release "political prisoners" who were IWW members. In taking that position, the court said, Smith had violated his oath to uphold the laws of the land.[31]

The court concluded that Smith's lumberjack and mule story "means that larceny and theft are justifiable," and it cited "Christians At War" as an example of the violent doctrines of the IWW. Over half of the court's written opinion consisted of quotations from IWW periodicals and pamphlets about direct action, sabotage, and strikes proving that the IWW "advocates the uses of criminal means for the accomplishment of its objects and purposes." Smith was free to advocate changes in the present form of government, the court ruled, "so long as his advocacy is confined to means sanctioned by law. But he oversteps permissible bounds when he advocates changes by criminal or other unlawful means, and this the evidence demonstrates he had done, both directly and indirectly."[32]

How the Washington Supreme Court reached its decision was not a public matter, but memoranda in court files reveal that the preliminary vote among the justices was against disbarment. The justices circulated a draft opinion arguing that there was no proof that Smith had advocated violence, criminal syndicalism, or sabotage. It quoted from Article I of the state constitution: "Every person may freely speak, write, and publish on all subjects, being responsible for the abuse of that right." The opinion concluded that there was no clear proof of the abuse of free speech in Smith's case. Accompanying this draft opinion was a draft of a minority opinion written by Justice Fullerton: "any person who advocates even the general principles of such an organization [IWW] is unworthy of the office of attorney-at-law."[33] Whatever the eventual reason for the change, it was Fullerton's opinion that gained a majority of the justices' signatures.

Vanderveer reported to Roger Baldwin:

> Frankly, both Elmer and I feel that the decision is purely a politi
> cal one. It was held up for many months prior to the election
> and came down shortly after the election as a punishment for
> our obnoxious political activity.

"The spirit of persecution never won a meaner triumph than the disbarment of Elmer Smith," said the *New Republic*. The *Nation* wrote:

> The true reason for Smith's disbarment was, of course, distinct
> from any pretext which his injudicious free speech afforded. It
> was to punish him for energetic professional services to I.W.W.

clients and to make it hard for such clients, in future, to feel that
they could get fair protection in their "day in court."

The *Federated Press Bulletin*, a news service for socialist and labor newspapers, commented: "By disbarring Elmer Smith, the attorney who has
defended I.W.W. cases when most other lawyers were afraid of business
and social ostracism, the supreme court of Washington arrays the law once
more on the side of the big lumber corporations and the business ring
of the states." The ACLU noted in a press release that four other radical
lawyers had been disbarred over the years for defending unpopular clients.
Washington's business community was pleased with the court's decision.
The Federated Industries, a statewide employers' lobby that had helped
secure witnesses against Smith, editorialized in its weekly business letter
that it was "proud of the fact the organization helped in the prosecution of
this case."[34]

Smith had until the end of March to petition the court for a rehearing, and he spent days in the law library in Olympia working under great
pressure to make a case that his constitutional rights had been violated.
On April 20, the court summarily denied Smith's petition and effectively
ended his career as an attorney.[35] Four days later, the police issued a warrant
for Smith's arrest for burglary for breaking into the home of Gus Masch-
key near Chehalis. No records are available to indicate what happened to
the case, but Smith may have been trying to get information to wrap up
one of his cases. Frustrated with their unwillingness to talk, Smith might
have pushed his way into the house to demand answers to his questions.
Whatever the story, it seems likely that the court decision weighed heavy
on Smith. It may have accounted for his unusual behavior.[36]

Smith did have one final hope in his disbarment case: an appeal
to the United States Supreme Court. But to make the appeal he needed
money and a good Washington, D.C., lawyer to argue the case. He asked
the ACLU for help, and his friend John Beffel wrote Roger Baldwin on his
behalf:

> I can tell you (which perhaps Elmer wouldn't) that he is laboring
> under a stiff economic handicap. . . . For five years he has given
> his energies to the cause of the Centralia boys without thought
> of self; I have seen him on the road while he was lecturing and
> collecting money for the defense, and I know the conditions
> under which he has lived; I know, too, that the family larder
> in the Smith home is frequently sparse. There is no danger that

you will ever be called upon to buy food for the Smith family—
but I want you to know what pressure is upon Elmer.[37]

Baldwin used the resources of the ACLU to look into a possible Supreme
Court appeal. ACLU lawyer Charles S. Ascher wrote a long letter to Smith
advising him of his chances. Ascher thought that Smith should have been
granted a rehearing in that the court relied almost entirely on evidence the
Board of Law Examiners had disregarded. "The color of the whole proceeding lends considerable support to your feeling that they were out to
get you—and they got you," he wrote.[38] But, Ascher said, an appeal to the
U.S. Supreme Court was not going to succeed on any of the constitutional
issues that Smith had raised in his petition. The only constitutional issue
that might have existed, Ascher advised, was that no evidence was introduced that showed that Smith violated his oath as an attorney; therefore,
the proceeding was held without due process. But the Supreme Court
could not hear arguments on this legal point because it had not been raised
by Vanderveer or Smith before the Board of Law Examiners.

Even if the Supreme Court did decide to hear Smith's case, Ascher
concluded, it would certainly rule against him. The most such an appeal
would do would be to serve as a forum to publicize the free speech issue
to a broader community. But because it did not present a clear enough
violation of civil liberties to be of good publicity value, Ascher believed
that Smith's case was not strong enough to appeal. He pointed out that
Smith did advocate a general strike, which amounted to a violation of the
criminal syndicalism law. Ascher concluded: "There is no doubt that you
got a raw deal. I do not see how you can expect the United States Supreme
Court, which is part of the same legal system as the Washington Supreme
Court to take a substantially different view of the case." Smith reluctantly
accepted Ascher's advice and agreed that it was "best to drop the matter."[39]
It was a demoralizing defeat.

The Conscience of the Legion

"Commonwealth of Toil"—Ralph Chaplin, *IWW
Songbook*, 1918,

But we have a glowing dream
  Of how fair the world will seem
When each man can live his life secure and free;
  When the earth is owned by Labor
And there's joy and peace for all
  In the Commonwealth of Toil that is to be.[1]

The mid-1920s moved slowly for the Centralia prisoners, as efforts
to release them through appeals to the governor and the parole board raised
hopes that were not realized. The public's hatred of the IWW had subsided somewhat, but the vigilance of the unforgiving American Legion and
the conservative Republican control of the statehouse still set the political
mood. As the years passed, both sides became more deeply entrenched in
their views. The IWW kept demanding that the authorities recognize the
innocence of the imprisoned men, but no one who counted was prepared
to admit that a mistake had been made. The case had long since ceased to
be about innocence or guilt. The Wobblies were clearly still in prison because they were members of an unpopular labor organization. Their release
would come in changing public opinion.[2]

Over the years, a number of committees had worked to release
the men. Smith's Centralia Publicity Committee was the most active and
had the closest ties to the prisoners. The Washington branch of the IWW
General Defense Committee remained the official support group, collecting money for the prisoners and their families. In early 1925, acting on

Smith's suggestion, the committee sent John Beffel to Seattle to organize a group of church people called the Seattle Citizens' Committee to make an appeal to the governor. After an unsuccessful effort, the group folded.[3] The ACLU, with early backing from the liberal, middle-class community, co-operated freely with the other defense committees but urged the prisoners to seek the most expedient means of gaining their freedom. This advice did not sit well with many Wobblies, who did not trust any organization that advocated political compromise. For a while, union women in Seattle and elsewhere in Washington formed Prison Comfort Clubs and sponsored fundraising events.[4]

In 1925, the American Communist Party formed the International Labor Defense (ILD) to aid "class war prisoners" and their families. The ILD waged its fight on behalf of the working class for non-Communist prisoners such as Tom Mooney and Warren Billings (radical leaders convicted in San Francisco of bombing a war preparedness parade in 1916), Nicola Sacco and Bartolomeo Vanzetti (Italian anarchists convicted of killing two guards during a payroll robbery in 1920), and IWW prisoners that included the Centralia men. Within a few years, the ILD formed the Centralia Liberation Committee. During the late 1920s, Adele Parker-Bennett from Seattle headed the Washington Conciliation Committee, a small collection of moderates funded by the ACLU, which made repeated efforts to organize prominent citizens to argue the case to the governor. The case even began to receive notice abroad when in late 1924 a trade union conference in England passed a resolution calling for an investigation into the matter.[5]

Although the efforts of these committees were important, Smith remained the soul of the release campaign. But the years of strenuous work were beginning to affect his health. He grew tired more easily and began to re-experience the pains in his stomach that he had first felt in the Montesano jail. To ease the pain, he bought a goat and began drinking its milk. He developed a tremendous appetite for rich foods, such as chocolate cake, gooseberry pie, and ice cream, all of which caused him to gain weight for the first time since he had left law school. He stubbornly ignored advice from Laura and his friends to see a doctor.[6] Smith scratched out a living by handling interviews and investigations for his partner, Alexander Mackel, who took over when the case went to court. Most of their cases involved workers' compensation claims, and the employers fought each one with tenacity.

In the fall of 1925, five of the jurors at the Montesano trial met with Governor Hartley on the sixth anniversary of the Armistice Day parade to make a personal appeal for the release of the prisoners. Two other jurors had also signed affidavits calling for their release. Hartley listened to the delegation but he gave them no encouragement. In June 1926, Smith organized a petition signed by relatives and friends of the prisoners and presented to the parole board by Mrs. Barnett, Mrs. Lamb, and two jurors. The petitioners hoped for favorable action by the board's September meeting, but many were skeptical that the board would be sympathetic. The September meeting passed without any action taken.[7]

The lack of any progress in the release campaign and his struggle to earn a living were Smith's constant worries. As his stomach troubles grew worse, he tried eating jello, raisins, and even sheep fat, but nothing seemed to work. When the gnawing pain became too great, he walked over to the Davis Cafe near his law office to satisfy his craving with a banana cream pie or a bowl of homemade soup. By August of 1927 Smith's condition had grown much worse, and he decided to enter the Nugent Hospital in Centralia for treatment. He remained conscious while the doctors operated on his ulcerated stomach, and was released after three weeks' recovery from the painful operation. His doctor ordered him to rest and relax, but Laura knew that the advice was "wasted words."[8]

Smith's recovery from the operation was slow. The doctor put him on a diet of oatmeal gruel, which had to be cooked for three hours and then put through a strainer lined with three thicknesses of fine cheesecloth. Laura worked hard to see that the gruel was properly prepared and that Elmer ate it while he was at home. Elmer called it his "willing diet" because "you had to be willing to eat it." But he still could not resist his trips to the cafe for a piece of pie. Once when one of his relatives saw him there, he made her promise not to tell Laura or his mother that he was breaking his diet.[9] In late September, Smith went to the Coffey Hospital in Portland, Oregon, where his problem was diagnosed as a duodenal ulcer. He was put on a stringent diet of bland food for three weeks before he was allowed to return home. But despite repeated warnings from his doctor, Smith refused to slow down and allow the ulcer to heal.[10]

On Washington's birthday 1928, Elmer took his family on a picnic and fishing outing on the Toutle River. While Laura prepared lunch, Elmer and the two children walked along the high banks of the swiftly running river. Elmer stopped to fish from a fallen log over the river and Virginia and Stuart launched pieces of wood into the water. Suddenly, Stuart slipped on the rocks and fell into the swirling stream. Virginia screamed "Daddy!" and Elmer jumped from his perch into the water ten feet below. He reached Stuart and pulled him to safety, but as he emerged from the stream he collapsed in agony on the ground, complaining of pains in his stomach. Virginia ran to get Laura, and they helped Elmer into the car. Laura did not know how to drive, so Elmer was forced to maneuver the car home, making frequent stops along the way to vomit blood into the wayside bushes as his two frightened children watched in horror from the back seat.[11]

When they got home, Laura arranged for Elmer to return to Coffey Hospital. Worried about how he was going to pay for his hospital stay, Elmer sent out letters to fifty of his clients who had not paid their bills, mostly bankruptcy cases in which he had put up the fifty dollar court fee himself. Explaining that he did not want to leave his family in debt in case something happened to him, Smith asked his clients for whatever they could afford. He showed the letter to a neighbor and Wobbly friend, Lucy Moore. "All of these are good, honest men," he told her. "They just happened to have some bad luck. I know I'm going to get some money." "I hope so Elmer," Moore replied, "but I don't think so." When he did not get a single answer from the fifty letters he had sent, Smith had a ready excuse. "They were ashamed to say that they didn't have any money," he explained to Moore. "They just had a bad background. They hadn't seen anything different. You can't blame them because they never saw anything good." Eventually, he had to borrow from his mother to pay his bills.[12] As Smith was in the hospital waiting to undergo a second operation for his ulcer, he made some notes to see what financial resources his family would have should he die. He valued his real estate at $2,500, and he owed money for some taxes and insurance. The Labor Temple owed him $300 for his building loan. The rest of the notes were a record of unpaid bills.[13]

Smith had a local anesthesia because he was so weak, and he was again conscious and in great pain during the operation. Resting afterward in his hospital bed, he sent out a spirited message through the Centralia Publicity Committee, telling his supporters to keep up the release campaign efforts and to "regain the old time enthusiasm in the class struggle."[14] Hundreds of Smith's well-wishers were relieved to hear the news of his recovery. Even Elizabeth Gurley Flynn, the famous IWW organizer and orator, visited Smith during his hospital stay to offer her support (a year later she would share the stage with him at a large Seattle rally for the prisoners).[15] After nearly a month in bed, Smith returned home, looking pale and weak.

By now, Smith's work on the CPC consisted of preparing information to present to regular parole board meetings. In June 1928, five of the Montesano jurors appeared before the board to renew their appeal for the prisoners. Before the hearing, Smith shared his expectations with

Lucy Moore: "They're going to come out. I know it." But she could only say, "I hope you're right, but I don't believe it."[16] Smith had organized a large contingent of supporters, including the jurors; representatives from the ILD; the Tacoma and Seattle Central Labor Councils (the first AFL councils to take a stand in favor of pardons); and Mrs. Barnett, Mrs. Lamb, and Mrs. McInerney and their children. The group presented new affidavits and a petition signed by two thousand residents of Centralia requesting that the prisoners be released. Smith pointed out that the Centralia petition was particularly impressive because there were only three thousand registered voters in the town. Mrs. Barnett was impressed by Smith's brief speech before the board: "Elmer Smith—always good, was at his best." He left the meeting optimistic as usual, wanting so much to believe that this time the parole board would make a favorable decision at its September meeting.[17] His efforts to free the prisoners had by now reached hundreds of thousands of people across the country. Norman Thomas, the Socialist candidate for president, called for the release of the men in a national radio broadcast that summer.

In July, Smith wrote "Elmer Smith Pleads for Liberty of Centralia Men," which was printed in the *Labor Defender* and published as a four-page leaflet by the Centralia Publicity Committee. "My heart bleeds for my brothers in Walla Walla and their families," he wrote. "Eight and one-half long years of grasping hope, with all the energy of despair, and still they wait; the families clinging to hope—yearning for their loved ones and counting the minutes of delay that seem like years."[18] When the parole board announced in September that it would not issue any paroles, Smith was deeply discouraged and the release campaign hit its low point.[19] The prospects of turning up any new material were bleak.

Unknown to Smith and everyone else working on the various re-lease committees, the arrival in Washington of a member of the American Legion in the spring of 1928 signaled the beginning of the last phase of the campaign to free the Centralia prisoners. Edward Patrick Coll, who had served as a captain in the army during the war, settled in Aberdeen, where he became the Legion service officer of the local Hoquiam Post. When Coll began to sell insurance in the area, he invited those he met to join the Legion, but he found that many men were disgusted with the part the Legion had played in the Centralia case. Coll was surprised by the undercurrent of criticism against the Legion. "My only knowledge of the Centralia trouble," he later wrote, "was the memory of former press reports stating that members of the I.W.W. had formed a plot and without the least provocation had brutally fired upon an Armistice Day parade of ex-servicemen and four veterans had been killed."[20]

Concerned about the disparaging remarks he heard, Coll was eager to prove the critics wrong, and he asked the Hoquiam Post to put on a program that would outline the American Legion view of the case. But the post cancelled the program after a prominent member told him that such a discussion would contain "enough dynamite to wreck the Post." It was better if the Centralia case was left alone.[21]

In August, the American Legion held its annual state convention in Centralia, where participants passed a resolution calling on the governor to oppose pardons for the Centralia prisoners. Coll was indignant; convention resolutions were supposed to summarize the individual decisions of each Legion post and yet no discussion had taken place at the post in Hoquiam. When Coll found out that C. D. Cunningham had introduced the resolution, he decided to visit Centralia to learn for himself what had happened. He talked to a number of Centralia Legionnaires and read accounts of the case, but he did not talk with Smith or anyone associated with his committee.[22]

Meanwhile, in a show of new support for the prisoners' cause, Methodists at a Puget Sound conference called for an impartial investigation of the case: "The evidence of guilt of these men is not as clear as it ought to be in a Christian conscience." The Legion post in Centralia was astonished by the Methodists' action and could only conclude that they had fallen for the IWW propaganda. But the Legion did agree to cooperate with any investigation to make sure it would have a balanced viewpoint. The official board of the First Methodist Church issued a resolution disapproving of the action taken by the Puget Sound conference, claiming that the trial had been conducted in a "fair and just manner." Members of the conference, the board judged, had acted "unwisely, indiscreetly and not for the best interests of the church, the community or the interests of justice in passing this resolution." The newspapers reported that Judge Wilson (who had tried the Montesano case) was a member of the church board.[23]

Later in September, Coll returned from Centralia and addressed his post, telling his audience that many veterans were refusing to join the Legion because of its hard-line attitude toward the Centralia prisoners. He issued an open letter to the post several days later, which concluded that the IWW was within its constitutional rights in protecting its hall. Wishing to separate the entire Legion from the acts of several local posts, he called on his fellow Legionnaires to show their courageous opposition to those who were guilty of mob violence. He ended the letter with the hope that someday the memorial statue in Centralia would be replaced by a memorial to Wesley Everest with an inscription reading, "Mobbed and lynched for upholding his Constitutional Rights."[24] Coll distributed one hundred copies of his letter among Legion members.

Smith was elated when he received a copy of the letter three days after its release. He realized that public support of the prisoners' cause by a member of the American Legion would inject the kind of interest and attention that was desperately needed. He immediately went to see Coll, and, after a long discussion, Coll authorized Smith and the CPC to print and distribute copies of his letter. Coll also agreed to conduct a further investigation into the case and to publicize what he learned. When he returned to Centralia, he talked with more eyewitnesses to the 1919 raid and shooting. He met with C. D. Cunningham, who got angry when pressed about the Legion's involvement in precipitating the raid. "Hell, I'm only wasting my time with you," he told Coll. "I think you're an I.W.W. already."[25]

November 11 marked the day of a statewide conference in Seattle, where representatives from the various release committees and church and labor groups met to plan a campaign strategy. The prisoners were glad to see all the committees working together. "We are here in the cause of labor," Barnett said in an interview with the *Labor Defender*, "and we want a united movement of all workers for our release. We do not see why all elements who are honestly devoted to the working class cannot unite on such an issue, even though they have differences on other questions." Bert Bland echoed Barnett's view in a letter to the *Defender*, saying that it "is exactly to our liking for anyone or any organization that will work in harmony with the champion of all. Elmer Smith can have our vote anytime. That red-headed fellow is the goods." After the conference, supporters of the Centralia Liberation Committee picketed the Supreme Court building in Olympia.[26]

In late November, just before the parole board was to consider a parole for Eugene Barnett, attorney W. H. Abel visited the prisoner. "I am going to help you get out," Abel told Barnett. "I never was sure that you were guilty. I hoped that you would get off at the trial." Abel said that he had recently written about his views to the parole board. Smith, Coll, a brother of the Blands, and Barnett were at the hearing. Coll spoke for all four, identifying himself as a member of the American Legion. He recalled that when he had first heard about the Centralia case, "I felt that no punishment could be severe enough for individuals who would fire upon a peaceful parade of ex-soldiers." Coll described how he had read about the case and had concluded "that a mistake has been made. . . . These workers are not guilty of firing upon an innocent parade. . . . Whoever incited that raid on that hall has got a lot to answer for. And it isn't the men in jail here."[27]

Coll presented the board with several new letters, including one from a Legion post, urging that pardons be granted. Two of the three board members indicated that they believed Barnett was innocent. After such encouragement, Smith and Barnett waited for an announcement that Barnett would be released, but the board reached no decision.[28]

Elmer Smith had always approached his defense work with a personal moral code that defined issues as either right or wrong; there was little middle ground. At times, he used these same inflexible standards in raising his children. On one occasion, Virginia told Laura that she wanted to join the Girl Scouts, but Laura knew that Elmer would not stand for it. Laura secretly made a uniform and on the day of the meeting helped Virginia sneak out of a bedroom window. Elmer saw her leave and ordered her back into the house. Laura argued that Virginia just wanted to be like all the other girls, but he stood firm. "She's not going to dress in a uniform as long as I'm her father," he said. Laura kept sneaking Virginia out to the meetings.[29]

When Virginia was ten, Elmer returned from work one day, upset because a young daughter of one of his clients had been seduced and was pregnant. It was time for Virginia to know "the facts of life," he said. Laura argued that Virginia was too young for such a discussion, but she finally volunteered to tell her. "*You'll* tell her!" exclaimed Elmer. "You don't know anything about it!" Virginia was on the stairs listening to the argument, and by the time Elmer came up to her room she was a very frightened girl.[30] Elmer also put a scare into his son Stuart, who went swimming in a nearby river during the flood season, which was forbidden. When Elmer found out, he told Stuart that he was going to put him in the reform school in Chehalis. Stuart was petrified, as Elmer loaded the family into the car and drove out and stopped in front of the school. With Virginia pleading with him not to take her brother away, Elmer pretended to get ready to leave Stuart inside. Finally, he turned the car around and brought everyone home, his point made to the extreme.[31] Despite such incidents, probably made worse by stress and his declining health, Elmer deeply loved his children. He was a warm, generous father, usually ready with a smile and big hug. As his children grew older, they began to idolize him.

Ed Coll's investigation into the Centralia incident and the Legion's opposition to his activities helped contribute to a reawakening of interest in the case. C. D. Cunningham was particularly upset with Coll's claims that the Wobblies did not get a fair trial, and the growing controversy within the Legion caused him to make a rare decision to discuss the case publicly. He agreed to debate Coll in January 1929 on the condition that only Legionnaires be in the audience.[32]

The debate did not produce any excitement until Cunningham described how Legionnaire McElfresh had died in his arms in the street on that Armistice Day. Coll quickly pointed out that since McElfresh was one of the raiders on the hall, Cunningham's description of events implied that Cunningham was also raiding the hall. Cunningham interrupted and called Coll a "red." Coll replied, "It is far easier to be considered as a 'red' than to have one's hands red with the blood of one's fellow man." At that, Cunningham refused to give any rebuttal and the meeting ended. Many in the audience were not impressed by Cunningham's failure to respond to Coll's charges directly, and some found his name-calling distasteful.[33]

The next morning, Smith drove to Coll's house to hear how the debate had gone. Smith told Coll that he badly needed a chocolate malt as it was "the only thing that soothes the gnawing in my stomach. After two operations I'm afraid the old trouble's come back again." The two drove around until they found a drugstore that was open. Smith's diet consisted mainly of potatoes, milk, flour, and grease, but the pain would not go away, so Smith turned to chocolate malts and chocolate cake for relief.[34] Pleased with Coll's report of the debate, Smith invited him to speak at the Seattle Eagles Hall in February.

In Seattle, Coll told the crowd of two thousand that he wanted to clear the good name of the American Legion, which could only be done by releasing the eight innocent men in prison. The meeting adopted the usual resolution demanding that the governor pardon the men. Coll's activities, Smith judged, were "a shot in the arm" for the prisoners' cause, but Coll would only continue his work on behalf of the prisoners as long as he received a monthly salary of $150. Smith and the CPC paid his way as long as they could, and then the ACLU and a wealthy liberal from California, Kate Crane Gartz, came through with assistance. Well-known men such as Charlie Chaplin and Upton Sinclair also responded to financial pleas from Smith and contributed money to the CPC over the years.[35]

In early March 1929, Smith, Coll, Mrs. Barnett, and several ministers attended yet another parole board meeting. The board had received enough information, Smith said, and he urged its members to make a decision. In an emotional appeal on behalf of the wives and children of the prisoners, Smith described how the CPC had been forced to cut payments to the families from forty to twenty dollars a month during the past winter. Although members of the board appeared to be increasingly sympathetic, they seemed reluctant to make parole recommendations to a governor who remained so strongly opposed to releasing the men.[36]

Governor Hartley had made it clear both privately and publicly that he was "perfectly satisfied of the guilt of the defendants and that they had a fair and impartial trial." Hartley had written to Cunningham, asking for help in responding to "this voluminous trash that comes to this office" about the Centralia case. He cited a letter he had received from Coll, whom the governor described as "one principal mischief-maker." Hartley wrote Coll:

> Appealing to class and group prejudices, spreading propaganda, getting petitions signed, and the like, have no just bearing in such affairs. . . . Justice is neither bought, sold nor coerced in the office of Governor. . . . The quicker these men at Walla Walla cut loose from the agitators and propagandists, the brighter their future.[37]

The lack of action by the parole board and the governor's opposition finally proved to be too much for Mrs. Barnett. Seeing little hope that her husband would ever be released, she filed for divorce in April 1929. Eugene Barnett wrote to Smith for help:

> It was a terrible blow. I'm afraid she has done this in a moment of despair, in an effort to get away from the misery of all these disappointments. I have planned so much on the happy home we would have on some little farm when I got out of here and now my house of cards has tumbled about my ears.[38]

Smith made a special, but unsuccessful, appeal to the governor on Barnett's behalf.

On Easter Sunday afternoon, Smith and Coll spoke in an open field in Centralia to a crowd of more than one thousand. Smith had invited Cunningham to appear at the meeting and debate him, but Cunningham had had enough of debates and declined. Smith began by telling a story about egotistical King Canute, who, drunk with power, believed that there was nothing he could not do:

He had his attendants carry him down to the seaside in order that he might command the tides to stand back. "Stand back, oh tides, stand back," he cried, but the tides came on in and the poor old fool was nearly drowned. The time has come in the Centralia case when the truth, having been driven home all these years, has today become a sweeping, surging tide. . . . There is nothing so strong in this world as the truth. They may cover it up for awhile, they may hide it, but in time it comes out, after nine long years it is coming out.[39]

But as it happened, the tide was coming in on the Centralia case and on Elmer Smith.

"I Have a Failing of Being Optimistic"

"The Prisoner's Song"—Guy Massey, 1924

Oh! I wish I had someone to love me,
Someone to call me their own.
Oh! I wish I had someone to live with,
'Cause I'm tired of living alone.

Now if I had wings like an angel
Over these prison walls I would fly
And I'd fly to the arms of my poor darlin'
And there I'd be willing to die.[1]

By 1929, the Centralia case had become the cause of the church community. In May, the Washington Congregational Conference voted to send a committee to assist in the Puget Sound Methodist Conference investigation begun the previous fall. At the request of these two groups, the Federal Council of Churches took charge; the council was joined by the National Catholic Welfare Conference and the Central Conference of American Rabbis.[2] The plan was to write a report and issue it in the name of the religious organizations, but there was no intention of following it with a campaign to release the men. It was uncommon for these groups to get involved in a criminal case, and when they did their action drew a lot of attention.

Later that year, these religious organizations hired an investigator, DeWitt Wyckoff, to gather information for the report. A graduate of Cornell University Law School and Union Theological Seminary, Wyckoff had worked for the American Bankers Association while giving much of his spare time to voluntary legal research for religious social action organizations such as the Fellowship of Reconciliation. Wyckoff traveled throughout Washington interviewing a wide range of people connected with the case: prisoners, Legionnaires, Wobblies, ministers, jurors, newspaper editors, Smith, and Edward Coll.[3] Smith was eager to help Wyckoff in any way possible, certain that the report would exonerate the IWW and lead to the quick release of the prisoners.

One of the prisoners, Ray Becker, did not look on the investigation with much hope. As the years passed, he grew increasingly hostile toward those working for his release, claiming that Vanderveer had deliberately mishandled the trial and accusing Smith of using the case to satisfy his own political ambitions and of deliberately obstructing his release. One by one, he denounced the release committees. Consumed with vindictiveness, Becker cultivated a fear and mistrust of everyone who tried to communicate with him. One of his visitors wrote: "Ray Becker is unquestionably the victim of prison psychosis. . . . The prison had broken him; there was a wild look in his eyes and he shook all over when he talked." Roger Baldwin wrote that Becker seemed to "hate everybody." Over the years, Smith chose to ignore Becker's rantings.[4]

A major controversy arose in June 1929 when all of the prisoners except Becker wrote an open letter repudiating the Centralia Liberation Committee (CLC).[5] The International Labor Defense, dominated by members of the Communist Party, had organized the CLC to focus on the Centralia case. To outsiders, both groups seemed to be run by the Communist Party, although one of the first organizers of the CLC denied that the ILD ever interfered with its work.[6] The prisoners were angry over a leaflet published by the Communist Party in Seattle that attacked Coll. The leaflet claimed that Coll was attempting to use the Centralia case "to further the ends of the Legion and not to win the freedom for these martyrs." It ended: "Speed up their return to the ranks of the workers' army Under the Leadership Of The Workers (Communist) Party." The prisoners objected to the CLC using "our plight as prisoners for self-advertising or party propaganda purposes." They also objected to the CLC's recent picketing of the state capitol.[7] Another leaflet by the Seattle Communists attacked Smith and his Centralia Publicity Committee for fooling the prisoners into allying themselves with "all reactionary elements, the A.F. of L., I.W.W., the Church and the State." The leaflet accused Smith of being "backed up by the murderers of Wesley Everest, the fascist American Legion, represented by Captain Coll, and by the corrupt reactionary officials of the A.F. of L."[8] The idea that the Legion was supporting his work was certainly news to Smith.

Smith had always been somewhat distrustful of the CLC and agreed with the general IWW view that the group was directed by the ILD and the Communist Party and did not have the release of the prisoners as its highest priority. Although he cooperated with the CLC in the beginning, Smith was influential in the prisoners' decision to denounce them (the prisoners' letter was released on stationery of Smith's Centralia Publicity Committee). In a letter to Baldwin, he criticized the CLC for injecting party propaganda into the pardon campaign. "I have hesitated to say this much to you," he wrote, "because I have always had a very sincere admiration for the work of the real Communists and I find it very difficult to harmonize the work being done by this committee with proper tactics."[9] Smith became disturbed when Communists and members of the CLC disrupted his meetings by holding up the passage of pardon resolutions while pushing for resolutions that supported their own political agenda. He opposed their efforts to use the Centralia case to build their own organization, and he clashed with them on the distribution of funds raised for the prisoners, charging that much of the money raised by the Communists and the ILD never reached the prisoners. That summer, actor Charlie Chaplin stopped giving money to the CPC and instead made donations to the ILD. After learning of this, Smith wrote Chaplin and sent a Wobbly friend to see him in Hollywood; Chaplin changed his mind.[10]

The Centralia Liberation Committee defended itself by saying that the ILD had organized picketing. It also claimed no responsibility for the leaflets, which it claimed had been written by the Communist Party. The CLC accused Smith of assuming that the organization was controlled by Communists simply because there were Communists on the committee. Nevertheless, as a result of the prisoners' letter, the CLC agreed to temporarily back off from pushing its program. The letter also caused the Seattle Labor Council of the AFL to withdraw its representatives from the CLC and give its money directly to the prisoners and their families. Without the backing of non-Communists, the CLC rapidly lost credibility and disbanded in 1930.[11] A majority of the prisoners, however, never repudiated the ILD, which continued to raise money for them. Lamb, Barnett, and Bert Bland regularly wrote letters of thanks to the *Labor Defender* for its help.[12]

That summer, Smith and Coll made another trip to Walla Walla. They had made the trip in March without success, and this time the parole board was not in any more of a receptive mood. "Well Smith," they said, "we've heard you before. I suppose it's the same old story, isn't it?" The board did allow Coll to say a few words and present the additional resolutions he and Smith had gathered. After the meeting, when the two visited with the prisoners, Smith told Barnett that he had persuaded his wife not to go through with the divorce.[13]

"I feel it's time wasted here," Smith told Coll on their way home, "but what other recourse do we have under the law?" Such meetings produced great frustration in Smith. Recent Wobbly activities in Centralia also revealed their anger and disappointment about the case. After the Legion had broken up a local railroad strike, two Wobblies went into a Legionnaire-owned restaurant, ordered a big meal, and walked out without paying. On another occasion, a Wobbly walked into a butcher shop owned by A. F. Cormier, the man who had led the 1919 parade. The worker ordered the best cut of meat in the shop and when it was wrapped up he said, "No, I'm not taking it. Send it over to the bridge," referring to the bridge where Wesley Everest had been lynched. Smith did not approve of such tactics, yet he could laugh when he repeated the stories to Coll. The Wobblies were crude in many ways, he said, but they were loyal to each other and to their families. "Someone must represent them, that's the purpose of the law," he told Coll.[14]

During this period, when he was in uncharacteristically low spirits, Smith thought increasingly about his own role in the Centralia case and for the first time expressed some second thoughts about his advice to the Wobblies in 1919. He wondered if the tragedy might never have happened if he had not told them about their right to defend themselves. He confided to a close friend:

> Maybe I just played God where I didn't need to. I thought then that I had the right to give that advice, but now I'm beginning to wonder because I didn't understand the circumstances. I believed in the letter of the law then. I'm beginning not to believe now.[15]

In early 1930 Smith had a new worry. Washington law required lawyers to take the bar examination over again if the attorney had not practiced for five years, which in Smith's case was April 1930. He believed that if the prisoners were released there was a good chance he would be reinstated. But he was afraid that if he pushed for reinstatement now it would have the effect of taking away valuable attention from the prisoners' cause. Roger Baldwin, to whom Smith often turned for advice, counseled Smith not to move until after the prisoners were released; but after a long deliberation, Smith decided to go ahead. He had received many hints from fellow lawyers that his application for reinstatement would be successful.[16]

To support his petition, Smith gathered nine letters of support from lawyers and judges. Judge J. M. Phillips, a former mayor of Aberdeen who had tried cases with Smith, wrote:

> I have always found him honorable, truthful and a man of good moral character. I feel thoroughly convinced that if Mr. Smith has been guilty of any indiscretion that justified his disbarment it was due to the passion and strain which he underwent during the time of his trouble.[17]

H. W. B. Hewen, a judge from South Bend, wrote:

> I have never seen anything that was not strictly honorable in his conduct; respectful to the Court, and from my personal acquaintance I think he is a gentleman. I do not hesitate to recommend him for re-instatement in the practice of law. His enemies, I think, are mostly due to political reasons, a subject on which I believe every person has a right to his opinion.[18]

There were more strong words of praise. One Centralia attorney said, "Within the hearts of a large percentage of the citizens of this county, who number over forty thousand, there lodges great respect for the honesty and sincerity of purpose of Elmer S. Smith." Finally, there was a letter of support from Judge W. A. Reynolds of the Superior Court in Chehalis. Reynolds had a reputation of extreme bias against the IWW, and every time Smith had had a case before him he had filed a motion of prejudice against him. Reynolds now wrote: "He was always respectful to the court, courteous, honorable and painstaking in the presentation of his cases, and had a high reputation for honest conduct and dealing with his clients." These letters indicated that Smith was respected by members of the legal profession as a man and as an attorney, not for his radical sympathies. By 1930, the perceived threat of the IWW had subsided to the point where lawyers and judges could tolerate public support for Smith.[19]

Smith filed his petition on May 31, 1930. He wrote that he had been "more than sufficiently punished for extreme utterances made during the fervor and heat of public speeches" and for other "indiscretions." He promised, if reinstated, to observe the "letter and spirit of his oath of office as an attorney."[20] Smith appeared before the Board of Law Examiners in Olympia on June 24. A week after the hearing—at the request of the Lewis County Bar, which wanted Smith to go on record as "renouncing the principles that caused his disbarment"—the board asked Smith to answer three questions.[21] First, did Smith approve of the ideas and principles of the IWW and were "such ideas . . . a desirable goal for society." Second, did Smith believe that changes in society "should be promoted by other than legal and peaceable means." And third, did Smith approve of the ideas in the IWW literature. Five years after disbarring him, the board was still primarily concerned about what the IWW believed rather than what Smith had done.

To the first question, Smith replied that he believed in the preamble of the IWW constitution, which advocated the organization of labor to accomplish "shorter hours, better working conditions and general improvement of the status of workers"; otherwise he did not approve of the IWW principles. "Absolutely no," was his answer to the second question, saying that change can be accomplished by peaceable and legal means. The last question was harder to answer, Smith wrote, because there was so much IWW literature. "There are many very beautiful ideas and principles set forth in some of the literature of the IWW," while some ideas were "vicious." He wrote that he did not approve of "sabotage, syndicalism, or any violation of law whatsoever in achieving social reform or changes." He believed that labor could achieve its worthy goals by organizing through unions under the law and with the ballot.[22]

Smith's answers showed that he had changed his views only slightly since 1919. He remained a strong supporter of IWW principles and its efforts to improve the lot of working people, although perhaps not as fervently as before. He had always denounced the use of violence. On his earlier speaking tours, Smith had sometimes been very outspoken in calling on workers to strike and take over control of industry, but he had always advocated peaceful methods.

In July, the board recommended to the Supreme Court that Smith be readmitted to the bar, noting that the great majority of the Lewis County Bar believed that Smith should be reinstated. The board was "satisfied" with Smith's answers to its questions and found that he had expressed his "disaffirmance of belief in the ideas and principles for which he was disbarred."[23] It was a strange conclusion to draw, for clearly Smith had not renounced his belief in the basic principles of the IWW. Perhaps the board simply no longer saw Smith as a threat to the social order.

There was also movement on two other legal fronts. A jury trial found Loren Roberts to be sane and thus eligible for parole. While prison officials recommended that Roberts be released, however, he stayed in prison while the prosecuting attorney, the brother of Warren Grimm, appealed the ruling.[24] For the remaining prisoners, Smith decided to try a new tactic, recognizing that appeals to the parole board and governor had reached a dead end. In a letter to supporter Upton Sinclair, he wrote:

> I felt that I had done all I could possibly do and by talking very plainly to them [parole board] I aroused their antagonism to such an extent that I believe others approaching the matter from a different angle can do more.[25]

After consulting with several other lawyers, Smith was convinced that the minimum legal sentence in the Centralia case was ten years for second-degree murder; and under state law, when a prisoner's conduct was good, release was mandatory after the minimum term was up. Prison officials had already reported to the parole board that the Centralia prisoners' conduct had been exemplary. Although the legal authority on this point was not clear, Smith hoped to capitalize on the idea when he learned that the governor and the parole board might consider recognizing ten years as the minimum sentence.[26]

Smith hired two conservative attorneys to pursue the theory, promising to pay only if they got results. He appealed to the ACLU for a loan, offering to guarantee it by taking out a mortgage on his house. "Personally I feel quite optimistic over the situation," Smith wrote to Baldwin, "but I realize that I have a failing of being optimistic. In any event, if it is a failing, it has helped keep up the fight which I believe is going to result in the release of the men." Baldwin and the IWW General Defense Committee came up with the loan, but the two lawyers were unable to convince either the governor or the parole board that the ten-year minimum applied in this case; the money was returned. "We must fight on regardless of how hopeless things may appear," Smith wrote to Baldwin.[27] While Smith waited to hear from the Supreme Court about his reinstatement, he also waited for Wyckoff to complete his long-overdue report. He wrote Baldwin: "It would surely be a powerful help to us in this matter [the pardon campaign]. It would also be a powerful help in the matter of my application for reinstatement to practice law."[28]

On August 6, Smith heard that James McInerney had died in prison of complications from spinal meningitis and tuberculosis. Eugene Barnett wrote to Smith: "I'm sorry about Mc. but eleven yea[r]s is a long time without air and sunshine." Smith addressed two thousand people at the graveside funeral on August 20 in Centralia: ".Don't mourn the dead; go ahead with the fight for the freedom of the workers." Coll and Wobbly leader James P. Thompson spoke about McInerney's life and the IWW. None of McInerney's fellow prisoners was allowed to attend, but representatives from nearly all of the defense committees gathered in solidarity by the gravesite. Only the ILD was denied a right to speak. Liberal IWW supporters also held a memorial service in New York.[29] On the day of the funeral, Loren Roberts became a free man, the first Centralia prisoner to leave Walla Walla alive. When Grimm failed to file an appeal of the jury's decision, the court declared Roberts to be legally sane. Roberts quietly moved to a small town outside Olympia, where he worked in the woods as a timber faller and bucker and hunted alone for deer. He died in 1976.[30]

On October 13, the religious groups released their forty-eight-page report, acknowledging that it was Coll's interest that had sparked their re-examination of the case. The report traced the background of the Centralia tragedy by describing working conditions in the woods, the 1917 lumber strike, and the 1918 Red Cross raid on the Wobbly hall. After describing the events of Armistice Day, the report addressed the question of who was the aggressor: "While a prior rush toward the hall is not conclusively shown, it appears more probable that this occurred than that the shooting took place first." The report also said that the weight of evidence tended to support Barnett's contention that he was not present in the Avalon Hotel that day and, therefore, did not fire the shot that killed Warren Grimm. The report blamed both the IWW and the Legion for the tragedy, but concluded: "The six I.W.W.s in Walla Walla Penitentiary are paying the penalty for their part in a tragedy, the guilt for which is by no means theirs alone. They alone were indicted; they alone have been punished." [31]

The *Christian Century* applauded the report as a

> judicious estimate of the case. . . . If our laws and institutions
> are worth defending against destructive radicals, they are worth
> respecting even when the legal rights of radicals are at stake or
> when radicals are brought to trial.[32]

But neither side was satisfied with the report. "Centralia Case Report Made by Church Bodies Indicates Bias of All Such Folk in Class War," reported *Industrial Solidarity*. The IWW was unhappy because the report did not declare outright that the prisoners were innocent. The *Seattle Times* called it "A Shameful Report," saying that the authors "ought to be ashamed of themselves" for blaming everybody but the IWW for what had happened. C. D. Cunningham faulted the report for not clearly recognizing that the prisoners were found legally guilty of murdering Warren Grimm.

And many Washington newspapers sharply attacked the report in their editorials.[33]

Smith was disappointed that the report did not come out more clearly on the side of the IWW, but he did feel that it could be used to help the prisoners and he welcomed the publicity that it generated. The report also received a warm welcome from the ACLU and other liberal supporters, who circulated copies widely. It represented the most impartial study ever made of the Centralia case, and the doubts it cast on the trial's fairness caused many church conservatives to become more active in the pardon campaign.

A month after the church report was released, Smith appeared before the state Supreme Court where his reinstatement hearing went smoothly. There was little opposition from the state attorney general's office, and three days later, on November 17, 1930, the chief justice announced the court's decision to reinstate Smith to the practice of law.[34]

Many people congratulated Smith on the news. The *Industrial Worker* announced on page one: "Every worker will join in rejoicing that this belated measure of justice has been done and in wishing well to a true-hearted and courageous advocate of social righteousness." The executive board of the ACLU wrote: "The Board fully recognizes your valued service in a cause which has needed courage and perseverance as well as ability of an unusual order." Upton Sinclair sent a letter offering "my profound admiration for the heroism you have displayed during these long years." He also sent a copy of his recent book *Mammonart*, inscribed "To Elmer Smith, hero, with admiration, Upton Sinclair." Even a stranger sent a letter: "Every friend of civil liberty has admired your courage and your steadfastness."[35]

Despite the good news, Smith's family and friends were growing increasingly concerned about his health. Looking older than his years, he had lost weight and his almost continual stomach pain robbed him of his usual high energy and enthusiasm.[36] He was also $5,000 in debt, and friends had to help him buy a modest home in town; until this time he could only afford to rent. Smith resumed his law practice during the Great Depression, when unemployment in the lumber camps and sawmills was high. By 1931, half of those who normally worked were out of a job. Smith could only get work handling minor criminal cases—defending workers charged with forgery, assault, and theft. In one case, his penniless client was charged with stealing a car. After a mistrial, Smith could only collect a small fee from the court. In another case, Smith won a judgment in back wages for a woman, but he did not charge her for his services, saying "Boy, I like to get my spurs

into those guys!"[37] After interviewing a new client, Smith would sometimes say, "I can straighten that out for you, I think, but bring a dollar with
you when you return, would you?" Many of his clients were small farmers
who paid their bills with chickens and vegetables. Once Smith got paid in
strawberries, and he spent the weekend making strawberry ice cream for
his family and friends. Clearly more was needed, so Laura helped out by
cultivating their vegetable garden, working wonders with little money to
make sure the children received proper nutrition. Once she managed to
get by on thirty-five cents a week by buying celery and using homegrown
potatoes for their meals.[38]

After Smith received his law license, he joined the International
Juridical Association, a progressive trade organization of lawyers head-
quartered in New York that dealt with the legal problems of union organizers and striking workers.[39] Edward Coll had decided to move on, even
though Smith asked him to stay on as an investigator for his legal cases.
In early 1931, Coll moved to California to accept another job offer.[40] Smith
decided to go into partnership with J. O. Davies, an association that lasted
until Smith's death.

In mid-1931, Governor Hartley granted Eugene Barnett an executive leave of absence to be with his wife, who was ill with cancer. At Christmas, Barnett and Commodore Bland received executive paroles. Barnett
became a fur rancher in Idaho, where he was an organizer for the CIO
International Woodworkers Union and was active in the Progressive Party.
Bland returned to Centralia, where he died in 1938.[41] Four of the men were
still behind bars.

Elmer was at his desk in his law office in early March 1932. He had
not been feeling well all day and had a slight fever, so when Laura came
down for a visit, he asked to be taken home. When he reached home, he
began coughing up blood. The doctor told Elmer that he must enter a hospital, but Elmer emphatically refused. He insisted that he be taken instead
to the Karsunky Sanitarium, a private naturopathic hospital in Puyallup. A
friend had told Elmer that the sanitarium's Dr. Karsunky could cure ulcers
with herbs and special diets. Elmer believed that his two previous operations had not helped, and after the last one he had told a friend, "I'm not
going to face the knife ever again. I'd die first." The sanitarium also cost
less than the hospital.[42]

Laura called Elmer's brother Jim, who drove them to Puyallup
with Elmer stretched out on the back seat. Laura worried that he might
not survive the trip. When they arrived, Karsunky gave Elmer a painkiller

and put him to bed. Laura remained at his side, and an extra cot was placed in his room for her. Elmer was not allowed to eat or even take water, and Laura sat with him and moistened his dry lips day and night with an ice cube wrapped in cloth. Elmer had been only semi-conscious since his arrival at the sanitarium, and when he did talk he spoke about a big case he was working on that he hoped would bring some money to the family. As the days passed he grew weaker. His mother asked the doctor to give her son a blood transfusion to help him regain his strength, but the doctor did not believe in blood transfusions. After seven days of steady vigil, Laura was exhausted and went to her parents' home in Tacoma for a night's sleep. At three o'clock the next morning, March 20, the doctor called to tell Laura that Elmer had slipped into a coma and died, bleeding to death from his hemorrhaging ulcer. He was forty-four years old.[43]

The Smith family was heartbroken as they gathered at Tom and Isabelle's home. Lucy Moore never forgot the day she heard the news: "I think that was one of the saddest days that I have ever known. We loved Elmer as a human being and man. He helped when help was needed. He could laugh when he felt like crying."[44] As the family made preparations for the funeral, letters of sympathy poured in. Even the hometown paper, The *Centralia Tribune*, praised Smith in a front-page editorial:

> Kindliness, generosity, understanding, and a sympathetic heart were outstanding traits of Elmer S. Smith. . . . If his friends gained through kindnesses he had bestowed during the course of his daily life could have rewarded him with dollars, Smith would have died a rich man.[45]

The *Industrial Worker* described Smith as a "brave and dauntless moral hero of the tragedy. . . . Smith died a martyr to principle."[46] An editorial column in a Seattle magazine said:

> The sad passing of Elmer S. Smith . . . brought to a close a valiant career which may not be recorded in our little history text-books but which has few equals for sacrificial devotion, perseverance and courage in the cause of Liberty, the ideal upon which the nation itself was founded.[47]

Roger Baldwin sent a telegram: "It is a tragedy to have a young man so valiant in struggle for civil liberty and working class rights die in midst of his labors." "Elmer Smith, that lion-like champion of workers rights; never faltering in his loyalty," wrote the director of the Seattle Labor College. The *Nation* reported: "A man named Smith died the other day with practically no notice by the press at large. He had been a courageous friend of the downtrodden and the persecuted, and he died a martyr to one of the most deserving but unpopular causes of recent years." "Our staunch and persistent fighter for justice to the downtrodden poor has passed away," wrote the secretary of the Centralia Publicity Committee.[48]

From Walla Walla, John Lamb grieved for "our dear friend," and a moving tribute came from Bert Bland:

> I am sorry and grieved and my words are inadequate to express my sorrow for the loss of that great fighting humanitarian who thought and acted first for his friends. It is hard for me to imagine that this great fighter has passed on.

Bland recalled Smith's words to the prisoners after the Montesano trial twelve years earlier, when he had promised: "Boys, I will never forget you, and as long as there is a breath in my body I will work for your release." Now Bland wrote: "Elmer has more than fulfilled that promise, giving his time, money, health, and even his life that he may help to free those whom he knew were framed to prison."[49]

On March 22, several hundred loggers, miners, sawmill workers, railroad men, and farmers filled the mortuary in downtown Centralia. Thousands more gathered outside in the chilly rain, clustered in small groups or waiting patiently in their black automobiles. Most of the crowd, dressed in overalls, dark suits, or grey dresses, lived in Centralia; hundreds more had driven or walked a dozen miles to be there. They had closely followed Smith's career, and some had cut Smith's picture out of the newspapers and tacked it on their living room walls. The funeral was the largest Centralia residents had ever seen. One of Smith's sisters-in-law recalled, "I don't think that I've ever seen any person mourned more than he was mourned by his loved ones and by his acquaintances."[50]

The Smith family sat together in the front two rows in the hall and stared in silence at the wooden coffin. Elmer's brothers openly sobbed throughout the service while Laura sat silently, stunned at the mass of people, most of whom she did not recognize.[51] Smith's mother, who had arranged the funeral, had insisted that no minister be present and no hymns be sung during the service. Nevertheless, before the service began the organist played "Beautiful Island of Somewhere": "Somewhere the sun is shining/Somewhere the songbirds dwell/Hush, then, thy sad repining/

God lives, and all is well." Isabelle took strong offense at the empty promises in the song and complained loudly to her family and friends. The song
showed no respect for the life her son had led, a life of uncompromis-
ing conviction and determination to improve the conditions of working
people.[52]

Judge J. M. Phillips gave the eulogy, and Connor Harmon, Smith's
brother-in-law, read "The Man With the Hoe" by Edwin Markham. It was
still raining when the mourners placed Smith's casket in the hearse. The
funeral caravan stretched out for three miles before arriving at the Mountain View Cemetery, just outside Centralia. At the grave, Judge Phillips
said that long after the enemies of Smith were dead his name would be a
symbol of honor for the future. He predicted that history would recognize
Elmer Smith as the greatest man ever to come from the state of Washington.[53] Phillips closed by reading the poem Smith had chosen to be read at
his graveside, "Mourn Not the Dead" by Ralph Chaplin:

> Mourn not the dead that in the cool earth lie—
>   Dust unto dust
> The Calm, sweet earth that mothers all who die,
>   As all men must!
> Mourn not your captive comrades who must dwell,
>   Too strong to strive—
> Within each steel-bound coffin of a cell,
>   Buried alive;
> But rather mourn the apathetic throng—
>   The cowed and the meek—
> Who see the world's great anguish and its wrong,
>   And dare not speak![54]

Epilogue: The Light at the End of the Tunnel

"The Big Rock Candy Mountain"

In the Big Rock Candy Mountain
The jails are made of tin
And you can bust right out again
As soon as they put you in;

Oh the buzzin of the bees in the cigarette trees
Round the soda-water fountain,
Where the lemonade springs and the bluebird sings
In the Big Rock Candy Mountain.[1]

Smith died without a will, having made no preparations for his family. At his death, he owned two pieces of property, some household furnishings, two pianos, a Chevrolet sedan, and some law books. The court appraisers set the value of his possessions at $2,266, and Laura was awarded the entire estate. In his last two years as a practicing attorney, Smith had accumulated unpaid promissory notes from twenty-seven clients totaling $1,540, but the appraisers estimated that only $68 of it was collectible.[2]

During the month of Smith's death, a Senate subcommittee of the Judiciary Committee held hearings in Washington, D.C., on the nomination of Judge Kenneth Mackintosh to the United States Circuit Court. Mackintosh had written the Washington Supreme Court decision that had disbarred Smith in 1925. One senator called Smith's disbarment "a most-arbitrary opinion, clearly without sanction," and the subcommittee affirmed that the IWW had a right to be defended. The Senate, influenced by the opposition of organized labor, eventually refused to confirm Mackintosh, partly because of his role in Smith's disbarment.[3] In June 1932, the Washington Supreme Court upheld a personal injury claim by Sam Baxter against the Ford Motor Company. A few months before he died Smith had argued the case, which would become a landmark decision in the field of negligence law. It also brought in several thousand dollars to Smith's family, by far the most money he had ever made from a single case.[4]

In 1933, Washington's new governor, Clarence Martin, took office. A conservative Democrat, he had no love for leftist groups, but the Centralia prisoners had become a politically nagging problem. Having promised to release the men if he was elected, he quickly paroled John Lamb, who moved back to Centralia, where he died in 1949. A few months later, the governor paroled Bert Bland and Britt Smith. Bland married and moved to Wisconsin, and Britt Smith went back to work in the woods and joined the CIO Woodworkers Union. He remained a radical until his death in the 1960s. Only Ray Becker remained in prison.[5]

Becker remained uncooperative to those working for his parole. "To hell with a parole," he wrote in 1933. "I want a full and complete pardon, or nothing at all." In 1934, he submitted a handwritten, 141-page brief to the Washington Supreme Court requesting a writ of habeas corpus. The plea was denied.[6] Support to help Becker was evaporating. The Centralia Publicity Committee had folded with the release of Bland and Britt Smith, and only the ACLU kept up the legal battle to free Becker. Roger Baldwin believed that Becker was foolish to hold out for a complete pardon, but Becker refused to accept anything less. During the next few years, he kept up his unsuccessful legal battle.

In 1936, the International Woodworkers of America took up Becker's cause and formed the Free Ray Becker Committee. Legal appeals centered on obtaining a commutation of sentence to time already served, and in 1939 Governor Martin commuted Becker's sentence on the condition that he leave the state. Becker was not told until the last minute, and after nineteen years behind bars he was forced from prison. He remained active in labor union projects and later opened up a leather goods shop in Vancouver, Washington. He died in 1950.[7]

With Smith's death, the Smith family began to break up. Laura took her children and moved out of Centralia. Her memories of the past remain painful:

> I always felt that the Wobblies were the direct cause of Elmer's death, and with the exception of a few who were very fine men, were not worthy of his sacrifice. They seemed to be un-

able to appreciate what he had done for them and truely never thanked him.[8]

For a while Laura taught school in Mendota, where her pupils included Eugene Barnett's son. She eventually remarried, divorced, and settled in Tacoma, all the while talking little about Elmer to her children. Virginia grew up to become a teacher in Tacoma, and Stuart worked for a short time for the Weyerhaeuser Timber Company and later became an oil geologist in Bakersfield, California. Both children held conservative views that were far removed from those their father believed and fought for.[9]

When Elmer died, his brother Jim was ill with cancer, but he did not tell the family until the pain became too great. He died in 1933 and was buried next to his brother. Isabelle and Tom moved on to Oregon, where they both died in the 1940s. Harry broke his hip while working in the mine, and his wife divorced him in 1937 because of his excessive drinking and gambling. He died in 1956 and was buried next to Jim and Elmer. Glen was also an alcoholic, and his wife divorced him before he died of the disease in a cheap boarding house in San Francisco in 1953. Dorothy contracted skin cancer and went into seclusion for several years before she died in 1962. The youngest brother, Bill, ran a gas station and became an oil distributer before he died of cancer in 1968.[10]

Traces of Smith's life are hard to find in Centralia today. His law office, long abandoned, was torn down in the late 1980s. His grave was almost lost to the weeds until Nora Beard, his law secretary, dug on her hands and knees until she recovered it and had a new headstone installed.[11] The bridge on which Wesley Everest was hanged has been replaced, but many Centralians still call it "Hangman's Bridge." The Legionnaires' statue in the city park still stands as the most prominent reminder of the events of 1919.

But Elmer Smith remains one of the most significant influences in the lives of those who knew him. Nora Beard remembered that his personality "just filled a room" and that he had a talent that made everyone around him feel better about themselves.[12] Smith was fiercely loyal to the Centralia prisoners and to the Smith family, but few people ever grew close to him. He appealed to peoples' emotions but kept his own feelings hidden. He always resisted asking for help for himself and never refused to lend assistance to others. Over time, this trait eventually wore him down. But despite the years of professional setbacks, family turmoil, lack of progress in the release campaign, and constant threats of violence against him, Smith somehow sustained an optimism about life that was his most enduring quality. "He seemed to be a man that saw the light at the end of the tunnel regardless of how dark it was in the middle," recalled one friend.[13]

The Centralia case ultimately takes on a larger meaning through the life of Elmer Smith. His lonely persistence kept the case alive and brought hope to the prisoners and their families. His personal sacrifice and commitment to nonviolence helped calm public hysteria. His honest and direct dealings with controversial issues were admired by participants on both sides. Probably no other person who was not a Wobbly was loved as much as he was by the rank-and-file members of the IWW, and his tireless efforts helped shield the union from some of the onslaught against their civil liberties. Although he cannot be admired for neglecting his finances, his family, and his health, Smith stands as a model of a consistent, principled, and courageous fighter for social justice. By fanning the fire of discontent during his lifetime, he helped keep the flame of justice alive for generations.

Notes

PROLOGUE

1. James Gilchrist Lawson, ed., *The World's Best Loved Poems* (New York; Harper & Brothers, 1927), 238. The poem appears in slightly altered form in Walker C. Smith, "Was It Murder?" Northwest District Defense Committee, Seattle (1922), 36. It was Elmer Smith's favorite poem.

2. For a description of the parade and shootings, see State v. Smith et al., No. 16354, Supreme Court of Washington (April 14, 1921), 770–8.

3. Copy of attorney's oath in Elmer Smith Disbarment and Reinstatement Records, No. 631, Supreme Court of Washington, Olympia [Disbarment Records].

4. Roger Baldwin to the author, May 14, 1973. Baldwin was the founder of the American Civil Liberties Union, an organization that often came to Smith's aid.

5. Herb Edwards, interview with the author, Seattle, Washington, October 1, 1972. A copy of the tape and transcript is in the Labor History Archives, Wayne State University, Detroit, Michigan. Edwards was a Wobbly and friend of Smith's.

"I'M LOOKING FOR TROUBLE"

1. The *Centralia Chronicle* gives a good picture of what the town was like during the early 1900s.

2. Oscar Osburn Winther, *The Great Northwest* (New York: A. A. Knopf, 1947), 326; Dorothy Johansen and Charles Gates, *Empire of the Columbia* (New York: Harper Brothers, 1957), 460.

3. Johansen and Gates, *Empire*, 463.

4. Mabel (Smith) Harris, interview with the author, Moses Lake, Washington, April 23, 1973; Grace (Smith) Skinner, interview with author, Seattle, October 2, 1972; Mary (Smith) Killen, interview with author, Olympia, Washington, September 30, 1972. All three women were sisters-in-law of Elmer Smith. Mabel married Glen, Grace married Harry, and Mary married Jim.

5. Census Report, June 12, 1900, National Archives, Washington, D.C.;

Edna (Smith) Nelson, interview with the author, Gresham, Oregon, September 30, 1972; Harris interview. Nelson married Elmer's brother Bill.

6. Harris, interview with the author, Moses Lake, Washington, September 21, 1974. Isabelle must have felt some loyalty for her heritage, however, when she gave Elmer his middle name of Stuart.

7. Elwyn Robinson, *History of North Dakota* (Lincoln: University of Nebraska Press, 1966), 229.

8. Elwyn Robinson, *The Themes of North Dakota History* (Grand Forks: University of North Dakota, 1959), 1–19.

9. Birthdate from Smith family Bible, in the possession of Edna Nelson. Harris interview, April 23, 1973.

10. Nelson, Killen, and Harris interviews.

11. Harris interview, September 21, 1974.

12. Skinner interview, October 2, 1972; Harris to the author, August 24, 1983.

13. No other records or family memories offer any further explanation.

14. From "Disguised Innocence," original essay in the possession of Virginia Smith Waddell, Tacoma, Washington. Waddell is Elmer Smith's daughter.

15. Henry D. Funk, *History of Macalester College* (St. Paul: Macalester College, 1910), 241–3.

16. Oakley Tripp, interview with the author, Minneapolis, Minnesota, March 9, 1972; Margaret Doty, interview with the author, St. Paul, Minnesota, June 23, 1970. Tripp was a college classmate of Smith's; Doty was a sister of one of Elmer's classmates.

17. Tripp interview; William Bell, interview with the author, Minneapolis, February 23, 1972; Wilbur Fisk, interview with author, South St. Paul, Minnesota, March 4, 1972. Bell and Fisk were classmates of Smith.

18. Bell interview.

19. *Macalester College Bulletin*, December 10, 1910.

20. *St. Paul Pioneer Press*, June 5, 1910.

21. Tripp interview; Bell interview; Fisk interview; Ann Elizabeth Taylor, telephone interview with the author, St. Paul, Minnesota, August 16, 1972. Taylor was a classmate of Smith's.

22. See Macalester yearbooks, 1908–10, for a description of sports activities at the college.

23. *Macalester College Bulletin*, July 1910, 1–2.

24. *Announcement of the St. Paul College of Law, for the year 1912–1913*, 12. In 1957, the school combined with several other law schools and was renamed William Mitchell College of Law.

25. Robert Esko, telephone interview with the author, March 17, 1972. Esko was the principal of South St. Paul High School.

26. John Drews, interview with the author, St. Paul, Minnesota, March 16,

1972; Abe Calmenson, telephone interview with the author, St. Paul, Minnesota, March 15, 1972. Both were Smith's classmates.

27. *Announcement*, 13.

28. Harris interview, September 21, 1974. Harry was a wild boy with a sharp though undisciplined mind. At eighteen he quit high school to join the Navy. As he grew older he earned a reputation as the family's black sheep. His father once told him, "Harry, you're going to die on the gallows." See also Nelson and Killen interviews.

29. Killen interview.

30. Frank Bertagnolli, interview with the author, Greyland, Washington, June 10, 1977; Nelson interview. Bertagnolli worked in the Smith mine.

31. Nelson interview.

32. Connor Harmon, interview with the author, Oregon City, Oregon, September 6, 1972. Harmon married Elmer's sister Dorothy. See also Ralph Winstead, "Evolution of Logging Conditions on the Northwest Coast," *The One Big Union Monthly* (May 1920), 22.

33. Loren Hurd, interview with the author, Olympia, Washington, September 21, 1972. Hurd was Smith's neighbor.

34. Smith's closing argument, "The People of the State of California v. J. H. Casdorf and Earl Firey, Defendants," Superior Court of California, Sacramento County, April 10, 1922, IWW Papers, Wayne State University, Detroit, Michigan; Killen interview.

TIMBER BEASTS AND SOLDIERS

1. Virginia (Smith) Waddell, interview with the author, Tacoma, Washington, June 14, 1977; Smith, "Murder," 36; Elmer Smith to Harry Smith, November 16, 1916, author's collection.

2. Elmer Smith to Harry Smith, November 16, 1916.

3. In one such case, Smith defended a man charged with grand larceny for stealing brass fittings and copper wiring from a logging company. See Case 177, Lewis County Criminal Files, Washington State Archives, Olympia [Criminal Files].

4. "The New Wild West," *The Liberator*, February 1920, 21; "Centralia Tragedy Has Roots in Young Lawyer's Struggle for Justice for Workingman," *Seattle Union Record*, November 13, 1919.

5. Herb Edwards, interview with Tracy Dalton, Seattle, Washington, February 12, 1972. Copy of the tape and transcript in the Labor History Archives, Wayne State University. Edwards was a logger and friend of Smith's. Joyce L. Kornbluth, *Rebel Voices* (Ann Arbor: University of Michigan Press, 1968), 252. For a general description of logging conditions, see Cloice R. Howd, "Industrial Relations in

the West Coast Lumber Industry," U.S. Department of Labor, *Bulletin of the U.S. Bureau of Labor Statistics*, no. 349 (December 1923), 38–44.

6. "Why I Am a Member of the I.W.W.," *Four L Bulletin* (October 1922), 9, 34. The Four L was a labor union begun by the War Department.

7. *IWW Songbook*, 34th ed. (Chicago: IWW, 1973), i.

8. *The Lumber Industry and Its Workers* (Chicago: IWW, 1920), 73.

9. For a general description of IWW-led strikes in Washington, see Robert Tyler, *Rebels of the Woods: The I.W.W. in the Pacific Northwest* (Eugene: University of Oregon, 1967); Philip S. Foner, *History of the Labor Movement in the United States*, Volume 4: *The Industrial Workers of the World 1905–1917* (New York: International Publishers, 1965), 214–25; Howd, "Industrial Relations," 64–67.

10. *Labor Defender*, November 1926, 191–2. The Wobbly was William F. Dunne, who later became chair of the Butte, Montana, American Legion.

11. *Centralia Chronicle*, February 5, 1915; *Centralia Daily Hub*, February 4–5, 1915; *Spokesman Review*, February 6, 1915.

12. W. H. Beal, interview with the author, Centralia, October 4, 1974. Beal was a lawyer who joined the "pick handle brigade." See also *Centralia Daily Hub*, February 4, 1915.

13. Walker C. Smith, *The Everett Massacre* (Chicago: IWW, 1917); Foner, *History of the Labor Movement*, 531–48; John McClelland, *Wobbly War: The Centralia Story* (Tacoma: Washington State Historical Society, 1987), 26, 19.

14. Loggers' cases, here and below, are from Harmon interview.

15. Ralph Chaplin, *The Centralia Conspiracy* (Seattle: IWW, 1920), 31–32.

16. Bertagnolli interview; Nora (Dishong) Beard, interview with the author, Centralia, Washington, September 19, 1972. Beard was Smith's legal secretary.

17. McClelland, *Wobbly War*, 23; Laura (Smith) Willits, interview with the author, Tacoma, Washington, June 12, 1977. Willits was Smith's wife.

18. Elmer to Grace Smith, May 31, 1914, copy in possession of the author.

19. Laura (Smith) Willits, letter to the author, April 4, 1981.

20. Willits letter; unpublished manuscript on Elmer Smith by Virginia (Smith) Waddell, in possession of the author.

21. Notes of an interview of Lucy Anne (Moore) Cloud by Harvey O'Connor, January 1962, in possession of the author. Cloud was a friend and neighbor of Elmer's. See also Willits letter.

22. Nelson interview.

23. McClelland, *Wobbly War*, 45.

24. William Haywood, quoted in John Gambs, *The Decline of the IWW* (New York: Columbia University Press, 1932), 41.

25. For two excellent accounts of the 1917 strike, see Claude W. Nichols Jr., "Brotherhood in the Woods: The Loyal Legion of Loggers and Lumberman, a 20 Year Attempt at Industrial Cooperation" (Ph.D. diss., University of Oregon, Eugene, 1959), 21–52; Howd, "Industrial Relations," 77–85.

26. Robert E. Ficken, "The Wobbly Horrors: Pacific Northwest Lumbermen and the Industrial Workers of the World, 1917–1928," *Labor History* 24 (Summer 1983): 325–42.

27. Melvyn Dubofsky, *We Shall Be All: A History of the Industrial Workers of the World* (Chicago: Quadrangle Books, 1969), 377.

28. Dorothy Nell Schmidt, "Sedition and Criminal Syndicalism in the State of Washington, 1911–1917" (Ph.D. diss., State College of Washington, Pullman, 1940).

29. Robert Bruere, "Following the IWW Trail," *New York Evening Post*, February 16, 1918.

30. Tyler, *Rebels*, 128–30.

31. "Report of the President's Mediation Commission to the President of the United States," January 9, 1918, Macalester College Library, St. Paul, Minnesota.

32. Robert S. Gill, "The Four L's in Lumber," *The Survey*, May 1, 1920, 166. See also Harold Hyman, *Soldiers and Spruce: Origins of the Loyal Legion of Loggers and Lumbermen* (Los Angeles: Institute of Industrial Relations, 1963), 179.

33. *Centralia Chronicle*, January 5, 1918.

34. David Kennedy, *Over Here: The First World War and American Society* (New York: Oxford University Press, 1980), 262.

35. For a general description of the wartime hysteria against the IWW, see Robert Murray, *Red Scare: A Study of National Hysteria, 1919–1920* (New York: McGraw-Hill, 1955).

36. Kennedy, *Over Here*, 83; William Preston Jr., *Aliens and Dissenters: Federal Suppression of Radicals, 1903–1933* (New York: Harper and Row, 1963), 116. See also Murray, *Red Scare*.

37. Willits interview. There are no records that identify what caused the scar tissue.

38. Smith to Laura Magill(1), August [?] 1917, original in the possession of Virginia Waddell.

39. Smith to Laura Magill(2), August [?] 1917, original in the possession of Virginia Waddell.

40. Robert I. Venemon, Lewis County auditor, to the author, February 6, 1975.

41. Beard interview; Marie Fusco, interview with the author, Centralia, Washington, September 19, 1972. Fusco was a former student of Smith's.

42. Willits, letters to the author, March 20, April 4, 1981; *Centralia Chronicle*, February 18, 1918.

43. A. Finan, interview with the author, Centralia, Washington, September 18, 1972. Finan was a student of Smith's.

44. *Centralia Chronicle*, December 30, 1919; Graham testimony, Washington State vs. Britt Smith, et al., trial transcript, Montesano, Washington, January–March 1920. Microfilm of transcript in University of Washington Library, Seattle [Montesano Trial].

45. *Centralia Chronicle*, December 30, 1919. The Chehalis Elks passed a resolution asking the school board to ban German from the schools. See Hollis B. Fultz, *Elkdom in Olympia* (Olympia: BPOE, 1966), 62.

46. *Centralia Chronicle*, December 12, 1919. Several newspapers later reported that Smith had been fired from his job for refusing to sign the oath. During the Montesano trial in 1920, the editor of the *Montesano Vidette* apologized in his column for printing this story after Smith testified that he quit his job. See *Vidette*, March 5, 1920.

LAWLESSNESS LEADS TO BLOODSHED

1. *Centralia Chronicle*, March 31, April 4, April 6, 1917.

2. Chaplin, *Conspiracy*, 24–25.

3. *Centralia Chronicle*, April 19, 1918, 8. Hubbard's uncle was the wealthy lumberman, F. B. Hubbard, with whom Smith had squared off earlier over Smith's homesteaded land. The *Chronicle* also printed long letters from Warren Grimm. See June 25, 1919, for an account of Grimm's experiences in Siberia.

4. *Centralia Chronicle*, March 4, March 28, 1919.

5. Chaplin, *Conspiracy*, 30.

6. *Centralia Chronicle*, April 6, 1918. The police never charged anyone for participation in the raid.

7. Willits letter.

8. Harry was the most extroverted member of the family. He played blackjack until he was broke, and Isabelle often had to buy food for Harry's wife and child. Elmer never gambled and tried unsuccessfully to get Harry to stop. See Grace (Smith) Skinner, interview with the author, Seattle, Washington, April 21, 1973.

9. Willits letter.

10. Killen interview.

11. Waddell manuscript; Killen interview; Willits letter.

12. See W. F. Dunn, "Crime of Centralia," pamphlet, Chicago, 1920, 4–6.

13. Case 344, Criminal Files.

14. Willits letter; Waddell manuscript.

15. "The New Wild West," *The Liberator*, January 1920, 21.

16. *Centralia Chronicle*, February 11, 1919.

17. Murray, *Red Scare*, 58–64; Harvey O'Connor, *Revolution in Seattle: A Memoir* (New York: Monthly Review Press, 1964), 125–45; *Centralia Chronicle*, February 11, 1919.

18. Kennedy, *Over Here*, 262; Philip S. Foner, *History of the Labor Movement in the United States*, Volume 8: *Postwar Struggles 1918–1920* (New York: International Publishers, 1987), 1–10.

19. Murray, *Red Scare*, 71, 75, 124, 153, 193.

20. McClelland, *Wobbly War*, 49.

21. *Centralia Chronicle*, April 11, 1919.

22. Floyd Kaylor, "Terrorists Ruling City of Centralia," *Seattle Union Record*, September 23, 1919; *Centralia Chronicle*, June 6, 1919; "Wild West," 21.

23. *Seattle Union Record*, June 14, 1919; Kaylor, "Terrorists," 1.

24. *Centralia Chronicle*, June 13, 1919; Disbarment Records; Kaylor, "Terrorists," 1.

25. "Speeches by Elmer Smith, Capt. Edward Coll," The Centralia Publicity Committee, March 31, 1929, 2, Hoover Institution on War, Revolution and Peace, Stanford, California; Chaplin, *Conspiracy*, 34.

26. Dunn, "Crime," 5; Chaplin, *Conspiracy*, 32, 34, 44.

27. Chaplin, *Conspiracy*, 35.

28. *Seattle Union Record*, September 23, 1919.

29. *Centralia Chronicle*, June 27, July 7, July 8, 1919.

30. Waddell manuscript; Willits letter, March 20, 1977; *Seattle Union Record*, September 24, 1919.

31. Smith testimony, 2148–2149, Montesano Trial; Chaplin, *Conspiracy*, 44.

32. *Seattle Union Record*, September 2, 1919; *Centralia Chronicle*, July 16, 1919.

33. Britt Smith testimony, 1600, Montesano Trial.

34. Jim Clowers, interview with William Knowles, Evergreen College, Washington, n.d. Clowers was a logger who worked with Britt Smith in the woods after Smith's release from prison.

35. Elmer Smith testimony, 2145–2150, Montesano Trial; Chaplin, *Conspiracy*, 40.

36. *Centralia Chronicle*, October 2, October 17, November 1, 1919.

37. *Centralia Hub*, October 20, 1919.

38. *Seattle Union Record*, October 24, 1919, 4; *Centralia Hub*, October 21, 1919; Smith, "Murder," 14, 34; J.M. Eubanks affidavit, June 10, 1936, Rayfield Becker Papers, Oregon Historical Society, Portland [Becker Papers].

39. Roberts supplementary statement, November 24, 1919, Charles D. Cunningham Papers, The American Legion Library Archives, Indianapolis, Indiana [Cunningham Papers].

40. Smith's legal advice was correct, but only if the Wobblies were in their hall at the time of the attack.

41. Copy of leaflet dated November 4, 1919, in IWW files, University of Washington, Seattle.

42. Smith, "Murder," 14, 36.

43. Testimony of Marie McAllister, 1640–44, Montesano Trial.

44. *Portland Oregonian*, June 26, 1913. Following his experience in Marshfield, Everest received a letter from the governor of Oregon, Oswald West, who decried his mistreatment at the hands of a mob and promised protection should he return: "Should it develop that you have violated any law, you can expect to

be prosecuted. Should it develop that you have suffered through the lawlessness of others, then they shall be prosecuted." Neither would happen to Everest in Centralia. See *Industrial Worker*, July 15, 1922.

45. Charles Everest, letter to author, September 21, 1978; Donald Capron, "The Centralia Riot of 1919: A Study of Pre-New Deal Labor Relations" (M.A. thesis, San Francisco State University, 1981), 136; Britt Smith testimony, 1635, Montesano Trial; Roberts confession of November 17, Cunningham Papers. See also Tom Copeland, "Wesley Everest, IWW Martyr," *Pacific Northwest Quarterly* 77 (October 1986): 122–9.

THE ESSENCE OF LAW AND ORDER

1. Smith printed this song on the back of his business cards. Copy in the author's collection. The author is indebted to Donald Capron and Albert Gunns for their help in analyzing the raid and lynching.

2. Elmer Smith testimony, 2139–2143, Testimony of R. F. Gardner, 812, Testimony of Leslie Johnson, 823, Montesano Trial.

3. For a description of the parade, see the Montesano trial transcript, University of Washington Library; Chaplin, *Conspiracy*, 53–54; Ben Hur Lampman, *Centralia, Tragedy and Trial* (1920; reprint, Seattle: Shorey Book Store 1965), 7–8; McClelland, *Wobbly War*, 72–73.

4. Confession of Loren Roberts of November 17, quoting Bert Bland, read into the trial record, 338, Montesano Trial.

5. There is much conflicting evidence about the actual sequence of events on Tower Avenue that day. This account of the events of November 11, 1919, is based primarily on the Montesano trial transcript and on newspaper articles from the *Centralia Chronicle* and *New York Times*, which had reporters on the scene. The stories of the Associated Press reporter on the scene were carried by the *Seattle Post-Intelligencer* and the *Portland Oregonian*, among other newspapers. See also State vs. Smith et al. (No. 16354), Supreme Court of Washington, April 14, 1921, 197 Pacific Northwestern Reports (1921), 770–8, for a summary of the day's events by the state supreme court.

6. *New York Times*, November 12, 1919; Tyler, *Rebels*, 160.

7. *The Seattle Post-Intelligencer*, November 12, November 13, 1919; *New York Times*, November 12, 1919; *Portland Oregonian*, November 12, 1919.

8. Testimony of Elmer Smith, 3003–3004, Montesano Trial.

9. Testimony of W. H. Graham, 830–836, Montesano Trial.

10. Testimony of physician Lee Scace, 259–273, Montesano Trial.

11. Bertagnolli interview; Letter of Archie Henderson, November 16, 1919, Luke May Papers, University of Washington, Seattle.

12. *New York Times*, November 12, 1919; *Portland Oregonian*, November 12, 1919; Claude Clifford affidavit, December 30, 1936, Becker Papers.

13. *New York Times*, November 12, 1919.

14. *Morning Olympian*, November 13, 1919; *Portland Oregonian*, November 12, 1919. See also the affidavits of eyewitnesses Charles Eagles and Dewey Lamb and the notes of an interview with eyewitness Bob Burrows in the Becker Papers.

15. *Industrial Solidarity*, March 13, 1920.

16. Skinner interview, October 2, 1972; Waddell manuscript.

17. *Centralia Chronicle*, November 12, 1919.

18. Beard interview.

19. *Centralia Chronicle*, November 13, 1919; *New York Times*, November 14, 1919; *Morning Olympian*, November 14, 1919.

20. *Centralia Chronicle*, November 13, 1919.

21. *Olympia Daily Record*, November 13, 1919. See also the *Morning Olympian*, November 13, 1919, for an editorial attacking Smith's role in the shootings.

22. *Portland Oregonian*, November 14, 1919; *New York Times*, November 14, 1919.

23. *New York Times*, November 13, November 14, 1919; *Portland Oregonian*, November 16, 1919.

24. Skinner interview, April 21, 1973; Lloyd Dysart, interview with the author, Centralia, Washington, September 20, 1972; Harris interview, April 23, 1973; Killen interview. Dysart led several of the posses searching for Wobblies.

25. Killen interview.

26. Lucy Anne (Moore) Cloud, interview with the author, Richmond, California, April 7, 1973.

27. *New York Times*, November 14, 1919; *Centralia Chronicle*, November 17, 1919; *Morning Olympian*, November 16, November 18, 1919; *Portland Oregonian*, November 17, 1919.

28. *Boston Evening Transcript*, as quoted in Murray, *Red Scare*, 186; *Post-Intelligencer*, November 12, 1919; newspapers quoted in Murray, *Red Scare*, 186; *Centralia Chronicle*, November 12, November 15, 1919; *New York Times*, November 13, 1919.

29. *Industrialisti*, November 14, 1919.

30. Smith, "Murder," 16; Albert Gunns, *Civil Liberties in Crisis: Pacific Northwest, 1917–1940* (New York: Garland Publishing, 1983), 42–48; Hart to President, November 25, 1919, Department of Justice Investigative Files, University Publications of America. Attorney General A. Mitchell Palmer replied to Hart's letter (December 2, 1919) by saying that there must be proof of specific overt acts of violence or anarchy to justify deportation. The Department of Justice's Bureau of Investigation made weekly reports on IWW activities in and around Seattle and sent them on to J. Edgar Hoover in Washington, D.C. Smith was later to become deeply involved in many criminal syndicalism cases. See Chapter 6 for a description of the law.

31. *Seattle Union Record*, November 12, 1919; Anna Louise Strong, "A

Newspaper Confiscated—and Returned," *The Nation*, December 13, 1919, 738–40.

32. *New Solidarity*, November 22, 1919, as quoted in Robert Murray, *Red Scare*, 186.

33. *Labor Defender*, November 1926, 191–2; Smith, "Murder," 44. The commander was a former Wobbly. In 1917, Wobbly Frank Little had been lynched in Butte.

34. "Rooting Out the Reds," *The Literary Digest*, November 22, 1919, 15.

35. Inquest evidence report, November 13, 1919, Cunningham Papers; *Centralia Chronicle*, November 14, 1919; *Portland Oregonian*, November 14, 1919.

36. *Centralia Chronicle*, November 12, 1919; Lampman, *Centralia*, 13, 16, 17, 15.

37. Pierce testimony, 1481, Montesano Trial. See motion by Smith and Sheehan for change of venue, May 5, 1920, Criminal Files; *Chehalis Bee-Nugget*, November 21, 1919.

38. *Chehalis Bee-Nugget*, November 21, 1919; *Centralia Chronicle*, November 17, 1919; Disbarment Records.

39. *Centralia Chronicle*, November 18, 1919.

40. Flyer dated November 24, 1919, in Luke May Papers.

41. *Centralia Chronicle*, November 21, November 29, December 2, December 3, 1919, January 8, 1920; *Montesano Vidette*, November 14, 1919.

42. *Centralia Chronicle*, December 15, 1919; Andrew and Lucretia Thompson affidavits, April 25, 1925, Becker Papers. Two weeks after the parade, Wilson also gave the main address in Bucoda at a meeting called to form an organization to promote "true Americanism" in the lumber mills where many immigrants worked. See the *Washington Standard*, November 28, 1919.

43. *Centralia Chronicle*, January 7, January 8, 1920.

44. Smith, "Murder," 7.

45. *Centralia Chronicle*, January 5, 1920.

46. *Centralia Chronicle*, December 22, 1919; Waddell interview; Willits interview; Edward Coll, interview with the author, Huntsville, Alabama, November 6, 1974. Coll was an investigator in the Centralia case in the 1920s.

47. *Centralia Chronicle*, December 12, 1919. In the same article, the *Chronicle* accused Smith of refusing to contribute to the Red Cross or any other fund drive in support of the war. Smith denied this charge on the witness stand in Montesano. During the time that Smith was in jail, the Woodsmen of the World cancelled his life insurance policy. See Willits letter.

48. *Chehalis Bee-Nugget*, November 14, 1919.

49. *Montesano Vidette*, January 2, 1920.

50. *Chehalis Bee-Nugget*, November 14, 1919.

51. Joe Murphy, interview with the author, Santa Rosa, California, July 27, 1981. Murphy was a Wobbly held in jail in Montesano following his arrest after the Centralia affair. During the 1920s, Murphy traveled with Smith on some of his speaking tours.

52. *Centralia Chronicle*, December 15, 1919; Murphy interview; McClelland, *Wobbly War*, 115.

53. *Centralia Chronicle*, January 23, 1920; *Montesano Vidette*, December 12, 1919.

54. Nelson interview; Willits interview.

ON THE PRISONERS' BENCH

1. *Seattle Union Record*, March 15, 1920. Strong wrote similar poems that were published in the *Record*. The author is indebted to Albert Gunns and Donald Capron for help in analyzing the Montesano trial.

2. *Centralia Chronicle*, December 12, 1919.

3. *Centralia Chronicle*, January 26, 1920; Becker Papers; Lampman, *Centralia*, 39; Smith, "Murder," 19; Report of A.W. Curtis, a special investigator for the defense, March 10, 1920, Labadie Collection, University of Michigan Library, Ann Arbor.

4. *Montesano Vidette*, January 30, 1920. During the first week of the trial, one Legionnaire from Montesano was reported to have said, "If the jury don't hang them, we will." See Report 17, January 30, 1920, Broussais C. Beck Papers, University of Washington Library, Seattle.

5. Lowell S. Hawley and Ralph Bushnell Potts, *Counsel for the Damned* (New York: J. B. Lippincott, 1953), 17.

6. Albert Gunns, "The Defense Strategy at the Montesano Trial" (paper delivered at the Pacific Northwest Labor History Association Conference, Seattle, Washington, May 15, 1976); Report of operative 165, February 3, 1920, Luke May Papers; Hawley and Potts, *Counsel*, 278.

7. Vanderveer motion to dismiss charges, 1180, Montesano Trial.

8. *Portland Oregonian*, January 31, February 2, 1920.

9. *Portland Oregonian*, February 21, 1920; *The New Solidarity*, February 28, 1920. One case was dismissed because of the flu and one was dropped for lack of evidence.

10. J.M. Eubanks affidavit, November 5, 1936, Becker Papers; Cunningham to Governor Hartley, February 18, 1927, Cunningham to C.B. Clausin, December 3, 1928, and Cunningham to Clarence Spencer, April 12, 1960, Cunningham Papers.

11. Lampman, *Centralia*, 16–17; *Centralia Chronicle*, January 26, 1920. See Luke May Papers. One of the five lumber companies was Hubbard's Eastern Railway and Lumber Company.

12. See Eugene Barnett, "A Rebel Worker's Life," *Labor Defender*, January 1927–March 1928 autobiography series.

13. For descriptions of the defendants, see the Luke May Papers and Chaplin, *Conspiracy*, 15, 21, 62, 68, 70, 72, 74.

14. Luke May Papers; Albert Gunns, "Ray Becker, the Last Centralia

Prisoner," *Pacific Northwest Quarterly* 59 (April 1968); 89. When asked for his draft card in Spokane, Becker threw his Wobbly card on the police desk, saying that was the only card he would ever carry. He added that he would rather die than join the army. See W. H. Turner to Luke S. May, December 26, 1919, Luke May Papers.

15. *Industrial Worker*, October 2, 1920.

16. *Centralia Chronicle*, January 29, 1920.

17. Opening statement by Allen, 1 and 11, Montesano Trial.

18. Statements by Allen, Vanderveer, and Abel, 22, Montesano Trial.

19. Vanderveer opening statement, 26, 42, 50, Montesano Trial.

20. Testimony, 124–157, Montesano Trial.

21. Court admits Roberts confession, 361, Montesano Trial. Roberts' November 18 statement has not survived.

22. Roberts November 17 confession, 331, Montesano Trial.

23. Roberts November 17 confession, 334–340, Bert Bland testimony, 2118–2119, Montesano Trial. Hansen was never captured.

24. Testimony of Morgan, 431–433, Montesano Trial.

25. Morgan's statement inexplicably appears in Cunningham's trial records that were later donated to the American Legion Library. See Morgan statement, November 24, 1919, Cunningham Papers.

26. *Centralia Chronicle*, January 29, 1920.

27. Willits interview; Willits letter.

28. Willits interview.

29. Killen interview; Skinner interview, April 21, 1973; *Seattle Union Record*, February 5, 1920. During the trial, Jim was arrested and fined for driving his car past a street car while it was discharging passengers. It is likely that the arrest was motivated by the trial, and Jim announced he would appeal the conviction. The results of any appeal are unknown. See the *Centralia Chronicle*, February 11, 1920.

30. Vanderveer motions and court ruling, 1176–1207, Montesano Trial.

31. Trial transcript, 1430 ff., Montesano Trial; Joe Murphy, interview. See reports of rumors by operatives in Luke May Papers.

32. Montesano Trial, 1433.

33. See juror affidavits from Frank Glen, January 11, 1936, Carl Hulten, July 20, 1936, P.V. Johnson, May 9, 1936, V. G. Robinson, January 11, 1936, Becker Papers.

34. *Industrial Solidarity*, March 13, 1920.

35. Testimony of Barnett, 1213–1214, Testimony of J.G. McAllister, 1337–48, Testimony of Marie McAllister, 1354–64, Montesano Trial.

36. Testimony of Elsie Hornback, 599–602, Montesano Trial.

37. Roberts' mother testified that her father and two cousins were insane. See testimony of Edna Roberts, 1526, Montesano Trial.

38. *Portland Oregonian*, March 11, 1920.

39. Testimony of Britt Smith, 1655–94, Montesano Trial.

40. Testimony of Mike Sheehan, 1939–52, Testimony of James McInerney, 1976–80, Montesano Trial.

41. Testimony of O. C. Bland, 2041–64, Testimony of John Lamb, 2087–98, Montesano Trial.

42. Testimony of Frank Bickford, 2015–24, Montesano Trial.

43. After the trial the charges were quietly dropped. See Testimony of Guy Bray, 2158–82, Testimony of J. Cook, 2184–2216, Montesano Trial.

44. Testimony of Mort Barger, 2299–2305, Montesano Trial.

45. Testimony of Mrs. T. W. Siddel, T. W. Siddel, Mrs. Nelson Hiatt, Serrena Armengrout, Maggie Stockdale, 2624–40, Testimony of Lucy Thrall, 2649–52, Testimony of T. H. McCleary, 3197–3200, Testimony of H. W. Thompson, 3221–3224, Testimony of B. H. Rhodes, 3227–32, Montesano Trial.

46. Statement by Vanderveer, 2934–2936, Montesano Trial. Without the test of cross-examination, this story cannot be accepted uncritically. We do know, however, that the lights went out.

47. See records of operatives spying on Vanderveer in Luke May Papers; Smith, "Murder," 18; Report of A. W. Curtis.

48. Smith later recalled that Graham had come to his office during the war to seek his help in claiming an exemption from military service. See testimony of W. G. Graham, 836–841, Montesano Trial.

49. Nelson interview; *Industrial Worker*, March 2, 1920.

50. Testimony of Elmer Smith, 2140, Montesano Trial.

51. Ibid., 2514–2520.

52. Ibid., 2530–35.

53. A report on the front page of the *Seattle Daily Times* on May 25, 1920, said that Ole Hansen (?), the IWW fugitive from Centralia, was found dead in the woods near Aberdeen of an apparent suicide. No confirmation of this has been found. Later rumors reported that Hanson was working on a ship in Hong Kong in 1921. See Cunningham Papers.

54. Lampman, *Centralia*, 68.

55. Chaplin, *Conspiracy*, 76.

56. *Seattle Post-Intelligencer*, March 14, 1920.

57. State v. Smith et al., 777.

58. See juror affidavits, W. E. Inmon, July 3, 1936, E. E. Sweitzer and W. E. Inmon, May 15, 1922, and P. V. Johnson, May 29, 1922, Becker Papers.

59. See juror affidavits, E. E. Sweitzer and W. E. Inmon, May 15, 1922, E. E. Torpen, June 5, 1936, Carl Hulten, July 20, 1936, and P. V. Johnson, May 9, 1936, Becker Papers; State v. Smith et al., 770–8.

60. *Portland Oregonian*, March 15, 1920; *Centralia Chronicle*, March 15, 1920; *The American Legion Weekly*, April 2, 1920; *Montesano Vidette*, March 19, 1920; Anna Louise Strong, "Centralia: An Unfinished Story," *The Nation* (April 17, 1920), 508–9; Lampman, *Centralia*, 64.

61. *Centralia Publicity Bulletin*, March 24, 1932.

62. *Spokesman-Review*, March 15, 1920.

63. *Portland Oregonian*, March 15, 1920; *Montesano Vidette*, March 19, 1920.

64. *Centralia Chronicle*, May 13, 1920. See statement of expenses in Cunningham Papers.

65. *Industrial Worker*, May 29, 1920.

66. Eubanks had been in attendance at the October 1919 Elks meeting, and he had testified at the trial for the defense.

67. J. M. Eubanks affidavit, June 10, 1936, Becker Papers; *Centralia Chronicle*, May 15, 1920; Willits interview.

LEST WE FORGET

1. This song was written to raise money for the prisoners' release committee efforts. See IWW Papers, University of Washington, Seattle.

2. Johansen and Gates, *Empire*, 551–628.

3. *Centralia Chronicle*, June 1, 1920; McClelland, *Wobbly War*, 178.

4. Ralph Chaplin, *Wobbly: The Rough and Tumble Story of an American Radical* (Chicago: University of Chicago Press, 1948), 301.

5. Chaplin, *Conspiracy*, 63.

6. Nearly every historian that repeats the Everest castration myth uses Chaplin as the source. In 1936, members of a committee organized to work for the release of Ray Becker, the last Centralia prisoner, obtained an affidavit from Claude Clifford who claimed to have witnessed the castration in the car. But without any supporting evidence, Clifford's story cannot be believed. That the affidavit was given seventeen years after the alleged event in response to defense efforts seriously reduces its credibility. It is further weakened by Clifford's claim that he was called to testify during the trial, although his name does not appear on the list of witnesses. For more detail about the castration story and other myths about Everest, see Copeland, "Wesley Everest," 122–9.

7. Paul Murphy, *The Meaning of Freedom of Speech* (Westport, Conn.: Greenwood Publishing Company, 1972), 44 ff.; Schmidt, "Sedition"; Gunns, *Civil*, 38–40.

8. *Session Laws of 1919 of the State of Washington*, Chapter 174, S.S.B. 236, 518–19. Two other related laws were passed on the same day. One made it a crime of sabotage to interfere or advocate interference with an enterprise that employed wage-earners or to injure or destroy any property. The other made it illegal to display any flag or banner of any group that advocated any theory or form of government antagonistic to the Constitution. Violating either law was a felony with a penalty of up to ten years in prison. *Session Laws of 1919 of the State of Washington*, Chapter 173, S.B. 181, 517–18, Chapter 181, S.S.B. 137, 555–6.

9. Eldridge Foster Dowell, *A History of the Criminal Syndicalism Legislation in the United States* (Baltimore: Johns Hopkins Press, 1939), 147.

10. *New York Times*, January 4, 1920; Hawley and Potts, *Counsel*, 285–6; *Seattle Post-Intelligencer*, February 2, 1920; Gunns, *Civil*, 46–55.

11. *Centralia Chronicle*, June 8–14, 1920; 1918 resolution quoted in *Industrial Worker*, January 3, 1920.

12. Letter from U.S. Army Recruiting Station in Seattle to Director of Military Intelligence, Washington, D.C., December 1920, U.S. Military Intelligence Report, Surveillance of Radicals in the U.S., 1917–1941, University of Minnesota Libraries, Minneapolis.

13. *Centralia Chronicle*, July 6, 1920.

14. *Seattle Union Record*, June 15, 1920.

15. *Industrial Solidarity*, July 3, 1920.

16. *Bellingham American Reveille*, June 22, 1920.

17. Broussais Beck Papers; Smith testimony before the Board of Law Examiners, October 15, 1923, Disbarment Records; *Seattle Union Record*, May 24, July 12, July 27, 1920.

18. See operative reports July 4, 1920, Luke May Papers.

19. J. Edgar Hoover took over the Bureau of Investigation in 1924. In 1935, the Bureau was renamed the Federal Bureau of Investigation. Elmer Smith's U.S. Department of Justice Bureau files, obtained through the Freedom of Information Act, contain 194 pages of reports, mostly verbatim accounts of his speeches, from operatives working out of the Seattle office primarily for the years 1922–23. Internal evidence suggests that these pages do not constitute his entire file. The files will hereafter be cited as Bureau Files. The author also obtained files on Ray Becker and Britt Smith, but the material in these files is of limited interest.

20. *Centralia Chronicle*, July 1, 1920.

21. Nathan Fine, *Labor and Farmer Parties in the United States, 1828–1928* (New York: Russell and Russell, 1961), 396; Hamilton Cravens, "A History of the Washington Farmer-Labor Party, 1918–1924" (M.A. thesis, University of Washington, Seattle, 1962), 107.

22. *Centralia Chronicle*, September 6, September 10, September 15, 1920.

23. *Centralia Chronicle*, September 15, 1920.

24. *Centralia Chronicle*, September 20, October 20, 1920; Robert Leslie Cole, "The Democratic Party in Washington State, 1919–1933: Barometer of Social Change" (Ph.D. diss., University of Washington, Seattle, 1972), 36.

25. *Seattle Union Record*, September 27, October 20, 1920.

26. Harvey O'Connor, letter to the author, August 31, 1972.

27. See copies of the *Farmer-Labor Call* in the Luke May Papers.

28. *Farmer-Labor Call*, October 22, 1920.

29. O'Connor letter; Harmon interview.

30. *Farmer-Labor Call*, October 22, 1920.

31. *Chehalis Bee-Nugget*, October 29, 1920.

32. *Farmer-Labor Call*, October 22, 1920.

33. Ibid.

34. *Centralia Chronicle*, October 5, October 11, 1920.

35. *Seattle Union Record*, October 12, 1920.

36. Beard interview; *Centralia Chronicle*, October 14, October 20, 1920.

37. *Farmer-Labor Call*, October 19, 1920; Harmon interview.

38. *Farmer-Labor Call*, October 19, 1920.

39. *Farmer-Labor Call*, October 22, 1920.

40. *Seattle Union Record*, October 26, 1920; Skinner interview.

41. For the Winlock incident, see Harmon interview; Beard interview; *Centralia Chronicle*, October 29, 1920; *Seattle Union Record*, October 28, 1920.

42. The boy was arrested but was later released by the police.

43. *Centralia Chronicle*, November 1, 1920. The newspaper in the neighboring town of Chehalis ran the same ad on October 29. See the *Chehalis Bee-Nugget*, October 29, 1920.

44. *Seattle Union Record*, November 3, 1920.

45. *Seattle Union Record*, November 22, 1920; *Chehalis Bee-Nugget*, November 5, 1920.

46. Harvey O'Connor to Harry Ault, November 25, 1953, Harry Ault Papers, University of Washington Libraries, Seattle. In Chehalis, Smith won only 18 percent of the vote, while gaining 31 percent for the entire county. See the *Chehalis Bee-Nugget*, November 5, 1920.

47. Cravens, "History," 134; Fine, *Labor*, 394.

48. *Seattle Union Record*, December 3, 1920, January 5, January 18, 1921.

49. *Seattle Union Record*, November 12, 1920, 2.

THE KICKING JACKASS

1. *Industrial Worker*, April 30, 1924.

2. Lucy Anne (Moore) Cloud, interview with the author, Richmond, California, August 24, 1972. Tape recording at Labor History Archives, Wayne State University, Detroit. See also Killen interview.

3. Operative C. Petrovitsky report, August 31, 1923, Bureau Files.

4. Smith testimony before the Board of Law Examiners, October 5, 1923, Disbarment Records.

5. Ibid.

6. *Industrial Worker*, September 3, 1921.

7. Fay Brabson, Assistant Chief of Staff for Military Intelligence, to Director of Military Intelligence, August 31, 1921, Military Intelligence Records.

8. Roger Baldwin, letter to the author, May 14, 1973.

9. Willits interview.

10. *Industrial Worker*, July 16, 1921; *Industrial Solidarity*, April 21, 1923.

11. *Industrial Worker*, July 15, 1922.

12. *Industrial Worker*, July 16, 1921, January 13, 1923, April 12, 1924; Plaintiff's exhibit of transcript of Smith's speech in Centralia on April 1, 1923, Disbarment Records.

13. McClelland, *Wobbly War*, 197; Agent Sausele report, August 4, 1921, Military Intelligence Records; Agent R. E. Skelly report, May 3, 1923, Bureau Files.

14. *Industrial Worker*, December 25, 1920.

15. Smith quoting Lincoln during disbarment hearing before State Board of Law Examiners, October 5, 1923, Disbarment Records; operative report from New York, August 30, 1921, Military Intelligence Records.

16. Cloud interview, August 24, 1972.

17. Agent R. A. Darling report, February 1, 1923, Bureau Files.

18. *Seattle Union Record*, January 31, 1922.

19. *Industrial Worker*, April 30, 1924.

20. Smith admired lecturer and agnostic Ralph Ingersoll because he stood up for his principles against strong opposition and because he had a wonderful speaking voice. Murphy interview.

21. In Portland, Oregon, and Raymond, Washington, city police blocked the entrance to Smith's meeting halls. Not to be intimidated, Smith later returned to both cities to give his talks. *Centralia Chronicle*, January 24, February 14, February 21, 1921; *Seattle Union Record*, March 22, 1921.

22. *Industrial Worker*, February 25, 1922.

23. Ibid.

24. *Industrial Worker*, February 25, 1922.

25. *Industrial Worker*, March 4, 1922.

26. *Centralia Chronicle*, February 20, 1922.

27. Woodrow C. Whitten, "Criminal Syndicalism and the Law in California 1919–1927," *Transactions of the American Philosophical Society* 59, part 2 (1969).

28. *The Humboldt Times*, March 19, 1922; Herb Edwards, letter to the author, January 16, 1972; *Industrial Worker*, April 1, 1922.

29. *Industrial Worker*, April 1, 1922.

30. *Seattle Union Record*, March 25, 1922; *Industrial Worker*, April 1, 1922; *San Francisco Call and Bulletin*, March 21, 1922; *The Humboldt Times*, March 19, 1922.

31. *The Humboldt Times*, March 19, 1922; Edwards letter; Edwards interview with the author; Edwards interview with Dalton.

32. Edwards letter; Edwards interview with the author; Edwards interview with Dalton.

33. Smith testimony before State Board of Law Examiners, October 9, 1923, Disbarment Records; Edwards interview with Dalton.

34. *The Humboldt Times*, March 21, 1922.

35. *The Humboldt Times*, March 21, 1922.

36. *San Francisco Call and Bulletin*, March 21, 1922.

37. Copy of letter in the author's possession.

38. Willits interview.

39. *Industrial Worker*, March 5, 1921; Willits interview; Laura Willits, letter, April 4, 1981.

40. Skinner interview, October 2, 1972; Harris interview, September 21, 1974; Waddell manuscript; Harmon interview.

41. Iver Grundfossen, interview with the author, Gresham, Oregon, September 6, 1972. Grundfossen was a logger and friend of the Smith family. See also Nelson interview.

42. Harmon interview.

43. *Seattle Union Record*, December 28, 1920; *Centralia Chronicle*, June 21, 1921; *New York Times*, June 23, 1921.

44. Coll interview; Murphy interview; Edward Coll, letter to the author, May 12, 1977.

45. *Defense News Service*, May 26, 1922, ACLU files. This news sheet for American labor editors was published by the IWW General Defense Committee in Chicago.

46. *Defense News Service*, June 10, 1922.

47. *Daily Washingtonian*, May 19, 1922.

48. Smith testimony, Disbarment Records; "C. S. Smith, Elmer Smith Wins Reinstatement," news release, n.d., Hoover Institution, Stanford University, Stanford, California; *Industrial Worker*, February 18, 1922.

49. *Seattle Union Record*, November 7, 1922.

50. William Haag, "Riot and Reaction," 1977, Olympia, Washington (unpublished paper). Haag was a resident of Centralia.

51. *Seattle Union Record*, November 8, 1922.

ACID IN A WOBBLY SHOE

1. Preston, *Aliens*, 258, 262–3. Smith admired Debs for his anti-war stand. See Harmon interview.

2. *Industrial Pioneer*, March 1921, 45; *Seattle Union Record*, March 11, 1921; *Industrial Worker*, March 26, 1921. That same month the U.S. Supreme Court refused to review the convictions of Chaplin, Bill Haywood, and other IWW leaders for violating the Espionage Act. Chaplin and the others began serving their time in prison, although some jumped their bail, including Haywood who fled to Russia where he died in 1928. See Dubofsky, *We Shall Be All*, 459, 461.

3. *Centralia Chronicle*, April 16, April 27, 1921.

4. *Centralia Chronicle*, April 27, May 30, June 3, June 6, June 9, 1921. "Footloose" was a common IWW term for someone who was unemployed.

5. *Industrial Worker*, June 11, 1921; *Centralia Chronicle*, June 9, 1921.

6. Austin Goodell, "Wobblies at Centralia See Change Come Over City and its Citizens," *Seattle Union Record*, June 13, 1921.

7. *Seattle Union Record*, June 16, 1921. Known for being pushy and somewhat of a hothead, Glen probably did not try very hard to avoid arrest.

8. Case 492, Criminal Files.

9. Plaintiff's exhibit GG, Disbarment Records.

10. Hiney Heathcote, interview with the author, Seattle, Washington, September 29, 1974.

11. Report of Operative, June 15, 1921, Luke May Papers. The Luke May agency was the same one hired by the prosecution at the Montesano trial. The name of the agent was Marion Karolchuck.

12. *Seattle Union Record*, June 18, 1921; *Centralia Chronicle*, July 5, 1921; Elmer Smith, "A Message from Five Jailed Workers in the Lewis County Jail," 1923, American Civil Liberties Union Files, selected papers in the University of Washington Library, Seattle [ACLU Files]; Affidavit by C. Austin Goodell, July 5, 1921, Criminal Files; Beffel to Baldwin, April 1, 1925, ACLU Files.

13. *Industrial Worker*, July 16, 1921; *Industrial Pioneer* (August 1921), 31.

14. George Kirchwey, "A Survey of the Workings of the Criminal Syndicalism Law of California," California Committee of the ACLU, December 1926. Out of 264 trials, 164 men were convicted. Later, 114 cases were appealed and 55 were reversed.

15. Kirchwey, "Survey," 9–10; Zechariah Chafee Jr., "California Justice," *The New Republic*, September 19, 1923, 97–100.

16. *Industrial Worker*, April 22, 1922.

17. Ibid.

18. Ibid.; Edwards interview with Dalton.

19. Smith's closing argument, Casdorf and Firey Defendants, Labor History Archives, Wayne State University.

20. Ibid.

21. As quoted in *Industrial Worker*, April 22, 1922; *The Nation* 144 (April 19, 1922): 456.

22. *Industrial Worker*, April 22, 1922.

23. *California District Defense Committee Bulletin*, March–April 1922, IWW Files, University of Washington, Seattle.

24. *Industrial Worker*, April 22, 1922.

25. *Industrial Worker*, June 10, 1922; *Industrial Solidarity*, July 15, 1922.

26. *Industrial Worker*, June 10, 1922; Agent Edward P. Morse report, June 3, 1922, Bureau Files.

27. *Industrial Worker*, June 10, 1922; People v. Eaton, 213 P 275, Pacific Reporter, January 26, 1923.

28. *Industrial Worker*, July 8, 1922.

29. Ibid.

30. Ibid.; Agent Edward P. Morse report, July 1, 1922, Bureau Files.

31. *Industrial Worker*, July 8, 1922.

32. Edwards interview with author.

33. *Seattle Union Record*, October 16, 1922; *Industrial Worker*, October 21, October 28, 1922; Gunns, *Civil*, 220–2. The following March, Smith won another criminal syndicalism case in Pasco, Washington, when the prosecutor announced that the charges would not hold. The March 24, 1923, *Industrial Worker* noted that convictions in such cases were extremely difficult to come by since the Montesano case.

34. Smith testimony, Disbarment Records. Many of the cases never came to trial. Smith handled preliminary motions for cases in Washington, Oregon, California, Montana, and Idaho. Between 1919 and 1932, Washington courts convicted eighty-six men under the criminal syndicalism laws. See Tyler, *Rebels*, 150.

35. Edwards interview with Dalton.

GET THOMAS JEFFERSON

1. *Seattle Union Record*, February 17, 1923; *Industrial Worker*, March 3, 1923.
2. *Industrial Worker*, February 24, 1923.
3. Agent T. N. Henry report, February 15, 1923, Bureau Files.
4. Smith to Baldwin, February 27, 1923, ACLU Files.
5. Copy of letter in agent T. N. Henry report, February 19, 1923, Bureau Files.
6. *Centralia Chronicle*, February 19, 1923; Smith to Baldwin, February 27, 1923, ACLU Files; *Industrial Worker*, February 24, 1923.
7. Testimony of James Compton and George Barner before the State Board of Law Examiners, October 2, 1923, Disbarment Records; *Industrial Worker*, February 24, 1923.
8. *Centralia Chronicle*, February 20, 1923; Smith to Baldwin, February 27, 1923, ACLU Files; *Industrial Worker*, February 28, 1923. Buxton was eventually paid by the court.
9. Baldwin to Barner, February 19, 1923, ACLU Files.
10. Barner to Baldwin, February 21, 1923, ACLU Files.
11. Baldwin to Barner, February 21, 1923, Baldwin to Smith, February 21, 1923, ACLU Files.
12. Smith to Baldwin, February 27, 1923, ACLU Files; *Centralia Chronicle*, February 24, 1923.
13. Bertagnolli interview.
14. *Centralia Chronicle*, February 26, February 27, 1923; *Seattle Union Record*, February 27, 1923; Agent T. N. Henry report, March 2, 1923, Bureau Files.
15. *Centralia Chronicle*, February 27, 1923.
16. *Centralia Chronicle*, February 24, 1923.
17. *Industrial Worker*, March 7, March 10, 1923.
18. Elmer Smith, "A Message from the City Jail of Centralia, Wash.," ACLU Files.
19. *Industrial Worker*, March 3, 1923; Smith to Baldwin, February 27, 1923, ACLU Files.
20. Baldwin to Smith, March 5, 1923, Smith to Baldwin, March 8, 1923, ACLU Files.
21. Agent T. N. Henry report, March 29, 1923, Bureau Files.
22. Robert Whitaker to Baldwin, March 19, 1923, ACLU Files; *Industrial Worker*, March 24, 1923.

23. Ibid.

24. Elmer Smith, "Education! Organization!" leaflet, ACLU Files. Although Smith tells this story in the third person in the leaflet, he made it clear in his speeches that it happened to him. See Edward P. Coll to J. M. McClelland Jr., September 25, 1972, copy in the possession of author. Coll was the American Legionnaire whose work on the Centralia case in the late 1920s contributed to the release of the prisoners (see Chapter 13). This was not the first time Smith had been arrested while citing the Declaration of Independence. A similar arrest occurred in Aberdeen in 1922. See the *Farmer-Labor Call*, February 16, 1922, ACLU Files.

25. Whitaker to Baldwin, March 19, 1923, ACLU Files.

26. *Seattle Union Record*, March 19, 1923.

27. Case 600, Criminal Files; *Seattle Union Record*, March 27, 1923.

28. Smith, "Education!" ACLU Files.

29. *Industrial Solidarity*, April 21, 1923.

30. Heathcote interview.

31. *Industrial Solidarity*, April 21, 1923.

32. Smith to Baldwin, April 2, 1923, ACLU Files; *Industrial Solidarity*, April 21, 1923; Agent T. N. Henry report, April 7, 1923, Bureau Files; Case 600, Criminal Files.

THE LUMBERJACK AND THE MULE

1. "In the Matter of the Proceedings for the Disbarment of Elmer S. Smith," Complaint Before the State Board of Law Examiners, ACLU Files.

2. Ibid.; *Centralia Chronicle*, July 6, 1923.

3. "The Disbarment of Elmer S. Smith," ACLU Files.

4. Plaintiff's exhibit GG, Disbarment Records.

5. Smith to Robert Dunn, June 18, 1923, ACLU Files.

6. Smith to Dunn, June 14, 1923, ACLU Files.

7. Dunn to Duncan, June 8, 1923, Dunn to Smith, June 8, 1923, ACLU Files.

8. Baldwin to Clarence C. Dill, June 12, 1923, ACLU Files.

9. Dill to Baldwin, June 18, 1923, ACLU Files.

10. Smith to Baldwin, July 7, June 14, 1923, ACLU Files; *The Nation* 117 (July 4, 1923): 2.

11. *Seattle Union Record*, April 26, 1923; *Centralia Chronicle*, April 25, April 27, 1923; Nichols, "Brotherhood," 127–8.

12. *Seattle Union Record*, May 2, 1923.

13. Agent R. A. Darling report, May 3, 1923, Bureau Files.

14. *Seattle Union Record*, May 8, 1923; Nichols, "Brotherhood," 128.

15. *Seattle Union Record*, April 27, 1923.

16. Smith testimony, Disbarment Records.

17. During the same speech, Smith called for a radical solution to eco-

nomic conditions under which workers suffered: "The next time anybody asks you how the workers are going to take over industry, I want you to tell them that you have paid for those industries a million times in blood, in sweat and in bent back in poverty stricken and hard old age, you have paid for it a million times. And I want you to ask him this question, 'If a man steals my watch and I find that watch in his possession and I am a bigger man than he is, how am I going to get back that watch?' That is an economic question." Plaintiff's exhibit G, Disbarment Records.

18. Vanderveer's Demurrer, June 25, 1923, board decision, July 5, 1923, Disbarment Records; *Centralia Chronicle*, July 5, July 6, 1923.

19. *Industrial Worker*, July 18, 1923.

20. Cloud interview, August 24, 1972; Willits interview, June 12, 1977.

21. Amended and Supplemental Complaint, August 1, 1923, Disbarment Records.

22. Albert De Silver to Dunn, July 13, 1923, ACLU Files.

23. Walter Nelles to Dunn, July 8, 1923, ACLU Files.

24. *Industrial Worker*, August 29, September 5, 1923; *Centralia Chronicle*, August 29, 1923; Agent C. Petrovitsky report, August 31, 1923, Bureau Files.

25. *Seattle Union Record*, September 4, 1923; *The Federated Press Bulletin*, September 1, 1923.

26. Clipping of the *Republic* of September 21, 1923, in Vanderveer's motion for a new trial, October 1, 1923, Disbarment Records.

27. Statement of Facts, Case 631 Before the State Board of Law Examiners, October 1, 1923, Disbarment Records; *Centralia Chronicle*, October 1, 1923.

28. Brief of Attorney General, May 27, 1924, quoting from "The Revolutionary IWW," Disbarment Records.

29. Ibid. Prosecutors had used the similar tactic of introducing songs from the *IWW Songbook* to try to show the violent nature of the IWW during a 1918 trial of Wobbly leaders in Wichita. See Foner, *History*, Vol. 8, 213.

30. Testimony and Vanderveer's motion, October 1, 1923, Disbarment Records.

31. Testimony of P. J. Welinder, October 3, 1923, Disbarment Records.

32. Testimony of Vanderveer, October 4, October 9, 1923, Disbarment Records.

33. Testimony of Smith, October 5, 1923, Disbarment Records. In a letter to the ACLU before the hearing, Smith commented on the sometimes inflammatory nature of the IWW publications: "there was a time when most of the literature on the IWW was handled on an open forum basis and a great many things were published which [were] to say the least rather crude and undiplomatic." Smith to Robert Dunn, June 14, 1923, ACLU Files.

34. Ibid. A few years later, Smith came home to find his children playing "Onward Christian Soldiers" on the record player. He yanked the record away and shouted that if he ever caught them playing it again, he would break it. See Stuart Smith interview.

35. Testimony of Smith, October 8, 1923, Disbarment Records.

36. Ibid; Testimony of Vanderveer, October 9, 1923, Disbarment Records; Letter of R. G. Sharpe (special agent quoted in Henry's report) to T. N. Henry, November 14, 1923, Bureau Files.

37. Report, Findings of Fact and Recommendations, January 24, 1924, Disbarment Records.

38. Ibid.

39. Ibid.

THE SPIRIT OF PERSECUTION

1. This song was a favorite of Smith's.

2. Preston, *Aliens*, 263; Dubofsky, *We Shall Be All*, 459–62.

3. *Seattle Union Record*, January 5, 1924.

4. Thomas Nash to Lucille Milner, November 3, 1925, ACLU Files. Milner was a field secretary for the ACLU. The criminal syndicalism prisoners refused to cooperate with the ACLU's efforts to free them, because the liberal organization argued that they should accept pardons.

5. The four criminal syndicalism prisoners were Thomas Nash, Frank Nash, William Moudy, and Fred Shuttle. Their principled stand cost them an extra three to four years in prison. Smith supported their decision, although he did try to get the governor to commute their sentences to time served. Eventually, the men accepted individual paroles and were released in 1926 and 1927. See Hart telegram to ACLU, December 19, 1923, Hart to Vanderveer, July 8, 1924, Smith to ACLU, March 6, 1924, Smith to Milner, December 7, 1925, John Turner (acting secretary of the IWW General Defense Committee) to Baldwin, September 22, 1926, ACLU Files; *Industrial Solidarity*, April 29, 1925; *Labor Defender* (April 1927), 62.

6. Dubofsky, *We Shall Be All*, 466–7.

7. Testimony of Elmer Smith before the Board of Law Examiners, October 5, 1923, Disbarment Records.

8. Barnett's book is in the possession of Donald Capron, San Francisco. Over the years, Smith and the Centralia Publicity Committee sold a variety of items to raise money, including ten-cent postcard pictures of Wesley Everest, special Centralia IWW stamps and IWW songbooks, bead necklaces, hair handbags, and dog collars and other items woven by the prisoners. See Becker Papers; Joe Murphy interview; *Labor Defender* (October 1926), 182.

9. Brief in Support of Respondent's Petition for Review, April 14, 1924, Disbarment Records; *Centralia Chronicle*, April 18, 1924; *Industrial Worker*, June 14, 1924.

10. Case number 659, February 17, 1924, Criminal Files; Cloud interview, August 24, 1972.

11. *Industrial Solidarity*, May 3, 1924; Coll interview; Willits interview; Murphy interview.

12. *Seattle Union Record*, June 17, 1924; Probate Records, Lewis County Clerk's Office, Chehalis, Washington; *Industrial Solidarity*, November 19, 1924.

13. *Seattle Union Record*, July 5, July 7, July 24, 1924; Cravens, "History," 222–5; *Industrial Worker*, November 12, 1924; Beffel to Baldwin, March 7, 1925, ACLU Files.

14. Smith to Beffel, n.d., Tamiment Library, New York University. See also Smith to ACLU, March 6, 1924, ACLU Files. Beffel was a reporter for the liberal newspaper *New York Call* at the Montesano trial and a long-time supporter of the IWW.

15. Cravens, "History," 203; Joseph Tripp, "Progressive Labor Laws in Washington State, 1900–1925" (Ph.D. diss., University of Washington, Seattle, 1973), 230.

16. *Industrial Worker*, July 26, August 23, 1924.

17. *Industrial Worker*, August 2, 1924.

18. *Industrial Worker*, August 30, 1924.

19. Cloud interview, August 24, 1972; Murphy interview; Nelson interview.

20. In the summer of 1925, Smith traveled to California with his family to visit a hotsprings health resort for treatment for his ulcer; they found that the place had been deserted for years. On the trip he also gave several speeches on behalf of the IWW in San Francisco and Los Angeles. See *Industrial Unionist*, July 19, August 1, August 8, 1925; Willits letter.

21. Cloud interview, April 7, 1973; Killen interview.

22. Cloud interview, August 24, 1972; Waddell manuscript; Willits interview.

23. Willits interview, June 14, 1977; Waddell manuscript; Waddell interview, June 12, 1977.

24. Waddell interview.

25. Skinner interview, April 21, 1973; Stuart Smith, interview with the author, Bakersfield, California, October 16, 1974. Stuart is Elmer's son.

26. Cloud interview, August 24, 1972; Waddell interview.

27. Willits interview.

28. Cravens, "History," 244–5; Tripp, "Progressive," 278; *The Federated Press Bulletin*, November 22, 1924.

29. In one affidavit, Ben Cassagranda's widow said that before leaving the house for the parade her husband had told her, "This may be the last time you will see me." See Florence Casagranda Mahar affidavit, October 17, 1924, Becker Papers.

30. *Industrial Worker*, November 19, 1924; *Seattle Union Record*, May 26, 1924; *Centralia Chronicle*, November 10, 1924; *Centralia Tribune*, November 13, 1924.

31. In the Matter of the Proceedings for the Disbarment of Elmer S. Smith, No. 631, En Banc. February 24, 1925, Washington Supreme Court, 288–9.

32. Many of these quoted articles had not been presented in evidence before the Board of Law Examiners. See ibid., 289–91. Justice K. Mackintosh, who wrote the majority opinion, had written a letter two days after the 1919 Armistice Day tragedy praising the returned soldiers. See *Industrial Worker*, April 12, 1924.

33. Draft of opinions, n.d., Disbarment Records.

34. Vanderveer to Baldwin, June 27, 1925, ACLU Files; *The New Republic* (August 19, 1925), 331; *The Nation* (July 8, 1925), 57; *The Federated Press Bulletin*, March 4, March 11, 1925; *Federated Industries of Washington Weekly Business Letter*, March 2, 1925, ACLU Files.

35. Petition for Rehearing, March 26, 1925, Disbarment Records.

36. Case number 714, April 24, 1925, Criminal Files.

37. Beffel to Baldwin, April 29, 1925, ACLU Files.

38. Ascher to Smith, June 19, 1925, ACLU Files.

39. Ibid.; Smith to Ascher, June 27, 1925, ACLU Files.

THE CONSCIENCE OF THE LEGION

1. Smith sang this song during the car trips to Walla Walla to appear before the parole board. See Coll interview.

2. For a good description of the state of the Centralia case in the mid-1920s, see George Moresby, "The Status of the Centralia Case," *Defense Bulletin*, vol. 1, no. 1, 4th quarter of 1924, IWW Papers, University of Washington Libraries, Seattle; *Seattle Union Record*, October 7, 1924.

3. Beffel to Welinder, March 11, 1925, John Beffel Papers, Tamiment Library, New York [Beffel Papers]. Welinder worked for IWW Defense Committee in Chicago.

4. *Industrial Pioneer* (April 1925), 45.

5. Theodore Draper, *American Communism and Soviet Russia* (New York: Viking Press, 1960), 180–2. See also *Labor Defender*, various issues, 1926–1932. In 1936, the Free Ray Becker Committee was formed by the International Woodworkers of America and eventually achieved its goal. See Gunns, "Ray Becker," 95–99.

6. Willits interview; Stuart Smith interview.

7. *Industrial Pioneer* (November 1925), 12; *Centralia Chronicle*, July 14, 1926; *Labor Defender* (December 1926), 215.

8. Willits interview; Cloud interview, August 24, 1972; *Centralia Publicity Committee Bulletin*, August 27, September 10, 1927, Becker Papers; Willits letter.

9. Cloud interview, April 7, 1973; Harris interview, April 23, 1973.

10. *Centralia Publicity Committee Bulletin*, October 29, 1927, Becker Papers; Harmon interview.

11. Waddell manuscript; Willits interview; Willits letter.

12. Cloud interview, August 24, 1972.

13. Notes in the possession of Virginia Waddell.

14. *Centralia Publicity Committee Bulletin*, February 18, February 22, 1928, Becker Papers.

15. Rosalyn Fraad Baxandall, *Words on Fire: The Life and Writings of Elizabeth Gurley Flynn* (New Brunswick: Rutgers University Press, 1987), 154; Elizabeth Gurley Flynn, *I Speak My Own Piece* (New York: Masses and Mainstream, 1955), 256.

16. Cloud interview, August 24, 1972.

17. *Centralia Publicity Committee Bulletin*, June 18, 1928; *Labor Defender* (August 1928), 177.

18. Elmer Smith, "Elmer Smith Pleads for Liberty of Centralia Men," in Centralia Publicity Committee pamphlet, July 1928, Labor History Archives, Wayne State University, Detroit.

19. *Centralia Publicity Committee Bulletin*, September 22, 1928, Becker Papers.

20. C.E. Payne, "Captain Coll-Legionaire," *The Nation* (July 10, 1929), 38; "Legion Officer and Over Seas Captain Demands Release of Centralia Victims," Centralia Publicity Committee leaflet, October 1, 1928, in possession of the author; Coll interview.

21. Coll interview; Coll letter to *Hoquiam Post*, September 28, 1928, reprinted in "Legion Officer" leaflet.

22. *Centralia Chronicle*, August 11, 1928; Coll interview.

23. *Centralia Chronicle*, September 17, September 21, October 2, 1928.

24. "Legion Officer" leaflet.

25. Coll interview.

26. James P. Cannon, "A Talk with the Centralia Prisoners," *Labor Defender* (June 1928), 134; *Labor Defender* (October 1928), 215, (January 1929), 12. Although the ILD and the CLC were becoming more active on behalf of the prisoners, they did give credit to Smith for his untiring work.

27. *Labor Defender* (February 1929), 36; Coll interview.

28. *Labor Defender* (February 1929), 36.

29. Cloud interview, August 24, 1972; Stuart Smith interview.

30. Waddell interview.

31. Stuart Smith interview.

32. Coll interview; Payne, "Captain," 39.

33. Coll interview.

34. Ibid.; Murphy interview.

35. Coll interview; Smith to Baldwin, February 2, April 22, April 27, 1929. See also correspondence between Baldwin and Adele Parker Bennett, February to November 1929, ACLU Files; Sinclair to Smith, August 6, 1926, Upton Sinclair Papers, Indiana University, Bloomington. The American Fund for Public Service, administered by the ACLU, also provided money for Coll.

36. *Centralia Publicity Committee Bulletin*, March 6, 1929, IWW Papers, Wisconsin Historical Society, Madison; Theodore K. Vogler, "Centralia's Prisoners Stay Behind Bars," *Christian Century* (April 4, 1929), 450–1.

37. Hartley to Coll, April 29, 1929, Cunningham Papers.

38. Barnett to Smith, April 16, 1929, Cunningham Papers. The letter was probably given by Smith to Cunningham to plead for his help.

39. "Speeches by Elmer Smith and Capt. Edward P. Coll," Centralia Publicity Committee pamphlet, March 31, 1929, 1, Hoover Institution, Stanford University, Stanford, California.

"I HAVE A FAILING OF BEING OPTIMISTIC"

1. From 33 *Prison and Mountain Songs* (New York: Shapiro, Bernstein & Company, 1932), 2–3. This was a favorite song of Smith's.

2. *Centralia Chronicle*, May 16, 1929.

3. D. Campbell Wyckoff, letter to the author, November 16, 1972. Campbell Wyckoff is Dewitt Wyckoff's son.

4. Becker to Smith, April 17, 1924, Becker Papers; John Beffel to Roger Baldwin, March 7, 1925, Beffel Papers; Baldwin to Adele Parker-Bennett, November 28, 1929, ACLU Files.

5. *Industrial Worker*, June 29, July 6, 1929.

6. Charlotte Todes Stern, letter to the author, September 20, November 16, 1982. Todes was the secretary of the Seattle branch of the ILD and one of the founders of the CLC. Of the seven members of the CLC executive committee, three were Communists. See Carl Brannin to ACLU, September 4, 1930, ACLU Files.

7. "Open Challenge to Capt. Coll," Communist Party, Seattle, leaflet, IWW records, University of Washington, Seattle; *Industrial Worker*, June 29, 1929.

8. *Industrial Worker*, July 20, 1929.

9. Smith to Baldwin, April 18, 1929, ACLU Files. For a description of Smith and Coll's work in urging the prisoners to repudiate the CLC, see Coll to Baldwin, July 12, 1929, ACLU Files.

10. Coll interview; Murphy interview.

11. *Industrial Worker*, August 17, 1929; *Labor Defender*, various issues, 1929–35; CLC Open Letter, July 3, 1929, Washington State Federation of Labor Papers, University of Washington Archives, Seattle. The CLC did give Smith credit for his work on behalf of the prisoners: "It is the work of Elmer Smith more than anything else which has kept the Centralia case alive," wrote James P. Cannon in the *Labor Defender* (June 1928), 135.

12. See *Labor Defender* (May 1930), 101; (September 1930), 189; (February 1931), 37; (June 1931), 119; (September 1931), 181; (January 1932), 11; (February 1932), 37.

13. *Centralia Publicity Committee Bulletin*, June 20, 1929, Wisconsin Historical Society, Madison; IWW papers, University of Washington, Seattle; Coll interview; Vogler, "Centralia's Prisoners," 450–1.

14. Coll interview.

15. Cloud interview, August 24, 1972.

16. Bennett to Bailey, January 17, 1930, Smith to Baldwin, April 8, 1930, ACLU Files; Smith to Upton Sinclair, November 28, 1930, Sinclair Papers. If Smith was reinstated, he would not have to take the bar examination.

17. J. M. Phillips to Smith, May 20, 1930, Disbarment Records.

18. H. W. B. Hewen to Smith, April 26, 1930, Disbarment Records.

19. W. H. Cameron to Smith, May 22, 1930, W. A. Reynolds to Smith, June 2, 1930, Disbarment Records.

20. Application for Reinstatement, 631, filed May 31, 1930, Disbarment Records.

21. State Board Report, July 14, 1930, Disbarment Records.

22. Dix Rowland to Smith, June 30, 1930, Smith to Dix Rowland, July 2, 1930, Disbarment Records.

23. State Board Report, July 14, 1930, Disbarment Records.

24. *Industrial Worker*, March 8, 1930; *Industrial Worker*, March 15, 1930.

25. Smith to Sinclair, November 28, 1930, Sinclair Papers.

26. Smith to Carl Benson, July 19, 1930. See correspondence between Smith and Baldwin, April–October 1930, ACLU Files.

27. Smith to Baldwin, May 12, July 5, 1930, and further correspondence between Smith and Baldwin, April–October 1930, ACLU Files.

28. Smith to Baldwin, July 5, 1930, ACLU Files.

29. Barnett to Smith, August 19, 1930, Washington Federation of Labor Papers, University of Washington, Seattle; *Centralia Publicity Committee Special Bulletin*, August 21, 1930, Washington State Federation of Labor Papers; Charlotte Todes, "Centralia, I.W.W. Misleaders," *Labor Defender* (October 1930), 206; *Industrial Worker*, September 6, 1930.

30. *Centralia Chronicle*, August 19, 1930; *Industrial Worker*, August 30, 1930; Loren Roberts, interview with William Knowles, Evergreen College, n.d.

31. Federal Council of Churches of Christ in America, National Catholic Welfare Conference, and Central Conference of American Rabbis, *The Centralia Case—A Joint Report on the Armistice Day Tragedy at Centralia, Washington, November 11, 1919* (New York: Federal Council of Churches, 1930), 16, 48.

32. *Christian Century*, October 29, 1930, 1299–1300.

33. *Industrial Solidarity*, October 21, 1930, as quoted in John M. McClelland Jr., "Terror on Tower Avenue," *Pacific Northwest Quarterly* 57 (April 1966), 71; *Seattle Times*, October 14, 1930; *Centralia Chronicle*, October 13, 1930.

34. Smith to James Taylor, November 15, 1930, Washington State Federation of Labor Papers; Supreme Court Order, In the Matter of the Application of Elmer S. Smith for Reinstatement as an Attorney at Law of This Court, November 17, 1930, Disbarment Records.

35. *Industrial Worker*, November 29, 1930; ACLU to Smith, November 28, 1930, ACLU Files; Sinclair to Smith, November 24, 1930 (the book is in the possession of Stuart Smith); copy of unsigned letter to Smith, November 22, 1930, ACLU Files.

36. Murphy interview; Nelson interview; Waddell manuscript; Stuart Smith interview.

37. *Industrial Worker*, November 29, 1930; Press release, by C.S. Smith, n.d., Hoover Institution, Stanford University, Stanford, California; Robert E. Ficken, *The Forested Land: A History of Lumbering in Western Washington* (Seattle: University of Washington Press, 1987), 188; Case 1059, October 17, 1930, Criminal Files; Orville Behrbaum, interview with the author, Chehalis, Washington, April 19, 1973.

38. Nelson interview; Waddell interview; Stuart Smith interview.

39. At the time of his death, Smith was serving on the executive committee of the association. Letter from *International Juridical Association Monthly Bulletin*, in the possession of Virginia Waddell; Ernest Goodman, letter to the author, November 8, 1977. Goodman is an attorney who is active in the National Lawyers Guild, a progressive legal organization formed in 1936.

40. Coll interview.

41. *Industrial Worker*, June 6, 1931; Gunns, "Ray Becker," 94–95. Barnett died in 1973. See McClelland, *Wobbly War*, 233.

42. Willits interview; Willits letter; Cloud interview, August 24, 1972.

43. Willits letter; Cloud interview, August 24, 1972; Certificate of Death, Elmer Smith, Olympia, Washington; Harmon interview; Willits interview.

44. Cloud interview, August 24, 1972.

45. *Centralia Tribune*, March 25, 1932.

46. *Industrial Worker*, March 29, 1932.

47. *The Town Crier*, March 26, 1932, Beffel Papers.

48. *Centralia Publicity Committee Bulletin*, March 24, 1932, Hoover Institution, Stanford University, Stanford, California; *The Nation* (April 6, 1932), 386.

49. *Centralia Publicity Committee Bulletin*, March 24, 1932, Hoover Institution, Stanford University, Stanford, California.

50. Julia (Godman) Ruuttila, interview with the author, Gresham, Oregon, September 7, 1972. Ruuttila worked on the campaign to release the last prisoner, Ray Becker. Copy of tape and transcript in Labor History Archives, Wayne State University, Detroit. See Nelson interview.

51. Cloud interview, August 24, 1972; Nelson interview.

52. Ibid.

53. *Centralia Publicity Committee Bulletin*, March 24, 1932; Coll interview.

54. *IWW Songbook*, 34 ed. (Chicago: IWW, 1973), 57.

EPILOGUE

1. From Alan Lomax, ed., *The Folk Songs of North America* (Garden City, N.Y.: Doubleday, 1960), 422–3.

2. Probate Records, Lewis County.

3. Hearings on the nomination of Kenneth Mackintosh, Senate Com-

mittee on the Judiciary, March 18–19, 1932, 72nd Cong., University of Washington Library, Seattle.

4. Baxter v. Ford Motor Co. et al., 12 Pac.2d 409 Supreme Court of Washington; Harmon interview.

5. Gunns, "Ray Becker," 95; Clowers interview.

6. Gunns, "Ray Becker," 95.

7. Ibid., 98–99.

8. Willits letter.

9. Willits interview; Stuart Smith interview.

10. Killen interview; Skinner interview; Harris interview; Nelson interview.

11. Beard interview.

12. Ibid.

13. Heathcote interview.

Bibliography

PRIMARY SOURCES

Interviews

Baxter, Sam, Centralia, Washington, September 18, 1972.
Beal, W. H., Centralia, Washington, October 4, 1974.
Beard, Nora (Dishong), Centralia, Washington, September 19, 1972.
Behrbaum, Orville, Chehalis, Washington, April 19, 1973.
Bell, William, Minneapolis, Minnesota, February 23, 1972.
Bertagnolli, Frank, Greyland, Washington, June 10, 1977.
Calmenson, Abe, St. Paul, Minnesota, March 15, 1972.
Cloud, Lucy Anne (Moore), Richmond, California, August 24, 1972, April 7, 1973.
        Tape recording, Labor History Archives, Wayne State University, Detroit,
        Michigan.
Clowers, Jim, Evergreen College, Tacoma, Washington, n.d.
Coll, Edward, Huntsville, Alabama, November 6, 1974.
Doty, Margaret, St. Paul, Minnesota, June 23, 1970.
Drews, John, St. Paul, Minnesota, March 16, 1972.
Dysart, Lloyd, Centralia, Washington, September 20, 1972.
Edwards, Herb, Seattle, Washington, October 1, 1972. Tape recording, Labor His-
        tory Archives, Wayne State University, Detroit, Michigan.
Edwards, Herb, Seattle, Washington, February 12, 1972.
Finan, A., Centralia, Washington, September 18, 1972.
Fisk, Wilbur, South St. Paul, Minnesota, March 4, 1972.
Fusco, Marie, Centralia, Washington, September 19, 1972.
Grundfossen, Iver, Gresham, Oregon, September 6, 1972.
Harmon, Connor, Oregon City, Oregon, September 6, 1972.
Harris, Mabel (Smith), Moses Lake, Washington, April 23, 1973, September 21, 1974.
Heathcote, Hiney, Seattle, Washington, September 29, 1974.
Hurd, Loren, Olympia, Washington, September 21, 1972.
Killen, Mary (Smith), Olympia, Washington, September 30, 1972.
Lipert, Helen, Centralia, Washington, September 17, 1972.

Murphy, Joe, Santa Rosa, California, July 27, 1981.

Nelson, Edna (Smith), Gresham, Oregon, September 30, 1972.

Ruuttila, Julia (Godman), Gresham, Oregon, September 7, 1972. Tape recording, Labor History Archives, Wayne State University, Detroit, Michigan.

Skinner, Grace (Smith), Seattle, Washington, October 2, 1972, April 21, 1973.

Smith, Stuart, Bakersfield, California, October 16, 1974.

Taylor, Ann Elizabeth, St. Paul, Minnesota, August 16, 1972.

Tripp, Oakley, St. Paul, Minnesota, March 9, 1972.

Waddell, Virginia (Smith), Tacoma, Washington, June 14, 1977.

Willits, Laura (Smith), Tacoma, Washington, June 12, 1977.

Legal Documents

Baxter vs. Ford Motor Co. et al., #23749 12 Pac.(2d)409, Supreme Court of Washington, June 20, 1932.

In the Matter of the Proceedings for the Disbarment of Elmer Smith, No. 631, En Banc (February 24, 1925), Washington Supreme Court, 288–91.

The People of the State of California vs. J. H. Casdorf and Earl Firey, Superior Court of California (April 10, 1922), Labor History Archives, Wayne State University, Detroit, Michigan.

People vs. Eaton, 213P275 Pacific Reporter, January 26, 1923.

State ex rel. Sheehan vs. Reynolds, #15910 190 Pacific Reporter, Supreme Court of Washington, June 8, 1920.

State vs. Smith et al. (No. 16354), Supreme Court of Washington (April 14, 1921), Pacific Northwestern Reports (1921), 770–8.

Washington State vs. Britt Smith et al., microfilm, University of Washington Library, Seattle.

Manuscript Sources

American Civil Liberties Union Papers, University of Washington, Seattle.

Harry Ault Papers, University of Washington, Seattle.

Rayfield Becker Papers, Oregon Historical Society, Portland.

John Beffel Papers, Tamiment Library, New York University, New York.

Broussais C. Beck Papers, University of Washington, Seattle.

Centralia Papers, Hoover Institution of War and Peace, Stanford University, Stanford, California.

Clifford D. Cunningham Papers, American Legion Library, Indianapolis, Indiana.

IWW Papers, Labor and History Archives, Wayne State University, Detroit, Michigan.

IWW Papers, University of Washington, Seattle.

IWW Papers, Washington State Archives, Olympia.

IWW Papers, Wisconsin State Historical Society, Madison.

Lewis County Criminal Files, Washington State Archives, Olympia.

Luke S. May Papers, University of Washington, Seattle.

Military Intelligence Records, National Archives, Washington, D.C.

Probate Records, County Clerk's Office, Chehalis, Washington.

Upton Sinclair Papers, Indiana University, Bloomington.

Elmer Smith Disbarment and Reinstatement Records, No. 631, Supreme Court of
   Washington, Olympia.

Elmer Smith Bureau of Investigation Files, United States Department of Justice,
   Federal Bureau of Investigation, Washington, D.C.

Elmer Smith manuscript, by Virginia Waddell, author's collection.

United States Military Intelligence Reports, Surveillance of Radicals in the U.S.,
   1917–41, University of Minnesota, Minneapolis.

Washington State Federation of Labor Papers, University of Washington, Seattle.

SECONDARY SOURCES

Books

Adamic, Louis. *Dynamite: The Story of Class Violence in America*. New York: Chelsea
   House Publishers, 1931.

Baxandall, Rosalyn Fraad. *Words on Fire: The Life and Writings of Elizabeth Gurley
   Flynn*. New Brunswick: Rutgers University Press, 1987.

Byrkit, James W. *Forging the Copper Collar*. Tucson: University of Arizona Press,
   1982.

Chaplin, Ralph. *The Centralia Conspiracy*. Seattle: IWW, 1920.

———. *Wobbly: The Rough and Tumble Story of an American Radical*. Chicago:
   University of Chicago Press, 1948.

Clark, Norman. *Mill Town*. Seattle: University of Washington Press, 1970.

———. *Washington*. New York: W. W. Norton and Company, 1976.

Churchill, Thomas. *Centralia Dead March*. Willimantic, Conn.: Curbstone Press,
   1980.

Dembo, Jonathan. *Unions and Politics in Washington State 1885–1935*. New York:
   Garland Publishing, 1983.

Dowell, Eldridge Foster. *A History of the Criminal Syndicalism Legislation in the
   United States*. Baltimore: Johns Hopkins Press, 1939.

Draper, Theodore. *American Communism and Soviet Russia*. New York: Viking
   Press, 1960.

Dubofsky, Melvyn. *We Shall Be All: A History of the Industrial Workers of the World*.
   New York: Quadrangle/The New York Times Book Company, 1969.

Federal Council of Churches of Christ in America, National Catholic Welfare
   Conference, and Central Conference of American Rabbis. *The Centralia*

Case—A Joint Report on the Armistice Day Tragedy at Centralia, Washington, November 11, 1919. New York: Federal Council of Churches, 1930.

Ficken, Robert E. *The Forested Land: A History of Lumbering in Western Washington*. Seattle: University of Washington Press, 1987.

Fine, Nathan. *Labor and Farmer Parties in the United States, 1828–1928*. New York: Russell and Russell, 1961.

Flynn, Elizabeth Gurley. *I Speak My Own Piece*. New York: Masses and Mainstream, 1955.

Foner, Philip S. *History of the Labor Movement in the United States*. Volume 4: *The Industrial Workers of the World, 1905–1917*. New York: International Publishers, 1965.

————. *History of the Labor Movement in the United States*. Volume 8: *Postwar Struggles, 1918–1920*. New York: International Publishers, 1987.

Friedheim, Robert L. *The Seattle General Strike*. Seattle: University of Washington Press, 1964.

Fultz, Hollis B. *Elkdom in Olympia*. Olympia: BPOE, 1966.

Funk, Henry D. *History of Macalester College*. St. Paul: Macalester, 1910.

Gambs, John. *The Decline of the IWW*. New York: Columbia University Press, 1932.

Gunns, Albert F. *Civil Liberties in Crisis: The Pacific Northwest, 1917–1940*. New York: Garland Publishing, 1983.

Hanson, Ole. *Americanism Versus Bolshevism*. New York: Doubleday, Page and Company, 1920.

Hawley, Lowell S., and Ralph Bushnell Potts. *Counsel for the Damned*. New York: J.B. Lippincott Company, 1953.

Haywood, Bill. *The Autobiography of Big Bill Haywood*. New York: International Publishers, 1929.

Holbrook, Stewart. *Holy Old Mackinaw*. New York: Ballantine Books, 1938.

Hyman, Harold. *Soldiers and Spruce: Origins of the Loyal Legion of Loggers and Lumbermen*. Los Angeles: Institute of Industrial Relations, 1963.

IWW Songbook, 34th ed. Chicago: IWW, 1973.

Jensen, Vernon. *Lumber and Labor*. New York: Farrar and Rinehart, 1945.

Johansen, Dorothy, and Charles Gates. *Empire of the Columbia*. New York: Harper Brothers, 1957.

Jones, Richard Seelye. *A History of the American Legion*. New York: Bobbs-Merrill Co., 1946.

Kennedy, David. *Over Here: The First World War and American Society*. New York: Oxford University Press, 1980.

Kornbluth, Joyce L. *Rebel Voices: An I.W.W. Anthology*. Ann Arbor: University of Michigan Press, 1968.

Lampman, Ben Hur. *Centralia Tragedy and Trial*. 1920; reprint, Seattle: Shorey Book Store, 1965.

The Lumber Industry and Its Workers. Chicago: IWW, 1920.

McClelland, John. *Wobbly War: The Centralia Story*. Tacoma: Washington State Historical Society, 1987.

Moley, Raymond, Jr. *The American Legion Story*. New York: Duell, Sloan and Pearce, 1966.

Murphy, Paul. *The Meaning of Freedom of Speech*. Westport, Conn.: Greenwood Publishing Company, 1972.

Murray, Robert. *Red Scare: A Study of National Hysteria, 1919–1920*. New York: McGraw-Hill, 1955.

O'Connor, Harvey. *Revolution in Seattle: A Memoir*. New York: Monthly Review Press, 1964.

Parker, Carleton H. *The Casual Laborer and Other Essays*. 1920; reprint, Seattle: University of Washington Press, 1972.

Preston, William, Jr. *Aliens and Dissenters: Federal Suppression of Radicals, 1903–1933*. New York: Harper and Row, 1963.

Renshaw, Patrick. *The Wobblies: The Story of Syndicalism in the United States*. Garden City, N.Y.: Doubleday and Company, 1967.

Robinson, Elwyn. *History of North Dakota*. Lincoln: University of Nebraska Press, 1966.

———. *The Themes of North Dakota History*. Grand Forks: University of North Dakota, 1959.

Salerno, Salvatore. *Red November Black November*. Albany: State University of New York Press, 1989.

Salo, Jenkins. *Timber Concentration in the Pacific Northwest*. Ann Arbor: University of Michigan Press, 1945.

Smith, Walker C. *The Everett Massacre*. Chicago: IWW, 1917.

Speeches by Elmer Smith, Capt. Edward Coll. Centralia: Centralia Publicity Committee, 1929.

Tyler, Robert. *Rebels of the Woods: The I.W.W. in the Pacific Northwest*. Eugene: University of Oregon, 1967.

Winther, Oscar Osburn. *The Great Northwest*. New York: A.A. Knopf, 1947.

Articles

Cantwell, Robert. "Hills Around Centralia." In *Proletarian Literature in the United States*. Edited by Granville Hicks. Seattle: University of Washington, 1935.

Chaplin, Ralph. "The Background of Centralia." *The One Big Union Monthly* (May 1920), 17–19.

Copeland, Tom. "Elmer Smith—Lumberjack's Lawyer." *William Mitchell College of Law Opinion* (November 1976), 9.

———. "Wesley Everest, IWW Martyr." *Pacific Northwest Quarterly* 77 (October 1986): 122–9.

———. "You Don't Look Like a Bad Guy, How'd You Get Into This? The Story of Elmer 'Red' Smith '10." *Macalester Today* (September 1972), 10–11.

Dunn, W. F. "Crime of Centralia." Pamphlet. Chicago: IWW, 1920.

Ficken, Robert E. "The Wobbly Horrors: Pacific Northwest Lumbermen and the Industrial Workers of the World, 1917–1928." *Labor History* 24 (Summer 1983): 325–42.

Gill, Robert S. "The Four L's in Lumber." *The Survey* (May 1, 1920), 165–170.

Gunns, Albert F. "Ray Becker, the Last Centralia Prisoner." *Pacific Northwest Quarterly* 59 (April 1968): 88–99.

Howd, Cloice R. "Industrial Relations in the West Coast Lumber Industry." *Bulletin of the U.S. Bureau of Labor Statistics* (December 1923), 38–44.

Kirchwey, George. "A Survey of the Workings of the Criminal Syndicalism Law in California." California Committee of the ACLU (1926).

"Legion Officer and Over Seas Captain Demands Release of Centralia Victims," October 1, 1928. Leaflet, Centralia Publicity Committee.

McClelland, John, Jr. "Terror on Tower Avenue." *Pacific Northwest Quarterly* 57 (April 1966): 65–72.

"The New Wild West." *The Liberator* (January 1920), 21–23.

Payne, C. E. "Captain Coll-Legionaire." *The Nation* (July 10, 1929), 38–39.

Pritchard, Barry. "Centralia, 1919: A Play." *The Minnesota Review* (Spring 1977), 71–118. Published in Bloomington, Indiana.

"Rooting Out the Reds." *The Literary Digest* (November 22, 1919), 15.

Smith, Elmer. "Education! Organization." Leaflet, ACLU files.

———. "Elmer Smith Pleads for Liberty of Centralia Men." Leaflet, Centralia Publicity Committee, 1928. Labor History Archives, Wayne State University, Detroit.

———. "A Message from the City Jail of Centralia, Wash." Leaflet, ACLU files, 1923.

Smith, Walker C. "Was It Murder?" Pamphlet. Seattle: Northwest District Defense Committee, 1922.

Strong, Anna Louise. "Centralia: An Unfinished Story." *The Nation* (April 17, 1920), 508–10.

Tugwell, Rexford. "The Casual of the Woods." *The Survey* (July 3, 1920), 472–4.

Tyler, Robert L. "Violence at Centralia, 1919." *Pacific Northwest Quarterly* 45 (October 1954): 116–24.

Vogler, Theodore. "Centralia Prisoners Stay Behind Bars." *The Christian Century* (April 4, 1929), 450–1.

Whitaker, Robert. "Centralia and the Churches." *The Christian Century* (December 3, 1930), 1478–80.

Whitten, Woodrow C. "Criminal Syndicalism and the Law in California 1919–1927." *Transactions of the American Philosophical Society* (1969).

"Why I Am a Member of the I.W.W." *Four L Bulletin* (October 1922), 9–35.

Winstead, Ralph. "Evolution of Logging Conditions on the Northwest Coast." *The One Big Union Monthly* (May 1920), 20–30.

Theses and Papers

Capron, Donald. "The Centralia Riot of 1919: A Study of Pre-New Deal Labor Relations." M.A. thesis, San Francisco State University, San Francisco, 1981.

Cole, Robert Leslie. "The Democratic Party in Washington State, 1919–1933: Barometer of Social Change." Ph.D. diss., University of Washington, Seattle, 1972.

Cravens, Hamilton. "A History of the Washington Farmer-Labor Party, 1918–1924." M.A. thesis, University of Washington, Seattle, 1962.

Gunns, Albert. "The Defense Strategy at the Montesano Trial." Paper read at Pacific Northwest Labor History Association Conference, May 15, 1976, Seattle, Washington.

Nichols, Claude W. "Brotherhood in the Woods: The Loyal Legion of Loggers and Lumbermen, a 20 Year Attempt at Industrial Cooperation." Ph.D. diss., University of Oregon, Eugene 1959[?].

Schmidt, Dorothy Nell. "Sedition and Criminal Syndicalism in the State of Washington, 1911–1917." Ph.D. diss., State College of Washington, Pullman, 1940.

Tripp, Joseph. "Progressive Labor Laws in Washington State 1900–1925." Ph.D. diss., University of Washington, Seattle, 1973.

Newspapers and Magazines

American Legion Weekly, 1919–20
Bellingham American Reveille, 1920
Centralia Chronicle, 1915–32
Centralia Daily Hub, 1915–20
Centralia Tribune, 1922–24
Chehalis Bee-Nugget, 1919–20
Daily Washingtonian, 1922
Defense News Service, 1922
Farmer-Labor Call, 1920
Federated Press Bulletin, 1923–25
Four L Bulletin, 1922
Humboldt Times, 1922
Industrial Pioneer (Chicago), 1921–25
Industrial Solidarity (Chicago), 1920–25
Industrial Unionist (Portland), 1925
Industrial Worker (Seattle), 1920–32
Industrialisti (Duluth), 1919–20
Labor Defender (New York), 1926–33
Morning Olympian, 1919

Montesano Vidette, 1919–20
New York Times, 1919
Olympia Daily Record, 1919
Portland Oregonian, 1913–20
San Francisco Call and Bulletin, 1922
Seattle Daily Times, 1920
Seattle Post-Intelligencer, 1919–20
Seattle Union Record, 1919–26
Spokesman Review, 1915–19
Washington Standard, 1919

Index

Made in United States
Orlando, FL
26 April 2023

32493775R00157